The
American Dream
in the
Great Depression

D0075142

CONTRIBUTIONS IN AMERICAN STUDIES

Series Editor   Robert H. Walker

Progress and Pragmatism: James, Dewey, Beard, and the American Idea of Progress
David W. Marcell

The Muse and the Librarian
Roy P. Basler

Henry B. Fuller of Chicago: The Ordeal of a Genteel Realist in Ungenteel America
Bernard R. Bowron, Jr.

Mother Was a Lady: Self and Society in Selected American Children's Periodicals, 1865-1890
R. Gordon Kelly

The *Eagle* and Brooklyn: A Community Newspaper, 1841-1955
Raymond A. Schroth, S.J.

Black Protest: Issues and Tactics
Robert C. Dick

American Values: Continuity and Change
Ralph H. Gabriel

Where I'm Bound: Patterns of Slavery and Freedom in Black American Autobiography
Sidonie Smith

William Allen White: Maverick on Main Street
John D. McKee

American Studies Abroad
Robert H. Walker, Editor

American Studies: Topics and Sources
Robert H. Walker, Editor

In the Driver's Seat: The Automobile in American Literature and Popular Culture
Cynthia Golomb Dettelbach

The United States in Norwegian History
Sigmund Skard

Milestones in American Literary History
Robert E. Spiller

A Divided People
Kenneth S. Lynn

The American Dream in the Great Depression

Charles R. Hearn

Contributions in American Studies, Number 28

GREENWOOD PRESS
WESTPORT, CONNECTICUT • LONDON, ENGLAND

Library of Congress Cataloging in Publication Data

Hearn, Charles R
    The American dream in the Great Depression.

    (Contributions in American studies ; no. 28)
    Bibliography: p.
    Includes index.
    1. United States—Civilization—1918-1945. 2. American literature—20th century—History and criticism. 3. Depressions—1929—United States.
    I. Title.
    E169.1.H32   973.9   76-56623
    ISBN 0-8371-9478-4

Copyright © 1977 by Charles R. Hearn

All rights reserved. No portion of this book may be reproduced, by any process or technique, without the express written consent of the publisher.

Library of Congress Catalog Card Number: 76-56623
ISBN: 0-8371-9478-4

First published in 1977

Greenwood Press, Inc.
51 Riverside Avenue, Westport, Connecticut 06880

Printed in the United States of America

HUGH STEPHENS LIBRARY
STEPHENS COLLEGE
COLUMBIA, MISSOURI

E
169.1
.H32

For Pamela,
Stephen,
and Melissa

162380

Contents

Preface

What happened to the American dream of success, one of our most compelling and tenacious cultural myths, when it collided with the reality of the Great Depression, the most disastrous economic crisis in our history? That, in its simplest form, is the question that provides the basis for this book. It is an important question because the myth of success, throughout our history, has been central to our value system and, in fact, has helped to define the very essence of what we conceive America to be as a culture. Posing the question, then, is a way of focusing a complicated set of larger questions involving the influence of the Depression of the 1930s on the attitudes, values, dreams, fears, and motivations of the American people. In seeking answers to the question, I have looked at a wide variety of sources, including how-to-succeed guidebooks and inspirational works, fiction and nonfiction from popular magazines, sociological studies, gangster, tough-guy, and proletarian novels, and the drama and fiction of major writers. I believe that the integration of these diverse sources, and particularly the inclusion of popular materials, provides a perspective on the Depression decade which is more balanced than the view that one finds in studies describing the period in terms of proletarian writings, social protest, and political ferment.

It would be impossible to mention everyone who helped with this study at one stage or another. But I would like to make several specific acknowledgments. Two professors at the University of Minnesota, where the study originated as a doctoral dissertation, deserve special mention: Joseph Kwiat, my adviser, who offered detailed criticisms through several revisions, and

Mary Turpie, who not only helped in countless ways as an administrator but also read the manuscript and offered suggestions for improvement.

I would also like to express my appreciation to the Grants and Research Funding Committee of Southeast Missouri State University, which provided funds for manuscript preparation, and to Diane Morgan, who typed the manuscript with such expertise.

In gratitude to my wife, Pamela, who inspired ideas, provided moral support, and did more of the grubby work than I like to remember, I can only say that she made the whole thing not only worthwhile but possible.

Charles R. Hearn

The
American Dream
in the
Great Depression

Introduction

Probably no idea has had a greater appeal to the American imagination than the American dream of material success. William James called "the exclusive worship of the bitch goddess Success . . . our national disease,"[1] while Lyman Abbott, in a more optimistic tone, described the ambition to succeed as "emphatically an American ambition; at once the national vice and national virtue."[2] In popular mythology, the self-made man has been one of our most admired heroes, and the rags-to-riches story one of our favorite fairy tales. From the beginning of our history, the New World was a symbol of unlimited opportunity for individual fulfillment in a fresh, new Eden. During periods of expansion and prosperity, particularly in the late-nineteenth century and the 1920s, the nation's great economic potential seemed to provide some factual basis for the widespread belief that the American dream would be fulfilled for those who pursued it with sufficient vitality and devotion. However, modern social scientists are generally agreed that, throughout our history, the rise of the self-made man has been the exception rather than the rule. Studies by Mabel Newcomer, Seymour Lipset and Richard Bendix, Pitirim Sorokin, Natalie Rogoff, and others have established the fact that, despite some spectacular instances of rags-to-riches success, the majority of the positions of leadership in American business were held, even in the late-nineteenth century, by men who had begun life with distinct social and economic advantages. Furthermore, a comparison by Seymour Lipset and Natalie Rogoff of social mobility in Europe and the United States has even challenged the traditional and virtually universal assumption that mobility is greater in America than in the older, presumably more rigid, societies of Europe.[3]

Whatever its basis in fact, however, the American myth of success has had remarkable vitality and persistence, especially on the popular level. The essential question underlying my analysis here is this: What happened to this deeply ingrained and wonderfully compelling dream of success during the Depression of the 1930s when the stark reality of an economic crisis seemed to belie the assumption that, in America, anyone who possessed the proper personal virtues (initiative, perseverance, frugality, industry, reliability) could raise himself from poverty to wealth? Historically, the myth of success has been identified with our most cherished cultural values, focusing, dramatizing, and supporting the very ideals that we consider most distinctively "American." Our belief in rugged individualism, equality of opportunity, laissez-faire capitalism, social classlessness, the gospel of work, self-reliance, material acquisitiveness, thrift, and ambition is nowhere more clearly illustrated than in the classic American success story—the story of the poor boy who raises himself to prominence through hard work, perseverance, and honesty. Thus, an analysis of the myth of success as it existed during the Depression years should provide important insights into what happened to our values during the worst economic crisis in our history.

This approach gives rise to a number of important questions. To what extent, for instance, did the conventional rags-to-riches myth persist during the Depression years? Certainly the mass-circulation magazines and other organs of popular culture continued to pander to the dream of success despite the reality of the Depression. Did the myth serve as pure romantic escape, or did it have other functions? What modifications and adjustments in the myth of success can be seen in the years when the Depression itself, as well as such broader developments as the expansion of the welfare state and the growth of big labor unions, was changing the fabric of American society? The popular magazines, how-to-succeed guide-books, and other sources concerned with the question of success could scarcely escape entirely the problem of adjusting the mythology of success to the reality of the times. But do these adjustments imply major changes in the goals and ideals of the ordinary American? To what extent, for instance, did the old ideal of individual aggressiveness give way to the ideal of conformity? Did economic security become more highly valued than mobility? Did the gospel of work become more sacred or less sacred as a result of high-unemployment ratios? These questions and others like them have important implications regarding the motives and goals that directed the lives of ordinary Americans a generation ago.

The Myth of Success in American History

The pervasive importance of the dream of success to the American imagination can be suggested by even the briefest sketch of the history of the myth of success in this country. This history extends deep into our Puritan past. As Max Weber pointed out in *The Protestant Ethic and the Spirit of Capitalism,* the pursuit of worldly success was given religious sanction by the Puritan doctrine of the secular "calling" with its assumption that God expected His servants to succeed in some worldly occupation and that He rewarded virtue with wealth. In theory, material success was not an end in itself for the New England Puritans. Man's purpose in the world was to glorify God, and in such sermons as John Cotton's "Christian Calling," the Puritan divines placed heavy emphasis on the "warrantablenesse" of the calling, on the necessity for the Christian to "depend upon God for the quickning, and sharpning of his gifts in that calling," and on the ideal of service to man and God through the calling.[4] Nevertheless, material success and even the accumulation of wealth were assumed to be an effective means of serving God and a clear sign of His favor. The most enthusiastic spokesman for material success among the early Puritans was Cotton Mather. In a document titled *Two Brief Discourses, one Directing a Christian in his General Calling; another Directing him in his Personal Calling,* he assured his readers that God expected them to prosper in their worldly endeavors. The Christian's general calling, according to Mather's reasoning, is to serve Christ, but salvation depends also on success in a personal, secular calling, "a certain Particular Employment by which his Usefulness in his neighborhood is distinguished."

> A Christian at his Two Callings, is a man in a Boat, Rowing
> for Heaven; the House which our Heavenly Father hath intended
> for us. If he mind but one of his callings, be it which he will,
> he pulls the oar, but on one side of the Boat, and will make
> but a poor dispatch to the Shoar of Eternal Blessedness.[5]

Judging from the metaphor used here, Mather wanted to insist that the personal calling be given as much emphasis as the general calling.

Implicit in Mather's theory of worldly success is the principle of stewardship—an idea that would be central to the philosophy of success expounded by late-nineteenth century moguls like Andrew Carnegie. Mather mentions in the same breath the Christian's "doing of Good for others" and his "getting of Good for himself." His assumption is that the two principles work together, that the Christian's pursuit of his own individual economic success will contribute to his social usefulness rather than clash with it. This assumption, of course, has been a key aspect of the Protestant ethic and a persuasive justification for American rugged individualism. The idea of stewardship is emphasized also in Mather's *Essays to Do Good* where he preaches that wealth is a gift of God, which provides those who have attained it with a wonderful opportunity as well as a heavy responsibility to do good for their less fortunate fellowmen.[6]

Since the moral and religious foundations for the American pursuit of success were laid in Puritan New England, it is not surprising that Benjamin Franklin, our first outstanding example of the self-made man and our most influential publicist of how-to-succeed maxims, grew up in a Puritan environment, where he was influenced by such teaching as Mather's *Essays to Do Good*. As a symbol of the American rise from obscurity to wealth and prominence, Franklin has had a more secure place in the American mythology of success than that of any other rags-to-riches hero with the probable exception of Lincoln. Appearing at a time when the aristocratic ideal of established social ranks and gentlemanly virtue was still dominant in many minds, Franklin became the archetype of the new American hero, not only exemplifying the self-made man in his own person, but articulating the ideal through his writings. The important differences between this new hero-image and the established, aristocratic ideal are implicit in the contrast between Franklin and his contemporary, George Washington.[7] Washington was admired as a great leader who symbolized stability, fatherly dignity, and extraordinary moral excellence. His outstanding qualities were inherent in his social position, not cultivated through pains-taking efforts toward self-improvement. Most portraits depicted him as somewhat aloof, larger than life, elegant in fine clothes. Franklin as hero affirmed the mobility of the ordinary man; he represented not inherited distinction but accomplishment based entirely on individual ability and character. The best-known portraits of Franklin show him as a rather chubby, unprepossessing figure, dressed in simple clothes, looking not elegant or refined but capable, kindly, and approachable. For the ordinary man, then, Washington was an ideal worthy of admiration and respect. Franklin, how-ever, was a successful man worthy of emulation.

Franklin's influence on the thinking of the American people is difficult to exaggerate. Irwin Wyllie has said that in *Poor Richard's Almanack, The Way to Wealth, Advice to Young Tradesmen,* and other writings Franklin "publicized prosperity maxims which have probably exerted as much practical influence on Americans as the combined teachings of all the formal philosophers."[8] It would be an injustice to Franklin to suggest that his career or his teachings reflect a narrowly materialistic conception of success. He emphasizes intellectual and moral growth, self-discipline, and public responsibility, as well as the acquisition of material wealth. It is true, however, that the maxims he is most remembered for are those outlining the way to wealth. The virtues he associates with success—industry, frugality, diligence, honesty, prudence, initiative—have remained at the heart of our mythology of success, and it has been traditional to assume with Franklin that the world is so ordered that "He that gets all he can honestly, and saves all he gets (necessary expenses excepted), will certainly become *rich.* . . ."[9]

By secularizing the teachings about worldly success inherited from his Puritan background, Franklin helped to provide the bridge to the cult of the self-made man which flourished so potently in the nineteenth century. By the second quarter of the century the cult of the self-made man was thriving, and Franklin, appropriately enough, was the first hero to be glorified by the cult. Printers published new editions of Franklin's works, prefaced by exhortations to young readers to follow Franklin's example. Public-spirited citizens inaugurated series of Franklin Lectures. Parents nurtured their children on Franklin's self-help maxims. Indeed, later in the century, Mark Twain observed satirically that young boys of Twain's own generation were hounded to death by Franklin's aphorisms:

> [Franklin] was of a vicious disposition, and early prostituted his talents to the invention of maxims and aphorisms calculated to inflict suffering upon the rising generation of all subsequent ages. . . . His maxims were full of animosity toward boys. Nowadays a boy cannot follow out a single natural instinct without tumbling over some of those everlasting aphorisms and hearing from Franklin on the spot. . . . That boy is hounded to death and robbed of his natural rest, because Franklin said once, in one of his inspired flights of malignity:
> "Early to bed and early to rise
> Makes a man healthy and wealthy and wise."[10]

Twain's irreverent exaggeration emphasizes Franklin's importance to the cult of success in the nineteenth century. But, of course, well before mid-century, other important figures had been added to the list of self-made heroes, and both political parties were capitalizing on the popular appeal of the image of the self-made man. The example of Old Hickory's enormous popular appeal set the Whigs to searching for log cabins or other symbols of humble origins in the backgrounds of their candidates. Daniel Webster flavored his eloquent speeches with memories of his childhood in a simple cabin in New Hampshire, and the cultivated, aristocratic Henry Clay became "the mill boy of the slashes." In the campaign of 1840 the effectiveness of the log-cabin, hard-cider rhetoric employed by Harrison's forces was demonstrated by the fact that Harrison won a four-to-one majority of electoral votes over Van Buren, who had been portrayed during the campaign as refined and aristocratic.[11] Later, the Republican party profited from the appeal of the rags-to-riches myth when the story of Abraham Lincoln's rise from rail-splitter to President became the supreme expression of the ideal of the self-made man.

In the atmosphere of expansion and industrialization that characterized the nineteenth century, it seemed self-evident that opportunities for individual mobility were boundless and that success depended solely on the character of each individual. The self-made man became a symbol of the triumph of democracy and equality over aristocracy and special privilege. In addition to political figures like Jackson and Lincoln, examples of self-made heroes could be found in the arts, the world of scholarship, and other areas. Chester Harding, a self-taught portrait painter, had many admirers and patrons in the 1820s, and Elihu Burritt, the self-educated blacksmith-philosopher, was esteemed as a true embodiment of the idea of self-improvement.[12] It was this kind of achievement that William Ellery Channing wished to emphasize in using the term "Self-Culture" as the title for his lecture to the Franklin Society in 1838. When he referred to the capacity "to discern not only what we already are, but what we may become,"[13] his main concern was with intellectual and moral development, not with political power or business success.

Nevertheless the chief arena of the self-made man has always been the world of business. At midcentury, names like John Jacob Astor, Peter Cooper, Cornelius Vanderbilt, and George Peabody were nationally known, and the average town could also boast of its own local self-made businessmen. It was in the context of business enterprise, in fact, that Henry Clay first used the term "self-made man." Defending his "American System" of protective tariffs and a central bank against the charge that the system would create a privileged industrial aristocracy, Clay argued that the protection of business enterprise would, on the contrary, support equality of opportunity and improve the chances for men of humble origins to rise to the top in business. He asserted that "In Kentucky, almost every manufactory known to me is in the hands of enterprising self-made men, who have whatever wealth they possess by patient and diligent labor."[14] The support which the myth of the self-made man would give to the American belief in the sanctity of business enterprise is clearly suggested in this statement. By arguing that any man willing to work could rise to the top in American business, Clay and later business apologists could justify giving business a free rein. To restrict business enterprise would limit free opportunity rather than safeguard democracy against special privilege. Implicit in Clay's statement was an attitude that prevailed throughout the nineteenth century—the belief that there was no cause to fear the concentration of economic power, provided that equality of opportunity was maintained at the bottom of the business hierarchy.

By the middle of the nineteenth century, popularizers of the rags-to-riches theme had created a considerable body of literature, fiction and nonfiction. In the 1850s, T. S. Arthur of *Ten Nights in a Barroom* fame called attention to the need, as he felt it, for biographies of America's successful men. Arthur believed not only that America's self-made men deserved to be celebrated, but that there was an obligation to outline their careers as models for young men.[15] Others felt the same need and were busily attempting to satisfy it. Freeman Hunt had founded *Hunt's Merchants' Magazine* in 1839 for the purpose of reporting the triumphs of American merchants. Later he collected biographical anecdotes and rules of success in *Work and Wealth* (1856) and *Lives of American Merchants* (1858). Similar inspirational biographies were John Forest's *Self-Made Men of America* (1848) and Charles Seymour's *Self-Made Men* (1858). The self-made man also received his share of attention in the popular fiction of the midnineteenth century. T. S. Arthur's *Sparing to Spend*, Mrs. S. A. L. Sedgwick's *Allen Prescott*, Timothy Flint's *George Mason, the Young Backwoodsman*, Mrs. E. D. E. N. Southworth's *Ishmael*, and T. H. Shreve's *Drayton: A Story of American Life* are all didactic sentimental novels portraying self-made heroes. Like the self-improvement handbooks, their nonfiction counterpart, these novels typically portray the self-made hero as a virtuous and industrious young man who rises above hardship and temptation to become wealthy and respectable.[16]

While popular writers celebrated the self-made man in fiction and biography, Ralph Waldo Emerson helped to provide a philosophical basis for the ideal of self-improvement. His transcendental belief in the essential divinity of all men served as the foundation of a highly individualistic emphasis on self-reliance and self-culture. This philosophy harmonized well with the popular ideal of the self-made man. In fact, one of the outstanding symbols of the free and self-reliant spirit, Emerson thought, was the vigorous and independent young self-made man who set out to build his own world. While Emerson was no worshiper of economic success for its own sake and while his concept of self-realization, like Channing's, was ultimately spiritual, he believed that the desire for wealth and power released energy and creativity necessary for progress. As he expressed it, "The pulpit and the press have many commonplaces denouncing the thirst for wealth; but if men should take these moralists at their word and leave off aiming to be rich, the moralists would rush to rekindle at all hazards this love of power in the people, lest civilization should be undone."[17] Always an admirer of vitality and creative energy, Emerson was practical-minded enough to realize that the ambition for wealth was a crucial source of this energy. He also makes the assumption, so basic to the American mythology of success, that success naturally comes to those who deserve it, provided that one does not tamper with natural economic laws:

> Do not legislate. Meddle, and you snap the sinews with your sumptuary laws. . . . Open the doors of opportunity to talent and virtue and they will do themselves justice, and property will not be in bad hands. In a free and just commonwealth, property rushes from the idle and imbecile to the industrious, brave and persevering.[18]

Like other advocates of self-help, Emerson was fearful of political action which might erect barriers against the natural flow of energy and ability. Buttressed by an optimistic faith in the potential divinity of man and the ultimate benevolence of natural laws, he did not fear inequitable concentrations of economic power, so long as the widest possible opportunities were open to all men.

Because of the compatibility of Emerson's economic ideas with popular American concepts of success, later exponents of self-improvement and economic success quoted freely from him and, in the process, almost always oversimplified and distorted his total views. The New Thought movement of the early twentieth century, for instance, borrowed heavily from Emerson, and in the 1920s, 1930s, and later, the writings of Roger Babson and Bruce Barton as well as those of Dale Carnegie, Norman Vincent Peale, and other advocates of positive thinking contain simplifications and popularizations of Emerson's thought.

In the midnineteenth century, the cult of the self-made man could refer with pride to Emerson as one of its philosophical spokesmen and to Abraham Lincoln as a spectacular example of one who rose from the honest poverty of a cabin to the Presidency of the United States. Nevertheless, the golden age of the American cult of success did not arrive until the latter decades of the century. This was the period of Horatio Alger, whose name has become synonymous with the rags-to-riches story, of Andrew Carnegie whose *Gospel of Wealth* (1889) became so influential as an argument for the stewardship of the wealthy, of Russell Conwell whose *Acres of Diamonds* (1887) was for many years a best-selling statement of the divine right of wealth, and of the McGuffey reader, which drilled self-improvement maxims into the heads of children. By the end of the century, men like Orison Swett Marden, editor of *Success* magazine, were making careers as specialists in the philosophy and techniques of success. As if these native materials were not enough, the American public also felt the influence of Samuel Smiles, the English self-help advocate who was internationally well known for a quartet of books titled *Self-Help* (1859), *Character* (1871), *Thrift* (1875), and *Duty* (1880).[19] How could a young man escape having his values shaped by a gospel of success that was taught in the schools, preached in the churches, dramatized in his light reading, and held up as a goal and a Christian duty by great men who had themselves succeeded? No popular ideal was expounded with such conviction or by so many sources. Kenneth Lynn has convincingly argued that even writers like Dreiser and Norris (he includes also Jack London, Robert Herrick, and David Graham Phillips), whose ideas are in many ways incompatible with or hostile to the success myth, were nonetheless shaped by it and never outgrew its impact on their imaginations. He writes that they "grew up on the success myth and in their maturity accepted it as the key to the meaning of American life."[20]

As John Cawelti has pointed out, the trend among apostles of success in this period was toward an increasingly frank and unqualified emphasis on the pursuit and use of wealth. Pre-Civil War exponents of success generally made an effort to balance the gospel of success against traditional moral and religious values. They were quick to point out the evils of excessive self-interest, speculation, extravagant spending, and other forms of corruption that lurked in the paths to success. In the post-Civil War era apostles of success concerned themselves less with the moral dangers of the pursuit of wealth. They still emphasized the importance of character and gave homage to such traditional virtues as industry, perseverance, honesty, and temperance. But they placed more emphasis on ambition, drive, confidence, and aggressiveness than earlier self-help advocates had done. Increasingly, they accepted the assumption that individualistic competition was the normal basis of human life. While the emphasis on the pursuit of wealth became stronger than ever, however, the basic rationale for success remained the same as it had been for Cotton Mather, Benjamin Franklin, Emerson, and others—that is, the assumption that individual success and the common good were in harmonious accord. Despite the objections of such reformers as Henry George, who argued that under the competitive system progress and poverty went together, the idea that the rugged individualist who created wealth was a power for good in the world had wide currency in the late nineteenth and early twentieth century. It was echoed in the pulpit, in such popular middle-class magazines as *Saturday Evening Post* and *Success,* and, of course, in the utterances of businessmen themselves. In "Wealth and Its Uses," Andrew Carnegie stated the principle bluntly: "It will be a great mistake for the community to shoot the millionaires, for they are the bees that make the most honey, and contribute most to the hive even after they have gorged themselves full."[21] Even assuming that wealthy men are greedy and self-interested, Carnegie suggests, they are still the community's most important benefactors, simply because they are doers and producers.

The gospel of success, as it was preached in this period of its greatest glory, incorporated a theory of failure and poverty which has been extremely important in conditioning American attitudes toward social-reform programs and welfare legislation. Due to the displacements caused by rapid and uncontrolled economic expansion, urbanization, industrialization, and immigration, poverty was a problem which could hardly be ignored. But it could be rationalized. Two attitudes toward poverty were an integral

part of the myth of success. One was the glorification of the poverty in
the backgrounds of those who later rose to wealth and prominence. Apostles
of success like Andrew Carnegie were convinced that a background of
"honest poverty" was indispensable to the training of great men. The self-
made man in the mythology of success struggled to redeem himself from
lowly beginnings like a sinner seeking salvation. As Irvin Wyllie has observed,
"In the religion of success poverty became the equivalent of sin in Calvinist
theology, an evil to be struggled against and overcome."[22]

Wyllie's theological analogy can be extended further to explain the
second attitude toward poverty. If poverty was a sin to be overcome, salvation depended upon each individual, acting alone and looking within himself rather than outside himself. Since the opportunity for success was
supposed to be available to everyone and not merely to the "elect," the
analogy partially breaks down at this point. And yet the attitude of the
prophets of success toward those who did not "make it" was often as
callous as the Calvinist attitude toward sinners. Since success was assumed
to depend upon inner character and not upon conditions external to the
individual, poverty could only be the result of laziness, wastefulness, a
failure of nerve, or other weaknesses of character. It was thus a moral
problem or a personality problem and not a social problem. Efforts to
change social, political, or economic conditions were considered pointless
and potentially harmful. Consequently, while some wealthy men like
Andrew Carnegie preached the idea of stewardship, other advocates of
self-help argued that no provision at all should be made for the poor.
One extremist—a man named John Heermans who titled his contribution
to the literature of success *Nuggets of Gold*—even suggested that the poor
should be systematically starved, arguing that, having deliberately chosen
a life of poverty, they deserved to suffer the consequences of their choice.[23]

In times of economic depression, as Wyllie has noted, exponents of
success have made special efforts to explain the plight of the unfortunate
in terms of personal delinquency. During the panic of 1873, for instance,
William Mathews explained that the straits of hungry poor people in
Chicago had resulted from their own wastefulness and lack of foresight.
He complained that "Instead of hoarding their receipts so as to provide
against sickness or want of employment, they eat and drink up their
earnings as they go, and thus in the first financial crisis, when mills and
factories stop, and capitalists lock up their cash instead of using it in great
enterprises, they are ruined."[24] Twenty years later Charles Kendall Adams,

president of the University of Wisconsin, cautioned students against assigning the wrong causes to the suffering that accompanied the Panic of 1893. "In a vast number, if not a majority of cases," he said, "suffering has come from improvidence, from extravagance, or from dissipation. Let us take care that we do not attribute results to wrong causes."[25] Similarly, the Panic of 1907 led Lyman Abbott to conclude that generally employers fired only those workers who made themselves dispensable by their laxness. As he expressed it, "As a rule men discharge themselves because they do not make themselves necessary."[26] In the Great Depression of the 1930s, as later chapters will demonstrate, the myth of success with its accompanying theory of poverty was invoked in a similar way by conservatives opposed to the use of social legislation as a method for relieving the suffering of those caught in the midst of the Depression.

Committed as they were to the belief that success and failure depended entirely on the character of the individual, late-nineteenth and early-twentieth century advocates of success frequently used the principle of self-help to attack Populism and Progressivism. By the same token, muckrakers and social critics of the Progressive era attacked many of the pieties of the myth of success. Henry George challenged the idea that individual fortunes and the social welfare were compatible. Ida Tarbell, in her *History of the Standard Oil Company,* provided evidence that unscrupulous business practices, more than honesty and virtue, accounted for the Rockefeller fortune. In his three-volume *History of the Great American Fortunes,* Gustavus Myers revealed a multitude of complex and devious methods by which America's wealthy men had achieved their success. Lester Ward, a liberal sociologist, pointed out the simple-mindedness of the self-help enthusiasts who ignored the influence of social factors in the struggle for success.

Despite some enmity between apostles of success and advocates of reform, however, it would be wrong to suggest that the myth of success had become the sole province of the conservative business class. It is true that the myth's function changed after the Civil War. Before the war, individual success was almost always viewed as a symbol of the triumph of the common man over aristocracy and special privilege. Self-made men were celebrated as fitting symbols of American democracy and opportunity. As the business class solidified its position of power in the years after the Civil War, however, the myth of success served increasingly as a conservative rationale by which big business might justify its position and preserve its control. But despite the fact that the ideology of success may have served the haves and the have nots unequally during this time, it never lost its appeal to the ordinary American.

One indication that the broad appeal of the myth of success had not weakened substantially is that, while businessmen invoked the myth of success to justify themselves, the Progressive reformers also used the rhetoric of success to serve their own ends. In *The Age of Reform,* Richard Hofstadter has pointed out that the Populists and Progressives, far from giving up the American dream of equal opportunity for individual success, were intent on insuring that everyone had an equal chance to enter the contest for success. Instead of attacking the values represented by the myth of success, they went on witch hunts for particular villains—eastern banks, railroad monopolies, and the like—which they felt were causing the inequalities and dislocations that weakened the ordinary man's chances of realizing the American dream. An important theme in Woodrow Wilson's *The New Freedom* is that the large corporation was crushing the individual and destroying the kind of self-made success so basic to the American conception of happiness. Wilson says that even businessmen themselves, if they could do it secretly, would admit

> . . . that the present organization of business was meant for the big fellows and was not meant for the little fellows; that it was meant for those who are at the top and was meant to exclude those who are at the bottom; that it was meant to shut out beginners, to prevent new entries in the race. . . .

> What this country needs above everything else is a body of laws which will look after the men who are on the make rather than the men who are already made.[27]

Because of the appeal of the rags-to-riches tradition, few of Wilson's contemporaries would have questioned his assumption that the proper order of things must include the possibility of mobility for the individual businessman. Though the myth of success was more commonly invoked to support a laissez-faire attitude, Wilson's passage illustrates how it was also used in support of progressive legislation designed to improve the little man's chances of competing against the big man. In fact, John Cawelti has suggested that the ideal of success was one of the important strains of con-

tinuity between the period of progressive reform and the "age of normalcy'
which followed it.[28] The ideal of business success was an article of faith
in both periods. In the progressive era, however, the emphasis was on safe-
guarding individual mobility against the threat of the trusts. In the twenties
the emphasis was on guaranteeing that the intervention of government
itself would not threaten the pursuit of success and prosperity.

The fact that elsewhere in *The New Freedom* Wilson appeals to the
workingman with essentially the same kind of rhetoric that he directed
toward the small businessman illustrates again the broad appeal of the
myth of success to all segments of American society. As Wilson understood,
even the relatively immobile American industrial worker was motivated by
the dream of individual success and not, generally speaking, by the desire
for class solidarity. Unlike the European worker, who has tended to develop
a sense of identification with a proletariat, the American worker has
identified with the symbols and goals associated with the myth of success
and has had only a vague sense of class differences or "class consciousness."
Thus, as socialist and communist organizers have complained, the American
worker has not been very responsive to radical ideas. As long as there is
hope, real or mythological, of climbing the ladder of success or of making
possible a better future for his children, the American worker does not
want to change the system radically. Robert and Helen Lynd found that
even in 1935, after six years of demoralizing depression, the Middletown
worker had little class awareness, though evidences of antagonism between
workers and owners were slightly more apparent than ten years earlier.[29]
To think of himself as a distinct class, set apart from other Americans and
motivated by different symbols, values, and objectives, would mean giving
up the American dream. It would mean conceding that America is not a
classless society offering equal opportunity for everyone to reach the top.
And this concession the American worker has never been willing to make.

While progressive reformers of the early twentieth century worried
about keeping open the channels of opportunity, increasing numbers of
inspirational writers were identifying themselves with a new concept of
success that stressed self-manipulation and the power of the mind. In the
early years of the twentieth century, this emphasis on mind power was
crystallized in the New Thought movement, a cult of success which made
its first appearance around 1890 and rapidly developed into a massive
movement with chapters or "centers" in every major city in the northern
states and Canada. As described by A. Whitney Griswold, New Thought
combined the Emersonian idea of self-reliance with the pseudo-sciences

of mesmerism and spiritualism to form a mixture that emphasized the ability of the individual to control things and people by the creative power of the mind. Emerson's influence is clear in the stated purpose of the New Thought Alliance: "To teach the infinitude of the Supreme One; the Divinity of Man and his Infinite possibilities through the creative power of constructive thinking and obedience to the voice of the Indwelling Presence, which is a source of Inspiration, Power, Health, and Prosperity."[30] In this new transcendentalism, Emerson's belief that the self-reliant individual could achieve greatness by uniting himself with universal spiritual forces is simplified and applied to the practical problem of gaining power and prosperity. Inherent in the New Thought creed was an early expression of certain new emphases concerning success that would become increasingly important as the century progressed. The emphasis on mind power was related to the growth in this century of psychology and psychotherapy and can also be seen, in part, as an effort to reaffirm the importance of the individual will in a world of increasing mechanization and corporate complexity.[31] Qualities of personal magnetism, self-confidence, mental manipulation, and positive thinking took precedence over the old virtues of honesty, industry, and frugality. Psychological health and adjustment were equated with the good life, and psychology and the new transcendentalism combined to suggest that man's link to the Infinite was the subconscious mind, which could be trained and controlled to serve the individual's ends.[32] In the twenties, this focus on psychology is observable in writings that stress personality and other direction, in the applied psychology fad, and in other trends. It was in the thirties, however, particularly in the personality and positive thinking dogma of Dale Carnegie, that the mind-power mystique reached a zenith of popular appeal. But that is a subject for a later chapter.

Sources and Approaches

There is no doubt that, throughout our history, the American dream of success has had an extremely important influence on the values of the ordinary American. W. Lloyd Warner refers to the myth of success as "the most powerful of American collective representations," not a mere fantasy to be dismissed but a dream that provides the motive power for much of what Americans do in their daily lives.[33] The vast quantity of success literature that Americans have produced and read is itself a measure of our devotion to the dream of success. Success manuals, magazine success stories, rags-to-riches biographies and autobiographies, Algeresque novels, and sermons on the gospel of success have been among the most widely read forms of popular literature in America. The values and aspirations inherent in this literature of success have been traditionally accepted as the quintessence of "the American way of life."

The Depression decade provides a dramatic focal point for an analysis of this important aspect of American culture because it was in those years that desperate economic conditions challenged the traditional myth of success as it had never before been challenged. My approach has been to bring to bear a large and diverse body of materials on the question of American attitudes toward success in the years surrounding the Great Depression. Many sources have been valuable in the study, but I have made most extensive use of four types: (1) manuals, guidebooks, and inspirational works on success; (2) popular-magazine biographies and other articles relating to the myth of success; (3) popular-magazine fiction; and (4) the fiction and drama of "serious" writers like Nathanael West, John Steinbeck, and Eugene O'Neill.

My use of these sources requires a word of explanation. I have distinguished between popular literature and serious literature because the two are generally related to such popular myths as the myth of success in quite different ways. Though it is impossible to draw a sharp line between the two, some valid distinctions can be made. In a mass society such as ours, popular literature can be considered literature as commodity. It is deliberately produced for a mass audience, and it appeals to that audience by catering to the tastes, attitudes, prejudices, dreams, stereotypes, and preconceptions of the average reader. In style and structure as well as ideas, popular literature relies upon the conventional and the expected. Whereas serious literature, or literature as art, is distinguished by fresh perceptions and original modes of expression, popular literature appeals to its mass audience by means of familiar formulas, stock situations, and language marked by clichés to which the reader can respond automatically and unthinkingly. Since it both reflects and helps to shape popular attitudes and values, popular literature can provide valuable insights into the motivations and aspirations that affect the behavior of the ordinary man. From this perspective, such sources as Dale Carnegie's best-selling *How to Win Friends and Influence People,* the highly popular detective novels of Raymond Chandler or Erle Stanley Gardner, and the articles and short stories appearing in a mass-circulation magazine like *Saturday Evening Post* have to be considered important to the present study.

If popular literature functions as an uncritical purveyor of conventional attitudes, popular myths, and stereotyped views, serious literature represents at once a more individual and a more universal level of perception. It is considered serious, or called "great" or given "major" status, largely because it rises above such stereotypes or provides a critique of them. The serious literary artist, no less than the popular writer, is a part of the cultural milieu. No writer works in a vacuum, and, in fact, some of the most illuminating clues to the deepest impulses and motivations of a culture (what Max Lerner called "the inner culture style") are to be found in the creations of its great writers and other artists. At the same time, the serious writer as opposed to the popular writer has a depth of vision that gives his work universality and allows it to transcend the stereotyped and superficial acceptance of the conventional values of a particular society. To the extent that a writer is gifted with sharp perceptions and superior imaginary vision, he is likely to challenge the stereotyped attitudes and the persistent myths that remain deeply ingrained in the popular mind. It is necessary, therefore, to maintain a distinction between popular literature and serious literature in generalizing about attitudes toward the myth of success. The stories in *Saturday Evening Post* and the novels of Nathanael West, for instance, represent very different levels of response to the myth of success.

In using the works of serious literary artists, then, I have not assumed that they necessarily reflect the attitudes and beliefs of the ordinary American, but have looked to them for deeper and more individualized insights than one finds in the popular literature.

Despite the gap that is likely to exist, however, between the attitudes and values of the serious writer and those ingrained in the popular mind, the works of the highly creative writer can be very revealing as a source of social history. A novelist who is a careful, perceptive, and imaginative observer of the social and human reality that he transforms into fiction is likely to portray a more detailed and vivid view of that reality than one could find in any other source. James T. Farrell's *Studs Lonigan* trilogy, for instance, reveals more about the dreams, aspirations, and frustrations of the lower-middle-class city dweller of the Depression era than one could hope to find in a sociological study, a success manual, or a political tract. In selecting serious works for use in the study, I have made no effort to include all the major writers of the period. Since my primary purpose is to throw light on a cultural phenomenon rather than to formulate a coherent interpretation of the literature of the period, I have chosen for close analysis only those works in which the dream of success is an important theme.

In attempting to get a reliable sampling of popular literature, I have placed heavy emphasis on popular-magazine fiction. Like other means of exploring popular attitudes, this source has its limitations. Editorial policy and the necessity of pleasing advertisers influence what a magazine prints, and subscribers do not necessarily read all parts of a magazine or agree with what they read. Yet the mass magazine can still be used as a reasonably reliable indicator of what the popular mind feeds on. The very fact that a magazine achieves mass circulation suggests that it reflects attitudes, tastes, and values appealing to a large number of people. Furthermore, it would seem safe to assume that in the thirties, before television, the mass magazines contributed much more significantly toward the shaping of public opinion than they do now.

In using magazine fiction as a source, my approach has been to make a systematic year by year sampling of a relatively large number of stories. Specifically, I have taken a random sampling of approximately two hundred short stories from four of the most widely circulated periodicals in the twenties and thirties. For purposes of comparison, I have included stories in the decade of 1920-29 as well as 1930-39, according to the following schedule: four stories per year in the *Saturday Evening Post* (a total of eighty), three stories per year in the *American Magazine* (a total of sixty), two stories per year in *Liberty* (beginning in 1924, for a total of thirty-two), and two stories per odd year in *Ladies' Home Journal* (a total of twenty).

Although I shall not rely heavily on the content-analysis approach, the size and nature of the sampling is intended to make possible certain statistical conclusions that will supplement a more impressionistic kind of literary analysis. A tabulation of the heroes according to their occupations, for example, provides clear support for the hypothesis that in the thirties, as compared to the twenties, the businessman hero was eclipsed by new popular idols, including the professional man and "the little man." In arriving at my generalizations, I have also analyzed and classified the stories with respect to the nature of the setting (city or country, modest or plush), the goals of the protagonist, the reward offered by the "happy ending" (whether material success, love, security, social status, or other rewards), the moral and character qualities of the heroes, and the plots, conflicts, symbols, and themes which recur in the stories. The relatively large year-by-year sampling of stories from both the twenties and the thirties provides a good foundation for tracing shifts in attitudes and noting continuities and changes in the accepted formulas for popular stories. While my general conclusions are based on a systematic study of a large number of stories, however, my specific discussions of the popular fiction will focus on a relatively small selection of typical examples. These selected stories will serve as concrete illustrations of my generalizations about the recurring themes, symbols, character types, attitudes, and formulas found in the stories as a group.

The concept of formula in popular fiction is a useful tool and deserves more elaboration.[30] Characteristic of popular literature is the repetition of safe, established, and marketable formulas. The dime novels of the nineteenth century follow a formula, Horatio Alger novels follow a formula, detective stories follow a formula, and true confession stories follow a formula. The popular-magazine stories of the twenties and thirties follow a broad formula requiring the hero's progression toward some kind of reward or happy ending, and they also treat such recurring themes as love and material success in a stereotyped, formulistic way. Thus, an analysis of dominant patterns and formulas can be a means of discovering some of the prevailing beliefs, dreams, and expectations of the reading audience. A predominant formula of the twenties, for example, is one in which the fictional hero must achieve material success before he can win the love of his dream girl. The numerous stories which follow this formula reflect the high premium that was placed on material success in the twenties. More importantly perhaps, violations or modifications of established formulas can be seen to reveal significant changes in attitudes or expectations. Among the popular stories of the thirties one finds variations in the conventional success-story formula which provide important insights into how popular attitudes toward success changed as a result of the economic crisis. One significant variation, for instance, is found in stories that replace the stock plot in which the hero rises to the heroine's economic level with one in which the heroine lowers herself to the young man's level. The rich girl who, in a story of 1935, takes a job as a waitress so that the young grocery clerk will feel worthy to marry her illustrates the adjustment of an old formula to suit new conditions.

In using nonfiction comments on success (primarily magazine articles and how-to-succeed manuals), I have attempted to determine the dominant patterns of ideas among those who set themselves up as authorities on the subject of success. The Dale Carnegie emphasis on personality selling and getting along with people, for example, is an important departure from the earlier emphasis on strong character and individual aggressiveness. More precise insights into the ways in which attitudes toward success changed during the decade of economic Depression can be derived from the many articles and features about getting ahead which appeared in the popular magazines. Tips on how to succeed, interviews with successful people, short biographies, articles about the influence of the Depression and the New Deal on the patterns of success in America, and thumbnail success stories under such headings as "Interesting People" and "How They Got That Way" were standard features in magazines like *Saturday Evening Post* and *American Magazine*. Thus, through these magazines one can quickly gain insights into popular attitudes on a wide range of subjects related to the pursuit of success. The subject of success and failure was a matter of deep concern to a nation plagued by economic ills, and the continuing discussion of the subject in the popular magazines provides one of the most direct means of tracing the patterns, continuities, and changes in the American public's attitudes toward the subject.

The stock-market crash which ended the 1920s provided an unusually dramatic line of demarcation between two decades. Since one was a decade of boom and one of depression, there is a convenient opportunity to contra the myth of success in two periods of opposite economic extremes. For the most part, I shall focus on the thirties and use the contrast with the twenties only as a means of clarifying generalizations about the Depression years. As a prelude to the discussion of the Depression years, however, Chapter 1 will focus on the myth of success in the prosperous years before the crash.

Notes

1. William James, Letter to H. G. Wells, September 11, 1906, in *The Letters of William James*, edited by Henry James, II, 260.

2. Lyman Abbott, quoted in Irwin G. Wyllie, *The Self-Made Man in America*, p. 1.

3. The Lipset and Rogoff study is "Occupational Mobility in Europe and the United States," in *Man, Work, and Society*, edited by Sigmund Nosow and William H. Form.

For a summary of the literature on social and occupational mobility in American history, see Seymour Lipset and Reinhard Bendix, *Social Mobility in Industrial Society;* Bernard Barber, *Social Stratification;* Pitirim Sorokin, *Social and Cultural Mobility;* Ely Chinoy, "An Evaluation of Some Recent Studies in Occupational Mobility," in *Man, Work, and Society*, pp. 354-59.

4. John Cotton, "Christian Calling," in *The Puritans: A Sourcebook of Their Writings,* edited by Perry Miller and Thomas H. Johnson, II, 320-22.

5. Quoted in A. Whitney Griswold, "Three Puritans on Prosperity," *New England Quarterly,* VII (1934), 475-93.

6. Cotton Mather, *Essays to Do Good,* pp. 89-90.

7. John Cawelti makes this contrast in *Apostles of the Self-Made Man,* p. 10.

8. Wyllie, p. 13.

9. Benjamin Franklin, "Advice to a Young Tradesman," in *A Benjamin Franklin Reader,* edited by Nathan G. Goodman, pp. 159-60.

10. Samuel Clemens, "The Late Benjamin Franklin," in *The Complete Humorous Sketches and Tales of Mark Twain,* edited by Charles Nieder, p. 138.

11. Cawelti, p. 40.

12. Ibid., p. 41.

13. William Ellery Channing, "Self-Culture," quoted in David Edgell, *William Ellery Channing,* p. 132.

14. Quoted in Wyllie, p. 10.

15. Ibid., p. 19.

16. Cawelti, pp. 55-63.

17. Ralph Waldo Emerson, "Wealth," *Conduct of Life,* in *The Selected Writings of Ralph Waldo Emerson,* edited by Brooks Atkinson, p. 699.

18. Ibid., p. 705.

19. See Kenneth Fielden, "Samuel Smiles and Self-Help," *Victorian Studies,* XII (December, 1968), 158.

20. Kenneth S. Lynn, *The Dream of Success: A Study of the Modern American Imagination,* p. 251.

21. Quoted in Edward Kirkland, *Dream and Thought in the Business Community,* pp. 156-57.

22. Wyllie, p. 22.

23. Ibid., p. 159.

24. Quoted in Wyllie, p. 157.

25. Ibid., p. 158.

26. Lyman Abbott, "Willing to Work," *Outlook,* LXXXIX (1908), 643.

27. Woodrow Wilson, *The New Freedom,* pp. 16-17.

28. Cawelti, p. 190.

29. Robert and Helen Lynd, *Middletown in Transition,* pp. 448-50.

30. Quoted in A. Whitney Griswold, "New Thought: A Cult of Success," *American Journal of Sociology,* XL (November, 1934), 310.

31. Richard Weiss, *The American Myth of Success,* p. 12.

32. Ibid., p. 217.

33. W. Lloyd Warner, *American Life: Dream and Reality,* p. 13.

34. For a very helpful discussion of the formula concept as an analytic tool, see John Cawelti, "The Concept of Formula in the Study of Popular Literature," *Journal of Popular Culture,* III (Winter, 1969), 381-90.

1 / The Dream in a Period of Prosperity: The 1920s

If the Depression years of the 1930s were a period of crisis for the American dream of success, the disillusionment resulted in part from the shocking contrast with the prosperous twenties. In the 1920s when, as Fitzgerald said, "America was going on the grandest, gaudiest spree in history," the cult of prosperity and the worship of success took on the proportions of a nation religion. America was viewed as a prosperous utopia where the opportunities for self-made success were virtually limitless. It was an atmosphere in which writers for popular magazines poured out success stories, businessmen were national heroes, and Christ was paid the ultimate compliment when Bruce Barton called him "the founder of modern business." Inspirationalists increasingly reflected the popular interest in psychology, and "systems" of "applied psychology" abounded—including the cult of Couéism, which reached considerable heights of popularity and absurdity by promising health and prosperity to those who would repeat the litany "Day by day, in every way, I am getting better and better."

Intellectuals and serious writers reacted against the philistinism and shallow materialism of American middle-class values, and the cult of success came in for its share of criticism. But the major novelists who treated the dream of success most extensively in the twenties and who will be emphasized in this chapter—Theodore Dreiser, F. Scott Fitzgerald, and Sinclair Lewis—responded ambiguously to the dream. These writers were disillusioned with many of their culture's myths and pieties and are generally considered penetrating critics of middle-class values. Yet to assume that they were totally alienated from traditional American concepts

of success would be to underestimate the extent to which their own imaginations were influenced by the values and aspirations inherent in one of the
dominant myths of their culture.

The Religion of Business Success

In the twenties, success was conceived almost invariably in terms of
business success, and the businessman was revered beyond belief. Business
publicists succeeded in creating a kind of mystique, not to say religion, in
which business was the salvation of the nation and the world. *Nation's
Business* declared effusively, "There is no doubt that the American businessman is the foremost hero of the American people today" and "the most
influential person in the nation . . . perhaps the most influential figure in
the world."[1] The only work of real importance, it was claimed, was the
pursuit of wealth. Politics, statesmanship, and other professions notwith-
standing, it was the pursuit of wealth that engaged the nation's most capable
men. *American Industries* assured its readers that since the late nineteenth
century "the men of real ability in the United States have devoted their
time, their energy, and their money to the pursuit of wealth."[2] One
business executive, in an article for the *Ladies Home Journal,* even pro-
claimed in his title that "Everybody Ought to be Rich." The wording of
this title not only implied that a fortune was available for anyone who
would pursue it, but also suggested that everyone had a moral obligation
to contribute to the prosperity created by the pursuit of wealth.

The most prominent apologists for big business were the three Presidents
of the decade—Harding, Coolidge, and Hoover. As a Presidential candidate,
Harding indicated his affinity for business ideals when he stated in an article
in *Nation's Business* that "This is essentially a business country. This is
why we need business sense in charge of American administration."[3]
Calvin Coolidge put it more bluntly in his often-quoted remark "The
business of America is business."[4] Coolidge's administration was hailed
in the business world as one in which government and business were more
completely fused than ever before. When Hoover was elected in 1928, less
than a year before the financial world collapsed, the fusion was even more
complete; a highly successful, self-made businessman was in the White
House. Hoover's concept of rugged individualism, echoing late-nineteenth-
century theories, assumed that the pursuit of success based upon the

"primary self-interest impulse of the individual to production" was absolutely essential if production were to keep pace with need:

> It is a certainty we are confronted with a population in such
> numbers as can only exist by production attuned to a pitch in
> which the slightest reduction of the impulse to produce will
> at once create misery and want.[5]

This assumption of the interrelation between individual acquisitiveness and the public good has traditionally been a key doctrine in the gospel of success in America.

It is not new or surprising that the apostles of business success should transform self-interest into service and success into a form of salvation. What is surprising to a later observer is the shamelessness with which Americans worshiped moneymaking and made the association between religion and business success. One popular journalist, Edward E. Purinton, a specialist in how-to-succeed articles and books, acclaimed business as "the finest game," "the soundest science," "the truest art," "the fullest education," "the fairest opportunity," "the cleanest philanthropy," "the sanest religion," and, in fact, "potentially, the salvation of the world." Why business is the "sanest religion" is vaguely explained, but it has to do with the fact that "the only ripened fruits of creeds are deeds." Why it is the "finest game" is explained in terms of the traditional ideals of the success cult:

> The rewards are for everybody, and all can win. There are no
> favorites—Providence always crowns the career of the man
> who is worthy. And in this game there is no "luck"—you have
> the fun of taking chances but the sobriety of guaranteeing
> certainties. The speed and size of your winnings are for you
> alone to determine. . . .[6]

Unabashed efforts were made on both sides to capitalize on the alliance between business and religion. The Swedish Immanuel Congregational Church in New York, for instance, was reported to have offered to those who made substantial financial contributions "an engraved certificate of investment in preferred capital stock in the Kingdom of God," and a Metropolitan Casualty Insurance Company pamphlet, *Moses, Persuader of Men,* described Moses as "one of the greatest salesmen and real-estate promoters that ever lived" and as a "Dominant, Fearless, and Successful Personality in one of the most magnificent selling campaigns that history ever placed upon its pages."[7] Proof that a large segment of the public could respond warmly to this kind of banality is the fact that the book which epitomized the efforts to associate business and religion, Bruce Barton's *The Man Nobody Knows* (1924), was the best seller in nonfiction for 1925 and 1926. In this life of Christ, Barton attempts to magnify Christ's appeal by describing him as a successful business executive. Rejecting the interpretation of Christ that portrays him as pale, weak, and delicate, Barton uses the magic language of the myth of success to transform Jesus into a magnetic and irresistibly inspiring character. In accordance with the Horatio Alger formula, he describes Christ as "a poor boy, growing up in a peasant family, working in a carpenter shop" until his ambition was awakened and he "picked up twelve men from the bottom ranks of business and forged them into an organization that conquered the world." Barton exclaims that "Stripped of all dogma, this is the grandest achievement story of all!"[8] The book's chapter headings sum up Barton's interpretation of Jesus as a successful businessman: The Executive; The Outdoor Man; The Sociable Man; His Method; His Advertisements; The Founder of Modern Business; The Master. Barton deemphasizes Christ's uniqueness and equates his "divinity" with that of other successful men who have started humbly and, through "the eternal miracle"—the awakening of the inner consciousness of power—discovered that their lives "might be bigger than [their] fathers'." God had spoken to Jesus, it is true. "But to *every* man of vision the Clear Voice speaks; there is no great leadership where there is not a mystic."[9] The influence of Emerson, whom Barton quotes throughout the book, is clear. As earlier mind-power inspirationalists had done, Barton takes the Emersonian concept of an indwelling spiritual presence and distorts it into an ideology of success. The potential divinity within all men is translated into practical terms and becomes a source of power which can be used by ambitious men to fashion successful careers.

Barton's philosophy of success reflects some of the newer ingredients in the success myth, particularly the impact of twentieth-century psychology, but it also has a clear attachment to earlier ideals. He attributes to Christ an ingratiating personality and a shrewd perception of people. But above other factors he emphasizes Jesus' passionate devotion to the ideal of

service—the same ideal that so many nineteenth-century advocates of
success had used to justify the veneration of individual acquisitiveness.
As Barton characterizes Jesus, he is essentially, to use David Riesman's
concepts,[10] an inner-directed man, though in several respects the characterization reflects the emphasis on other-direction that became increasingly apparent in the twenties and thirties. Barton's Christ is other-directed
in his sociability and skill in handling people. He is described as "the most
popular dinner guest in Jerusalem," a jolly-good-fellow capable of being
the life of the party. His first miracle, Barton says, was to make wine out
of water at a wedding feast when the wine ran out, thus winning friends
and proving his conviviality. If Christ was a sociable man, he was also
"The great advertiser of his day," a man of remarkable persuasive powers
who was particularly skilled in appealing to basic human emotions by
means of simple stories or parables. Barton places more emphasis, however,
on Christ's inner-direction. He portrays Him as a magnetic and aggressive
man, having a sublime disregard of public opinion as "all achieving characters
do" and constantly shocking His followers by His unconventionality. His
motto, Barton suggests, might well have been, "Never explain; never retract;
never apologize; get it done and let them howl."[11]

    In his final chapter, Barton pays homage to the Protestant ethic by
arguing that business *is* religion. Literally interpreting Christ's statement
"Wist ye not that I must be about my father's *business*?" to support his
argument, Barton explains that there is no difference between business
enterprise and religious work. Business activities, he says, are not selfish,
but a part of God's plan for the world. "Thus *all* business is his Father's
business. All work is worship; all useful service prayer. And whoever works
wholeheartedly at any worthy calling is a co-worker with the Almighty
in the great enterprise which He has initiated but which He can never finish
without the help of men."[12]

Success Formulas in Popular
Magazine Stories

    Apologists for business and self-styled authorities on success, like Barton,
were in their glory in the twenties. At the same time the mass-circulation
magazines suggest that the devotion to business success and prosperity
was a widespread popular obsession in the twenties and not a phenomenon
limited to the realm of business. Articles on successful men and on how

to succeed are extremely common, but the obsession with material success is shown more indirectly and interestingly in the fiction that occupied much of the space in the popular magazines. Almost all the stories in my sampling are somehow concerned with economic success, and the majority of them have some problem involving success in a career as a major theme. The heroes cover a fairly wide range of occupations, but almost half of them are successful businessmen or aspire to be in the future. By far the most common kind of happy ending in the stories is one in which the hero is rewarded with material success. Sometimes the material reward is accompanied by other rewards such as love, prestige, or contentment, but it seems that economic success must be present as a kind of minimum requirement before any other kind of reward can be fully realized or enjoyed.

A typical formula used in the stories follows the outlines of the conventional rags-to-riches myth, that favorite American fairy tale which panders to the dreams of the reader by showing how success can come even to the most humble. The details vary but the formula is essentially the same in story after story. In one example a flunky in a movie studio with a great ambition to be a movie magnate is given the opportunity to act temporarily as general manager after the old manager is fired. He shows a flair for the job and eventually gets it.[13] In another story the hero is a humble tailor who unexpectedly learns that he is an English earl. He disapproves of the aristocracy and is terrified at the prospect of living as a nobleman. But the author satirizes his foolish hesitation and provides the story with a happy ending in which the character finally accepts his new status and goes to England.[14] The childlike, fairy-tale atmosphere created in these stories is even more obvious in "No Questions Asked," a story in which a struggling young Broadway actress is preyed upon by an evil stock-market speculator who uses her hard-earned money in shady manipulative schemes. A young admirer, who understands the stock market, comes along and helps her double-cross the villain by selling when he advises her to buy. The villain is ruined; the heroine, suddenly rich, marries the "prince" and escapes to France where they live gloriously "with all kinds of money, and servants, and pleasures . . . as rich Americans of that kind often do."[15] The greedy speculator is portrayed as the villain and the loser, but the extravagantly materialistic revels of the hero and heroine are fully approved. To the popular writers the fulfillment of the American dream means, above all else, the accumulation of money and the indulgence in pleasure.

It would be misleading to imply that "easy money" success based on luck is admired above other kinds of success in the popular stories. Actually, one of the most common morals in the stories is that lasting success will come only if one has the conventional, solid, middle-class virtues—ambition, aggressiveness, industriousness, and true ability rather than surface flash or big talk. The Puritan ideal of an honorable calling and the gospel of work that derives from it are reaffirmed frequently in the stories. If a character gets ahead in some worthwhile occupation, his success is generally a sure sign of his virtue. Rarely is a character portrayed as both successful and morally imperfect. Hard work and success are not only signs of virtue; they are redeeming influences which help to produce virtue. In one story based on this assumption, "Mart Gets an Even Break," an escaped criminal has settled in Wyoming with his wife and son—"Two poor humans . . . off here in a little shack under the sky with their kid trying to scrape themselves a livin' and get ahead." When the U.S. marshal who has come to arrest Mart finds that he "has settled down, hard working and steady and determined to amount to something," he decides not to arrest him for the old crime.[16] In this story there is a very real reward for hard work and getting ahead. The marshal seems much more impressed by Mart's material success than by any other signs of his reform. The character's economic success is ample proof of his moral regeneration.

Many of the stories are cautionary tales having as their theme the wrongness, even sinfulness, of not having any particular ambition. "Treasures," a story by Nelia White, dramatizes this moral in a typically heavy-handed way. A boy in his teens has vague dreams of discovering treasures in Mexico or South America, but he has no specific career in mind and no particular desire to work. Hoping to be free and independent, he plans to run away from home and merely drift until he discovers some goal or cause worth committing himself to. Before he can leave, however, his little blind brother falls down a bank, and the young hero rescues him. This incident awakens his sense of responsibility, and he decides that "he'd go to the city as his father wanted him to do, go into an office, learn to make a living right away—then he'd be able to take care of Peter better."[17] This is the same concession that Harold Krebs has to make in Hemingway's "Soldier's Home" ("He would go to Kansas City and get a job and she [his mother] would feel all right about it"),[18] but of course Hemingway's story questions the small-town, middle-class values that the popular-magazine story didactically affirms.

The hazards of insufficient ambition are frequently dramatized by means of a standard plot in which a character loses, or almost loses, a girl because of his lack of drive. In a typical rendering of this recurring plot, titled "A Combination That Couldn't Be Beaten," the action begins directly after the easygoing hero has experienced a business failure, a setback dreadful enough in itself but compounded by the fact that he knows the girl he wants to marry will reject him if he remains a failure. Worse still, his rival, much admired by the girl, is a model self-made man who talks in the clichés of a success manual and has a foolproof "system" for success. The only course open to the hero, if he wants to keep the girl, is to use his rival's system. He does so, and the girl decides that the "system," coupled with the hero's natural kindliness, is an unbeatable combination.[19] Occasionally, even the heroine must have strong ambition and an honorable calling before she can win the hero. "A Blossom in Waste Places," for instance, features a model and social butterfly in Manhattan, who becomes engaged to an ambitious young doctor. The engagement is broken off because he disapproves of the purposelessness of the heroine and her friends. Only after she decides to become a nurse can they be married, and by this time she has decided, " 'I think I want most—to go on with it [her nursing work] !' "[20] Not only has she found a useful "calling," but she has come to value it above even love and marriage. Contrary to the stereotyped conflict between a career and a marriage, her work makes marriage possible instead of clashing with it.

Generally, the tone of these stories in which the boy almost loses the girl is one of rather ominous warning. The reader is informed of what can be lost if the proper ambition is *lacking.* An equally familiar pattern, however, is one which emphasizes what is to be gained if the ambition is *present.* In the stories illustrating this pattern, the hero begins with the ambition but not with the girl, and the girl becomes his reward for turning ambition into success. As in Dreiser's *An American Tragedy* or almost any of Fitzgerald's works portraying the dream of success, the dreams of the popular-fiction heroes frequently focus on a Golden Girl who symbolizes all that is beautiful and glittering and desirable in the world. The typical Golden Girl story has a hero who is irresistibly attracted by the glitter of the girl and her world, but too poor to court her. One story of this type concerns a young accountant who has "two vaulting ambitions: One was to be office manager of the Goddard Manufacturing Company and to sit at a desk with a telephone and a fancy calendar. The other was to stand beside Gladys Marie Tobin and sniff gently of orange blossoms."[21] Characteristically, the two goals are inextricably interrelated; the young man must achieve the first, success in his job, before he can hope to achieve the second, a love affair with his dream girl. Of the two ambitions, the author apparently feels that the former is the more significant and interesting, for he focuses his plot around the hero's pursuit of economic success and ends the story before the love affair has a chance to develop. For the popular writer of the twenties, this emphasis represents the proper order of things. Success must precede love, and once the details of the successful career have been worked out, the details of the love affair can be taken for granted.

As many of Fitzgerald's works illustrate, it was possible to take the basic ingredients of the poor boy-dream girl formula and create out of them an intense dramatic conflict and even a sense of tragedy. But in the popular stories, the conflict is almost always resolved very simply and predictably. Occasionally, the glamour girl turns out to be either not so remotely above the hero's status after all or willing to come down to his level. Most often, the hero simply achieves material success and lays his spoils at the girl's feet, and she is his.

In a substantial majority of the popular stories, the fulfillment of the dream of success is simply a necessary condition for happiness, and the values clustered around the myth of success—ambition, hard work, money, mobility—are taken for granted. There are a few exceptions to this generalization. An occasional story raises questions about the propriety of the scramble for success and, thus, deserves credit for providing penetrating comments on a national obsession instead of merely adding to the mythology surrounding the pursuit of success and prosperity. One story, for instance, attacks the cult of prosperity through the characterization of a woman who longs with bitter jealousy for a new house like her friend's but who eventually comes to view all the straining for success and possessions as vicious and devouring, like "snarling, menacing animals."[22] Other stories follow Sinclair Lewis' lead in satirizing "boosterism," compulsive materialism, and other forms of Babbittry. A *Saturday Evening Post* story, for example, portrays a banker with a heart condition who is ordered to stop hustling and learn to enjoy himself, but finds it impossible to free his mind of business and financial matters even when he sets about planning a vacation trip. The author comments that "His idea of fun was to post the price of the stamps used in corresponding with the hotel keeper and cottage agents."[23] But such criticisms are infrequent, and as in the latter example, the satire is usually light. Popular stories which effectively and unequivocally attack the shallowness and banality of the cult of success are extremely rare in the twenties.

A stock situation in the stories is one in which the conflict is between love or family relations and the worship of success. This introduces an area in which one might expect a clear-cut rejection of the "bitch goddess success." But rarely does even love win an unqualified victory over material success. The resolution of the conflict between love and success is almost invariably a have-your-cake-and-eat-it-too resolution. Events are contrived so that in the end the hero can have both love and success. In one story, the businessman hero cannot even forget moneymaking long enough to propose. When he does work a proposal into a thirty-minute interval before a business trip, his intended bride refuses him. She objects that he is already married to his business and challenges him to prove his love by missing the train. He seems willing to do it, and this is enough for the heroine. She jerks him up, says he hasn't a minute to lose, sends him on his trip, and promises to be waiting when he returns.[24] The story is daring enough to suggest that it may sometimes be necessary to take a few minutes of time out of the business day to attend to matters of love, but it falls well short of presenting a true dilemma in which a character must live up to the consequences of a choice between love and business.

In another portrayal of the love-success conflict, titled "The Great Man's Son," the hero is living in the shadow of a very prominent father who "was so busy making himself a success that he forgot he ever *had* a son." The hero disappoints and almost loses his fiancée when, unable to reconcile himself to being the undistinguished son of a successful man, he begins to use the selfish methods his father had taught him. But he finally reneges on a shady land deal that would make his fortune because, he says, "I know what love is because I've had so little of it. It's worth whatever you have to pay for it."[25] Again, however, as in the preceding story, the story's happy ending is contrived so that the character can have both love and material success. In an ending reminiscent of a Horatio Alger novel, the hero is rewarded for his honesty and integrity by an appointment to a lucrative and prestigious government position. Thus, unscrupulous means of gaining success are condemned, but material success must ultimately be present as a reward. Love and personal integrity are important values in the story, but in the final analysis the author does not ask his readers to believe that love without material success would be sufficient to guarantee the character's happiness.

The overwhelming impression left by the popular fiction is not only that the subject of success had a vast appeal in the twenties but also that material success as the central American value was virtually never questioned with any depth or conviction. The magazine stories supplied the popular mind with a mythology of success different in some details but similar in basic outlook to the orthodox gospel of success preached by such men as Benjamin Franklin, Russell Conwell (*Acres of Diamonds*), Andrew Carnegie, Horatio Alger, and in the twenties, Roger Babson and Bruce Barton. The outlook is one of comfortable optimism and bourgeois materialism. That America is a land of opportunity where everyone's dream can be fulfilled is never questioned. That material success is equivalent to happiness is rarely questioned. That virtue, ambition, industry, and ability rather than self-interest, superior strength, and cunning are the keys to success is piously believed. That the pursuit of success could be shallow, standardized, and mechanical is never suggested as a possibility. That the successful businessman was the great benefactor of mankind is taken for granted.

Dreiser, Fitzgerald, and Lewis— an Ambiguous Response to the Dream

Clearly, the mythology of success reflected in the popular magazines contains much of the middle-class crassness and banality that the intellectuals and serious writers were so critical of or alienated from. Certainly the three novelists who treated the American dream most extensively in the twenties—Dreiser, Fitzgerald, and Lewis—portray a very different world from that of the popular fiction. And yet their very fascination with the subject suggests the powerful impact of this favorite American myth on their own imaginations. They find perversion and tragedy in the pursuit of the dream, but its attraction for them is too great to allow an unambiguous rejection of all that it represents.

Theodore Dreiser's preoccupation with the dream of success is no less obvious than that of the popular writers. While *An American Tragedy* is his most explicit and detailed comment on success in America, virtually all of his important novels touch on the theme in one way or another. A part of the reason, no doubt, is biographical. His early responses to life were being formed in the late-nineteenth century (he was born in 1871) when the myth of rags-to-riches success was most popular. Like Clyde Griffiths of *An American Tragedy,* he began to dream at an early age of escaping the life of poverty and misery that he was born into, and at the age of sixteen he followed the pattern of many a Horatio Alger hero when he went to the city to seek his fortune.[26] Later, after becoming successful in newspaper and magazine work, he contributed to our mythology of success as a free-lance writer who interviewed successful men and women and wrote stories about them for Orison Marden's magazine, *Success.*

While Dreiser's fascination with success is quite apparent in his novels, however, it is equally apparent that his conception of success and failure in America is far from the optimistic view of the Alger myth or the popular fiction of the twenties. His first novel, *Sister Carrie,* shocked and angered a complacent public by implicitly attacking one of its favorite pieties— the belief that success is assured by industry and virtue. Carrie moves from poverty to phenomenal success as an actress, but not because of virtue or persistent hard work; she has a desire for pretty things, luck, and a willingness to drift amorally into relationships with men who can help her. If her career dramatizes the possibilities for success open to the hopeful, the lucky, and the amoral, her condition at the end of the novel dramatizes the truth (similarly contrary to popular mythology) that material success is not necessarily equivalent to happiness. Carrie's values are the shallow ones of a success-oriented, materialistic society. Once material success is achieved in such a society, Dreiser suggests, there is nothing left, no further prize to strive for. For Carrie, all that remains are vague, empty dreams: "In your rocking-chair by your window, shall you dream such happiness as you may never feel."[27] The sympathy Dreiser betrays for his character, despite his effort to maintain the detachment of the naturalist, derives partially, no doubt, from his personal understanding of the difficulty of escaping the limitations of the values inherent in the dream of success.

What it means to fail in a society that worships success is shown by the contrast between Hurstwood's precipitous decline and the spectacle of Carrie's rise. Chance can bring bad luck as well as good, and one can suddenly become one of the weak in the struggle for survival. A starkly symbolic scene near the end of the book forces the reader to consider the careers of Hurstwood and Carrie in relation to each other. Hurstwood has been kicked into the slush while trying to get into Carrie's dressing room; he is seen lying under the glaring lights that spell her name. According to this dark vision of life in America, success means glamour, dazzle, and a suite in the Walforf, if not contentment, while failure means begging on the streets, misery, and death.

In *Jenny Gerhardt* Dreiser portrayed a generous and sensitive heroine who lacks Carrie's desire for material success. Dreiser's interest in the problem of success and failure in America is seen in the novel's contrast between the wealthy Kane family and the poverty-stricken Gerhardt family, but the dream of success is not the dominant motivating force in this work. In the Cowperwood novels, however, Dreiser returned to the theme of success with a hero who represents the aggressive and powerful rugged individualist par excellence. In *The Financier,* which treats Cowperwood's boyhood and early rise to wealth and prominence, Dreiser shows a fascination for the strong man who succeeds because of his superior toughness, cunning, and magnetism. Cowperwood frankly espouses the lobster-eat-squid morality of the social Darwinists, and it serves him well in the late nineteenth-century business world in which Dreiser places him. Once he has absorbed the lesson of the lobster and the squid, Cowperwood develops into a kind of superman who considers himself exempt from the ordinary standards of morality. By virtue of his shrewdness and magnetism, he moves confidently from financial conquest to sexual conquest to financial conquest. Against his vital, magnetic, amoral ambition, ordinary men can offer but trifling opposition. Dreiser's attitude toward these exploits is in large part one of fascination. He does not gloss over the hard facts of his hero's unscrupulous methods, and yet his admiration of Cowperwood's superior cunning and strength is sufficiently evident that the novel can be taken as essentially a celebration of business success. In *The Titan* Dreiser elevated Cowperwood to even greater heights of power and prestige, piling financial and sexual conquests on top of each other in what Stuart Pratt Sherman called a club-sandwich structure, and describing his hero along the way as a Prometheus, a Renaissance prince, a Hannibal, a colossus, and a "half-god or demi-gorgon." Having told this story of monumental achievement, Dreiser apparently did not know how to complete the Cowperwood saga, for he did not publish the final novel of the trilogy, *The Stoic,* until 1947.

In *An American Tragedy,* Dreiser left the robber baron hero and focused on a character type that he quite astutely considered more representative of the twentieth century—the white-collar hero. The era of the rise of individual entrepreneurs to personal ownership of large enterprises had given way to the complex bureaucracy of the corporation, making the Cowperwoods of America a phenomenon of the past. As C. Wright Mills has said, America had become by the middle decades of the twentieth century "a great salesroom, an enormous file, an incorporated brain, a new universe of management and manipulation."[28] Dreiser's white-collar hero, Clyde Griffiths, is no less dominated by the dream of success than Cowperwood is, but he is an ineffective as Cowperwood is effective. He lacks Cowperwood's ability and strength of character, as well as the vastness of his opportunities. The contrast between the two characters reflects a major shift in the mythology of success—one that had begun to appear in some of the how-to-succeed manuals and popular stories of the twenties but would become much more pronounced in the thirties and later with such works as Dale Carnegie's *How to Win Friends and Influence People* and Norman Vincent Peale's *The Power of Positive Thinking*. The shift is from an emphasis on domination through strength of character to an emphasis on manipulation through personality. The psychology of mental maneuvering and adjustment to others takes precedence over aggressive individual action. As Mills states it, "Now the stress is on agility rather than ability, on getting along in a context of associates, superiors and rules, rather than getting ahead across an open market; on who you know rather than what you know, on loyalty to your firm rather than personal entrepreneurship."[29]

Quite obviously Clyde Griffiths relies on personality rather than character, on getting along rather than getting ahead. He exemplifies Riesman's other-directed man while Cowperwood is the inner-directed hero. It is significant that while Cowperwood's lobster-eat-squid tactics bring him fabulous success, Clyde's career is a colossal botch. Clyde's first efforts to get ahead on his own end in disaster and failure. He is able to escape from the squalid life he has with his parents by getting a job as a bellboy in a hotel. But instead of working himself up from that position to a better one, as the hero of a popular-magazine story might, he becomes involved in a hit-and-run accident in which a little girl is killed. As a result he not only fails to advance his career, but is forced to flee the city. His first opportunity for real mobility comes not through what he knows or does, but through whom he knows—an uncle who owns a collar factory. He gets some acceptance in the social class above him not primarily by promotion in the factory and accumulation of money but by making himself agreeable and pleasant in manners. His real desire is to bypass the more demanding channels of success and advance himself socially and economically by marrying into a wealthy family. Throughout his scramble to improve himself, Clyde tends to relate monetary success with sexual success, and in the glittering and elusive person of Sondra Finchley, he sees the symbol of the glamorous life he wants for himself. As in many of Fitzgerald's stories as well as many of the popular magazine stories, there is an aura of romance surrounding the female embodiment of the protagonist's dream. She is the Golden Girl, intriguing, irresistibly enticing, and just out of reach. In Clyde's case, however, Sondra is not only a desirable object in her own right but also a means to a more important end. His marriage to Sondra would fulfill the dream of economic success that has dominated his life. In this version of the interrelation of material and sexual success, Dreiser seems intent on exploding the romantic myth of popular fiction in which the hero, through strength of character and his own persistent effort, raises himself to the Golden Girl's level. Dreiser creates instead a character who hopes that his ingratiating personality will make it possible for him to use the Golden Girl as a means of gaining other rewards.

These considerations lead to the crucial question of Dreiser's attitude toward his unfortunate character, toward the society in which the character grows up and which frustrates him so much, and particularly toward the dream that dominates his character's life. The term "tragedy" in the title can be interpreted in various ways. Does Dreiser mean to suggest that in the opulent twenties, when opportunities were supposed to be virtually unlimited, it was a tragedy for anyone to fail as Clyde does? Does he mean to criticize the rags-to-riches myth which is partly responsible for the intensity of Clyde's desires and consequently his sufferings? More broadly, does he mean to castigate the kind of capitalistic society in which a person can grow up with a set of values as shallow as Clyde's?

There is no question that the novel is to a certain extent an indictment of the American dream of success. But again Dreiser's ambivalent attitude toward the dream introduces an important complication. Clyde Griffiths is victimized by a society that produces aspirations which are not only shallow but often impossible to fulfill. Despite what Dreiser may have intended, however, the same fascination with success which led him to betray considerable admiration of his earlier successful characters causes him to despise Clyde Griffiths for his weakness and ineptitude. It is difficult not to get the impression that an individual, personal deficiency of character is the primary reason for Clyde's failure. Lacking the strength and ability of earlier Dreiser characters, he attempts precisely the sort of easy shortcuts to success, including his effort to marry Sondra, that the popular fiction moralizes against. No less self-interested than Carrie or Cowperwood, as his treatment of his family and Roberta indicates, he has limitations of imagination and will which ruin him. He yields to temptations (getting involved with Roberta, for instance) that could damage his career, and finds himself incompetent to handle the consequences. He is too devoted to his dream to marry Roberta when he gets her pregnant, and yet he can imagine no solution to the dilemma except abortion or murder. He has no moral scruples against abortion, but he is ineffectual in his efforts to arrange one. He is capable of coldly premeditating Roberta's murder, but incapable of either performing the act or taking decisive action to save Roberta once he has changed his mind.

In other words, he is a "born loser," a weakling, and thus can only be pitied or despised, not admired. This is not to say that Dreiser is totally unsympathetic toward Clyde or approving of the success-worshiping society in which Clyde fails. Indeed, in the early chapters of the novel particularly, Dreiser's sympathy with his character is the same kind of sympathy that he had for Carrie; in both cases it appears to derive from the projection of his own youthful dreams into the character. Furthermore, Dreiser was always sensitive to the human problems existing in a society which created aspirations that could not be realized and made promises that could not be kept. But this sympathy reflects only one side of Dreiser's ambivalent attitude toward American society and the American dream of success. He was also capable of saying, in the opulent twenties, "I like this sharp, grasping scheme of things. Plainly it produces all the fine spectacles I see." No other society was "so wonderful, so fully representative of the natural spirit of aspiration in man, his dreams, hopes, superior constructive possibilities."[30] When he wrote *An American Tragedy*, Dreiser was still too attracted to this version of the promises of America to attack America's cult of success unequivocally. The tragedy he portrays is not so much that Clyde is duped by his society into playing a foolish game that he cannot win, but that he plays the game so weakly and ineptly. In Clyde's situation, Frank Cowperwood would have played the game shrewdly and assured himself of victory. Thus, from one perspective the tragedy is that American society had stopped creating supermen like Frank Cowperwood and had started creating weaklings like Clyde Griffiths. To a large extent, it seems to me, Dreiser shares with the popular writers the assumption that the key to success is within the man, though he is not simpleminded enough to identify honesty, industry, and virtue as the personal qualities necessary for success.

One must certainly conclude that Dreiser was capable of perceiving and dramatizing much of the emptiness and tragedy inherent in the dream of material success. The vision he presents of American capitalistic society is often a dark one, in which the polarities of success and failure, luxury and poverty imply that success for some can come only at the expense of misery for others. His work repeatedly contrasts the fortunate with the unfortunate, the shrewd with the inept, the strong with the weak, the winners with the losers. Carrie and Cowperwood are spectacularly fortunate, but Hurstwood, Jennie Gerhardt, and Clyde Griffiths are pathetically unfortunate. In making the contrast, however, he does not lavish sympathy on the losers and heap contempt on the winners. He has the socialist's compassion for the downtrodden, but also the social Darwinist's admiration for the strong, the crafty, and the lucky who achieve success. His philosophical determinism led him to portray characters who are powerless to control their fate in an indifferent universe, but his imaginative sympathy with the myth of success caused him to praise those who were strong enough to make their own happiness. In a story titled "Free," published in 1918, Dreiser describes how his main character comes to the realization that

> Nature, unless it were represented by some fierce determination within . . . cared no whit for him or any other man or woman. Unless one acted for oneself, upon some stern conclusion nurtured within, one might rot and die spiritually. Nature did not care. "Blessed be the meek"—yes. Blessed be the strong, rather, for they made their own happiness.[31]

Here Dreiser suggests that to discount the part played by individual weaknesses is to falsely blame one's failure on an indifferent universe or on "society." To be a self-made man who forges his own happiness is not easy, the passage implies, but it is possible, and it depends on the character and will of the individual.

Thus, at least until after the crash of 1929, Dreiser did not totally reject the values associated with the myth of success. In his book, *Dreiser Looks at Russia,* published in 1928, many of his criticisms of Communism reflect his sympathy with the rags-to-riches view of success. He expresses the belief, for instance, that "the elimination of the old-time creative or constructive businessman, with all his self-interest and consequent industry, ingenuity, etc. . . . was likely to result in a kind of slowness" of development. About Moscow he says, "there appeared to me to be a kind of trudging resignation, based, I felt, on an absense of that 'kick' which lies, for so many, in the hope of financial advancement or dread of failure."[32] After the crash of 1929, Dreiser was less certain that the fear of failure was a healthy stimulant of productivity. But that is another story.

Like Dreiser, F. Scott Fitzgerald was concerned with the subject of success almost to the point of obsessiveness, and his response to the dream of success, like Dreiser's, was an ambivalent one. Less crudely than Dreiser perhaps but no less deeply, Fitzgerald was fascinated with wealth and success, and the theme of realizing a dream is found again and again in his novels and stories. But at the same time, Fitzgerald was acutely aware of the pernicious and illusory aspects of the dream, and he exposes these qualities more effectively, it seems to me, than Dreiser was ever able to.

Characteristically, Fitzgerald's fictional treatment of the myth of success corresponds to one of the recurring plot formulas in popular-magazine fiction. A poor but ambitious boy is attracted to a Golden Girl, and his efforts to improve his economic and social status are inseparably interwoven with his romantic quest of the girl. The dual theme of monetary and sexual success is prevalent in Dreiser's fiction also, as we have seen, but with a difference. Dreiser tended to think of sexual success in terms of conquest and mastery. Economic success provides his characters with the splendor to attract and master the sexual objects of their desires, or perhaps the same magnetism that brings economic success gives them an irresistible power over women. At any rate sexual transactions, like business transactions, involve one character's overpowering domination of another. Even Clyde Griffiths, the loser, has the stature to conquer and master the lowly Roberta, while he attempts to use Sondra as a means of achieving economic and social success. In Fitzgerald's fiction, sexual success is usually not a matter of conquest and mastery; the Fitzgerald hero *wins* the dream girl by achieving the economic success that makes him worthy of her.

Although *The Great Gatsby* is Fitzgerald's fullest and most suggestive treatment of this characteristic theme, versions of it are dramatized in several of his short stories written during the twenties. A very simple example is a story entitled "The Sensible Thing" (1924). The hero of the story, George O'Kelly, is poor but ambitious. One of his dreams is to be an engineer; another is to marry one of the dream girls that Fitzgerald evokes so frequently and so compellingly. When the story opens, she refuses to marry him because he is earning only forty dollars a week, and they part. A year later he returns, successful as an engineer, having "stumbled into two unusual opportunities." "In this short time he had risen from poverty into a position of unlimited opportunity," Fitzgerald says. But this success is not an end in itself. "There was no triumph, after all, without a girl concerned, and if he did not lay his spoils at her feet, at least he could hold them for a passing moment before her eyes."[33]

Up to this point, my terse account of "The Sensible Thing" resembles a synopsis of almost any Horatio Alger or *Saturday Evening Post* story. However, while the typical popular-magazine story ends happily with the hero's triumph, Fitzgerald's main interest is in the circumstances that follow his triumph. He echoes the formula of the fairy-tale success story up to its conclusion, but instead of living happily ever after, his characters find themselves disillusioned. In "The Sensible Thing," the hero returns with his spoils only to find that the freshness of his love is gone, and there is no spark left. He will marry the girl; yet in the process of realizing his dream, he has lost his youthful and romantic sense of its meaning. In telling the story, Fitzgerald treats summarily the details of how the hero works his way up to the dream girl's level. What he lingers on is the description of the original intensity of the dream and the contrasting disillusion when the dream becomes reality. The problem is the old one of how to enjoy the fruits of the dream once it has been realized. Fitzgerald understood, as had Dreiser, that the romantic pursuit of a dream can become an end in itself, a quest motivated by imaginary enticements whose glamour could never be matched in the real world. Alexis de Tocqueville had observed as early as the age of Jackson that for Americans the achieved goal is never as magical as the dream, and it is this truth that Fitzgerald dramatizes in "The Sensible Thing" and other works.

Fitzgerald returns to this same essential idea so frequently that the dream motif emerges as one of the dominant patterns in his fiction. In "Winter Dreams" his treatment of the theme is very similar to that in "The Sensible Thing." Again in the case of Dexter Green, dreams of romance and dreams of material and social success are closely interrelated. The glamorous and elusive Judy Jones is one of the catalysts in arousing Dexter's winter dreams, but she is not their only content. His dreams also involve accumulating money, and his success story, like George O'Kelly's, is narrated in two brief paragraphs which read like a success story in a popular magazine. After college, at the age of twenty-three, Dexter borrows a thousand dollars and buys a part ownership in a laundry. Having an abundance of American initiative and industry, he specializes in a process for washing woolen golf stockings without shrinking them. The result is that "Before he was twenty-seven he owned the largest string of laundries in his section of the country."[34]

Dexter's financial achievement does not end his dreaming and take the meaning out of his life because for years the glittering Judy Jones remains just beyond his reach, serving as an object on which he can focus his dreams. He never wins her, and eventually she marries someone else, but his disillusion does not come until he learns, by accident, that in the years since he has last seen her, her beauty has faded. This discovery takes the spark out of Dexter's life and leaves him without feeling: "A sort of dullness settled down upon Dexter. . . . The dream was gone. Something had been taken from him. . . . Even the grief he could have borne was left behind in the country of illusion, of youth, of the richness of life, where his winter dreams had flourished."[35] To Fitzgerald, life without a dream is scarcely worth living. The capacity for dreaming nurtured by a relatively open and fluid society is one of the features of the American character that Fitzgerald finds most appealing and interesting. But in the case of Dexter and other Fitzgerald heroes, there is tragedy inherent in the dream. Having focused his entire capacity for dreaming on the surface beauty of Judy Jones, eventually Dexter must face the inevitable truth that physical beauty, like other material things, is mutable. Her glitter, not any depth of character, has attracted him, and her glitter does not last. The implication is that the American attempt to combine idealism and materialism is destined to failure. Materialistic idealism does not work.

These stories demonstrate Fitzgerald's ability to begin with a situation which is commonplace in popular fiction and penetrate much more deeply into its implications than the popular writers do. But it is in *The Great Gatsby* that Fitzgerald makes his most probing analysis of the subject, and perhaps the most suggestive and artistically satisfying treatment of the American dream in all of American fiction. In Jay Gatsby, Fitzgerald has created a legendary character who must be viewed in relation to the American experience as a whole. Gatsby's leading traits are the characteristically American traits of innocence (even naïveté) and romantic idealism. He is a modern and extreme version of the American Adam, with "an extraordinary gift for hope, a romantic readiness" which controls all his actions and responses to life. Fitzgerald gives Gatsby a legendary, myth-

ological quality not only by associating him with great American myths
such as the Adamic myth and the success myth, but also by cloaking him
in mystery and leaving the outlines of his character somewhat hazy.
Gatsby's own distortions, along with the rumors about his past that
circulate among the party guests, have the effect of blurring his character
so that he comes across as half legend and half man. As a symbolic, mythological character, he serves as the vehicle through which Fitzgerald records
his ambivalent response to the American dream. The ambivalence is seen
in the fact that, while Gatsby is corrupted by the shallow materialism of
the dream, he is the only decent and halfway admirable major character
in the novel with the exception of the narrator. The Buchanans and the
party guests who sponge off Gatsby are "a rotten crowd"; he is "worth
the whole damn bunch put together."[36]

Fitzgerald emphasizes the fact that the content of Gatsby's dream is
materialistic and corrupt. Like Dexter, Gatsby has a goal beyond material
success, but that goal itself (Daisy) is symbolic of shallow, materialistic
glitter. Gatsby understands perfectly that the charm of Daisy's voice comes
from the fact that it is "full of money." Nick agrees, "that was it. I'd
never understood it before. It was full of money—that was the inexhaustible
charm that rose and fell in it, the jingle of it, the cymbals' song of it. . . .
High in a white palace the king's daughter, the golden girl. . . ."[37] Gatsby's
method of realizing his dream is no less corrupt than the content of the
dream itself. He cannot even be given credit for the open and honest
ruthlessness of the robber baron of a generation before him; his fortune
has come from bootlegging, gangsterism, and unexplained shady deals.
The extent of Gatsby's corruption of the ideal of the self-made man is
emphasized in the last chapter by the irony of his father's comment that
" 'Jimmy was bound to get ahead. He always had some resolves like this
or something.' " He has just shown Nick a daily "Schedule" and a list of
"General Resolves" that Gatsby had drawn up as a boy. Included are
resolves to save money, avoid wasting time, study needed inventions,
read one improving book or magazine per week, and conform to other
strictures modeled on the self-improvement regimens of Benjamin Franklin
or Andrew Carnegie.[38] The effect of Fitzgerald's use of these details is
to force the reader to view Gatsby's corrupt career in relation to the tradition of self-improvement that extends deep into the American past.

Looked at from a slightly different angle, Gatsby can also be taken to
represent an American idealism that, paradoxically, has grown both illusory
and materialistic. In a passage connecting Gatsby to his transcendental

roots, Fitzgerald describes Gatsby as springing "from his Platonic conception of himself." He "invented just the sort of Jay Gatsby that a seventeen-year-old boy would be likely to invent, and to this conception he was faithful to the end."[39] He is a self-made man, then, in the full sense of the term. The tragedy is that his imagination has had such meager nourishment that he has been able to invent nothing more substantial than a Gatsby surrounded by shallow, insincere people and by false, glittering things, including imitative architecture and real but unread books. It is an idealism bounded by the possession of material things. In another sense, Gatsby's idealism is so naïve as to be totally detached from reality. Not only does he misjudge Daisy, but, more importantly, he is under the illusion that he and Daisy can step out of time and not only recapture the past but even do away with what has happened between past and present. Not content to recapture the relationship that he had established with Daisy five years earlier, he wants Daisy to wipe out four years by telling Tom she never loved him. To Nick's warning that you can't repeat the past, his only answer is an incredulous "Why of course you can!"[40] He sincerely believes he can remake the world as well as himself. This colossal optimism is in a sense a simple logical extension of Gatsby's self-creation; if it is possible to create oneself, it should be possible to create the kind of world one wants. Thus, having succeeded in creating himself, Gatsby assumes that he can also make the world conform to his idealized version of things as they should be.

And yet, in spite of the fact that his dreams become grotesquely corrupted, it is his very capacity for dreaming that makes Gatsby superior to the other characters. As a representative of the American newly rich self-made man, he has a sense of direction that solidifies his character. Surrounding the Buchanans, who represent the old, idle rich, is an aura of European decadence even though, like Gatsby, they are originally from the West. Along with their wealth, they have inherited a lack of direction and a certain ennui, the opposite of Gatsby's "heightened sensitivity to the promises of life." They have been cheated of the values inherent in the process of earning their own money. In other words they suffer, as do other Fitzgerald characters (cf. "The Rich Boy," for example), from what has been called the problem of the second generation—the problem of adjusting to inherited wealth in a culture that places a premium on making one's own fortune. It is their arrogance and lack of responsibility, however, that Fitzgerald considers most damning: "They smashed up things and creatures and then retreated back into their money or their vast carelessness . . . and let other people clean up the mess they had made. . . ."[41] In *Gatsby,* as in the sharply satirical story "The Diamond as Big as the Ritz," there is little ambiguity in Fitzgerald's treatment of the rich

Through this story of Jay Gatsby, then, Fitzgerald has made a major comment on the American dream of success and the cluster of values associated with it. He hints at some of the Puritan and Transcendental roots of the dream and dramatizes its materialistic corruption in the twentieth century. And yet, in spite of the corruption and the unviable combination of romantic idealism and crass materialism represented in Gatsby, Fitzgerald is clearly sympathetic to him in the end. He cannot ultimately reject the major impulse at the heart of Gatsby's character, that "heightened sensitivity to the promises of life" which comes in large part from an absolute belief in the possibilities open to the individual in the New World. The rhetoric of Fitzgerald's final page is almost spellbinding:

> And as the moon rose higher the inessential houses began to melt away until gradually I became aware of the old island here that flowered once for the Dutch sailors' eyes— a fresh, green breast of the new world. Its vanished trees . . . had once pandered in whispers to the last and greatest of all human dreams; for a transitory enchanted moment man must have held his breath in the presence of this continent, compelled into an aesthetic contemplation he neither understood nor desired, face to face for the last time in history with something commensurate to his capacity for wonder.[42]

Here Fitzgerald connects Gatsby with the very earliest American past. Gatsby has inherited the capacity for wonder inspired by the New World. But by his time the world he finds himself in is corrupt and not new, not commensurate to his capacity for wonder. He is the American Adam thrown out of the garden of Eden into a distorted and grotesque world of materialism and decadence.

In turning to another important social novelist of the twenties, Sinclair Lewis, we would perhaps expect to find an archenemy of the American myth of success. On the surface, Lewis seems to be one of our most scathing critics of middle-class values, an iconoclast of the Mencken type, a mythsmasher. But as Maxwell Geismar has pointed out, while Lewis appears to be critical of the middle-class society he portrays in his novels, he is actually so at one with it that he can only briefly escape from its fundamental values, pieties, and illusions.[43] One test of the validity of this interpretation of Lewis is his treatment of the theme of success. In several novels, he attacked many of the stupidities and excesses inherent in the cult of success, and yet his criticism is never the kind that could rock the foundations of the traditional ideal of the American self-made man. Indeed, in *Dodsworth,* his most extensive treatment of the success theme, the self-made man has his full sympathy.

It could be said that a part of the burden of *Babbitt, Arrowsmith,* and *Elmer Gantry* is that the drive toward material success gets in the way of personal fulfillment, integrity, and any really worthwhile achievement. A true scientist, Lewis says over and over in *Arrowsmith,* must devote himself to science, not to success. Dr. Max Gottlieb, the model of the dedicated scientist, tells Arrowsmith:

> To be a scientist is like being a Goethe: it is born in you. Some-
> times I t'ink you have a liddle of it born in you. If you haf, there
> is only one t'ing—no, there is two t'ings you must do: work
> twice as hard as you can, and keep people from using you. I will
> try to protect you from Success. It is all I can do.[44]

In *Elmer Gantry* those who make a "success" out of the clerical life, the "spiritual magnates" who earn huge salaries as pastors of large congregations, come in for Lewis' most biting sarcasm. It is the commercialization of so many aspects of life that Lewis objects to in these and other works.

In *Babbitt,* this commercialization and the frantic struggle of the up-and-coming middle-class businessman for more possessions, more rank, more camaraderie are effectively satirized. Except for his short-lived rebellion, when he decides to quit the rat race and become a man instead of a machine, Babbitt gives up everything for material success and social rank. He can have no security because of the constant need to make more money and become accepted by the social class above him. At one point, as he approaches his office, he finds himself walking faster and faster, muttering, " 'Guess better hustle.' " Lewis adds, "All about him the city was hustling, for hustling's sake. . . . Men who made five thousand, year before last, and ten thousand last year, were urging on nerve-yelping bodies and parched brains so that they might make twenty thousand this year."[45] In this atmosphere of feverish hustling, which Lewis intensifies as Babbitt

moves toward his revolt, personal relationships, self-knowledge, and spiritua
contentment all take second place to boosterism and success.

In a sense, then, Babbitt is a victim of his own success, and his abortive
rebellion against his hectic and unsatisfying life indicates that he realizes
the fact (however vaguely) himself. Lewis describes Babbitt's existence
as a standardized, machinelike conformity to a materialistic society:

> He beheld, and half admitted that he beheld, his way of life as
> incredibly mechanical. Mechanical business—a brisk selling of
> badly built houses. Mechanical religion—a dry, hard church,
> shut off from the real life of the streets, inhumanly respectable
> as a tin hat. Mechanical golf and dinner parties and bridge and
> conversation. Save with Paul Riesling, mechanical friendships—
> back slapping and jocular, never daring to essay the test of
> quietness.[46]

In describing the effects of creeping mechanization, Lewis is dealing with
one of the recurring themes of the serious writers in the twenties, though
the subject almost never appears in the popular fiction. In *Poor White*
(1920) Sherwood Anderson had written, as he phrased it, "a novel of the
coming of industrialism" in which the hero is, even more literally than
Babbitt, a victim of his own success since as an inventor he actually helps
to create the industrial world that he later finds so barren. In *Poor White,*
the emphasis is on the transition from an agrarian to an urban-industrial
society; in *Babbitt* Lewis produced what has been called "the first America
novel of any importance to regard industrialism not as a monstrous encroac
ing force . . . but simply as an enveloping all-pervasive condition of modern
life."[47] Gloomier and more deterministic in tone are two important plays
of the decade, Elmer Rice's *The Adding Machine* and Eugene O'Neill's
The Hairy Ape, in which industrialism is not only an all-pervasive condition
but one which reduces human beings to the level of ciphers or caged anima
Rice's Zero discovers that the impersonal corporation can replace him with
an adding machine, while O'Neill's Yank eventually is seen as a lost and
alienated creature, caged in by steel like an ape in a zoo.

If Babbitt is not as completely victimized and trapped as Zero or Yank,
he is nevertheless a far cry from the superman who molds and controls
his destiny. Like Dreiser's Clyde Griffiths, Babbitt represents the small
man hustling for success. He is not the complete loser that Clyde Griffiths

is, but he is a middle-class hero who lacks the magnetic and awesome strength of character usually attributed to the old entrepreneurial hero. Certainly he is a clear example of the shift in emphasis from character to personality, from inner direction to other direction. He is so worried about getting along and being well liked that even his employees frighten him. The contrast between him and what Lewis calls "those Victorian financiers who ruled the generation between the pioneers and the brisk 'sales engineers' " is made by Lewis himself through the character of Eathorne. In the face of the dignity and the power of this old plutocrat, even Babbitt doubts himself and begins to wonder if hustling and booster-ism are the true keys to success.

In several of his novels of the twenties, then, Lewis does attack the problem of conformity to a set of materialistic values which emphasize hustling for success above all else. Also, a theme running through almost all his novels is that the large organization is a corrupting influence be-cause it encourages the pursuit of wealth and power and destroys the integrity of the individual. Among the novels of the twenties, this theme is particularly apparent in *Arrowsmith* and *Elmer Gantry*. However, Lewis' satiric criticism of boosterism, conformity, the scramble for money, and other middle-class failings represents anything but an unequivocal rejection of the American dream of success. He by no means strikes at the foundations of the American capitalistic system. As he admitted himself, he was no more of a radical than George Horace Lorimer of *The Saturday Evening Post*. In an article for *The Nation*, which he titled "Mr. Lorimer and Me," Lewis professed half seriously to be essentially in accord with the values of Lorimer and the Babbitts:

> I am frequently credited with being the worse crab, next to
> Father Mencken and Father Nathan, in our Beloved States.
> I am informed by innumerous preachers and editorial writers
> that I'm all for anarchism and bombing and general hell to pay.
> Actually, I like the Babbitts, the Dr. Pickerbaughs, the Will
> Kennicotts, and even the Elmer Gantrys rather better than
> anyone else on earth. They are good fellows.[48]

Lewis could feel affection for the Babbitts and still see through their foibles, of course, but he portrays their foibles as an insider rather than an outsider.

The values he would substitute for the middle-class inanities he describes are not new or foreign, but deeply rooted in the American traditions of self-reliance, inventiveness, independence, honest work, and individualism, all of which are central to the myth of the self-made man. In describing the hustling of the Babbitts, he laments not that the individualistic pursuit of success is a destructive force, but that individual initiative and self-realization are curtailed by mechanical conformity and by the organization. He implies that the spurious values—the other-direction, the conformity, the boosterism—created by the burgeoning mechanical-industrial-corporate system are unfortunate departures from the old tradition of self-reliant individualism.

At the end of the twenties, Lewis created a character who serves as a standard by which to measure his Babbitts. Significantly the standard, Sam Dodsworth, is the prototype of the American self-made man. He is the entrepreneur, the big businessman who has risen above the petty strivings of the Babbitts.

With his sympathetic portrayal of Sam Dodsworth, Lewis clearly aligned himself with the solid middle-class virtues most emphasized in the inspirational literature and popular fiction of the twenties. Sam is not only industrious and dependable but also inventive and pioneering. He succeeds in the American way, starting not at the bottom but, nevertheless, as a relatively poor man. He is a producer rather than a manipulator or an advertiser, a rugged individualist rather than an organization man. He has the entrepreneurial willingness to gamble, and the gamble he takes in going into the Revelation Automobile Company pays off in a substantial fortune largely because, being a dreamer, he creates original designs for automobiles. His work is his religion and he takes great pride in it until a corporation, again the villain, absorbs his company and leaves him with the feeling that he is an unnecessary appendage. Dodsworth has his faults, and it is clear that his success is responsible for some of his limitations, but by and large he is a sympathetic character, representing Lewis' reaffirmation of the worth of the self-made man.

The main problem Lewis analyzes in the novel is how to enjoy the fruits of economic success once it has been achieved. Dodsworth has earned his fortune honestly by his own effort, but he has not prepared himself to live with the leisure time and the money made possible by his success. He is a latter-day Christopher Newman (and the novel is similar in many ways to James's *The American*) who retires before he reaches fifty and

HUGH STEPHENS LIBRARY
STEPHENS COLLEGE
COLUMBIA, MISSOURI

goes to Europe to learn to live. His devotion to moneymaking has left him intellectually impoverished, and his flighty, pseudo-sophisticated wife, Fran, never lets him forget it. He says at one point, "I'm a good citizen. I've learned that Life is real and Life is earnest and the presidency of a corporation is its goal. What would I be doing with anything so degenerate as enjoying myself?"[49] In Europe, separated from his work and having nothing but Fran to absorb him, Sam at first feels that he has no reason for being. Like Dreiser's Carrie Meeber or one of Fitzgerald's characters, he feels a vague discontent and a certain disillusion after realizing his dream of success.

However, Dodsworth, like Christopher Newman, is sensitive and intelligent, and he is eventually capable of absorbing what Europe has to teach him without losing his own integrity and sense of values. His wife, who considers herself European and constantly reminds him that he is a plodding businessman, looks for sophistication, art, and gracious living in Europe but finds only pseudo-sophistication, decadence, and corruption. Sam ultimately rejects her, and the reader knows that, in his solidity of character, he is immeasurably superior to his shallow wife and her European friends. He learns much from Europe about how to enjoy life, and he learns to place moneymaking in its proper perspective, but he by no means rejects his American values in favor of European values. He achieves a synthesis of character which gives him fulfillment and self-assurance. He is left at the end planning to marry an American widow living in Europe. They will return to the Midwest to live, and Sam will occupy himself with a creative moneymaking scheme involving the building of tasteful and unpretentious garden suburbs, which he hopes will contribute to the beauty of America. This resolution of Sam's conflict is strikingly similar to the characteristic resolution found in the popular fiction of the day, in which ultimately the character enjoys both material success and other rewards. Sam has overcome some of the limitations of his narrow worship of success, but ironically he is rewarded at the end by the possibility of more work and more material achievement. Through his characterization of Dodsworth, Lewis reaffirms rather than rejects the commitment to individualism, work, and material productiveness which has always been at the heart of the American dream.

Thus, while Lewis presents a dark view of the impoverishment resulting from a mechanical, standardized worship of material success, he does not reject the fundamental values associated with the self-made-man concept of

162380

success. On the contrary, the main problem he portrays is that of the individual becoming swallowed up in the complex machinery of twentieth-century corporate life. The individualism, the initiative, the inventiveness of the old entrepreneurial type, like Dodsworth, are rare but highly desirable qualities in the shallow, mechanical world Lewis describes.

It seems clear that in the boom years before the crash of 1929, the devotion of Americans to material success and prosperity was in many ways more open and less qualified than at any time in our history. The alliance between business and government, the idolization of the businessman, the popularity of success prophets like Bruce Barton, and the outpouring of success stories (fictional and nonfictional) in popular magazines suggest that Americans had forgotten other values in their worship of material success. It is not surprising that the period produced tireless critics and satirists of the culture as well as a lost generation of writers and intellectuals who were so alienated from their society that they became expatriates. To a large extent the literary renaissance which came to fruition in the twenties was animated by a spirit of rebellion and alienation. Sherwood Anderson, T. S. Eliot, Ernest Hemingway, William Faulkner, John Dos Passos, Sinclair Lewis, F. Scott Fitzgerald, H. L. Mencken, E. E. Cummings, Eugene O'Neill, and many other writers derive much of their power from a profound sense of disillusionment with their culture's materialism, philistinism, bourgeois conformity, and spiritual sterility.

At the same time it is not really surprising, considering the importance of the myth of success as a vehicle for conveying and perpetuating a major set of cultural values, that the three important social novelists emphasized here reflect the influence of the myth on their own imaginations. The fact that the three were so deeply interested in economic success as a literary theme suggests a strong personal attraction to the rags-to-riches tradition, as well as a realization that the question of success is of central importance in fiction which treats social life in America. Certainly the differences between these novelists and the specialists in popular-magazine fiction who did so much to perpetuate the myth of success should not be slighted. The popular writers treat the theme of success in a stereotyped way, didactically reinforcing the conventional pieties regarding ambition, work, business, and the gospel of prosperity. On the other hand, the serious writers, as we have seen, found crudeness, conflict, perversion, and tragedy in the American dream and treated the subject with a depth and complexity not to be expected in the popular fiction. Whereas to

Dreiser material success is a result of luck or superior strength and shrewdness, the popular stories reflect the conventional assumption that success
results from ambition, industry, and virtue. Whereas Fitzgerald portrays
the disillusionment that can come after the dream of material success and
romance has been realized, the popular stories seldom betray a doubt
that material success is the key to happiness and complete contentment.
Whereas Lewis satirized the Babbitts who allowed themselves to become
trapped in an empty and mechanical scramble for success, the popular
stories rarely portray the American businessman as anything less than a
dignified and admirable hero. Yet, despite these differences, it is difficult
not to be impressed by the obsessions, values, and assumptions which
these major novelists share with the popular writers of the decade.

In a sense the specific keys to success urged in the popular-magazine
fiction of the twenties are even more traditional and conservative than
those of the popular philosophers of success like Bruce Barton. Barton,
as we have seen, emphasizes the traditional ideals of service, individual
achievement, and hard work, reaffirming the Protestant ethic to the
point of insisting that business *is* religion. But he also reflects the influence
of the new psychological orientation toward success—at least to the extent
that he blends an other-directed emphasis on personality with a more
traditional, inner-directed emphasis on strong character. This contradictory
mixture of other direction and inner direction was typical of many inspirational works of the post-World War I period. The growing pressures
toward conformity to the corporation encouraged the newer emphasis on
self-manipulation and adjustment to others, and yet the inner-directed
rugged individualist could still be venerated as the creator of prosperity.
Despite the ambivalence of some success writers, however, the popular-
magazine fiction of the decade was unequivocal in its emphasis on the
time-honored character qualities of ambition, industry, and individual
self-assertion.

As we shall see in later chapters the business collapse and extended
Depression following these prosperous years helped to change many of
the emphases and undermine many of the values associated with the myth
of success. But an interesting phenomenon of the thirties was the attempt,
particularly in popular literature, to perpetuate or reaffirm traditional
faiths concerning success even as actual conditions widened the gap
between myth and reality and rendered the dream more illusory. It is this
reaffirmation that will be developed in the next chapter.

Notes

1. *Nation's Business,* XIV (July, 1926), 120; XIII (November, 1925), 52.
2. *American Industries,* XXV (October, 1924), 7.
3. Warren G. Harding, "Business Sense in Government," *Nation's Business,* VIII (November, 1920), 13-14.
4. Quoted in William Allen White, *A Puritan in Babylon: The Story of Calvin Coolidge,* p. 253.
5. Herbert Hoover, *American Individualism,* p. 36.
6. Edward Earle Purinton, "Big Ideas from Big Business," *Independent,* April 16, 1921, pp. 375-76.
7. Quoted in Frederick Lewis Allen, *Only Yesterday,* pp. 178, 180.
8. Bruce Barton, *The Man Nobody Knows,* p. 8.
9. Ibid., pp. 12, 17-18.
10. See David Riesman, Nathan Glazer, and Reuel Denney, *The Lonely Crowd,* pp. 13-20.
11. Ibid., p. 76.
12. Ibid., p. 179.
13. George R. Chester, "The Boy Wonder," *Saturday Evening Post,* May 26, 1923, pp. 8-10, 130.
14. Don Marquis, "Once an Englishman," *Saturday Evening Post,* Oct. 12, 1929, pp. 19, 90, 94, 99.
15. George K. Turner, "No Questions Asked," *Liberty Magazine,* Aug. 15, 1925, pp. 8-13.
16. William D. Pelley, "Mart Gets an Even Break," *American Magazine,* Nov., 1925, pp. 23-25, 90.
17. Nelia White, "Treasures," *American Magazine,* Jan., 1927, pp. 44-47, 143.
18. *In Our Time,* p. 101.
19. C. H. Markey, "A Combination That Couldn't Be Beaten," *American Magazine* April, 1923, pp. 31-33, 168-72.
20. Alice G. Steele, "A Blossom in Waste Places," *American Magazine,* Aug., 1920 pp. 57-59, 157-62.
21. Everett Rhodes Castle, "Greenback Luck," *American Magazine,* April, 1924, p. 22.
22. Bess Streeter Aldrich, "The Nicest House in Town," *American Magazine,* Feb., 1923, pp. 40-42, 94.
23. William Allen White, "Teaching Perkins to Play," *Saturday Evening Post,* Aug. 6, 1921, pp. 12-13, 69.
24. Walter Raleigh, "Only a Matter of Minutes," *Liberty Magazine,* Dec. 5, 1925, pp. 51-53.
25. Holworthy Hall, "The Great Man's Son," *American Magazine,* Nov., 1921, pp. 21-23, 119.
26. Kenneth S. Lynn develops the Algerlike quality of Dreiser's own early career in his *The Dream of Success: A Study of the Modern American Imagination.*
27. Theodore Dreiser, *Sister Carrie,* p. 554.

28. C. Wright Mills, *White Collar: The American Middle Class*, p. 259.
29. Ibid., p. 263.
30. Quoted in Lynn, p. 68.
31. Theodore Dreiser, "Free," *Saturday Evening Post*, March 16, 1918, p. 90.
32. Quoted in Lynn, p. 70.
33. *The Stories of F. Scott Fitzgerald*, ed. Malcolm Cowley, p. 154.
34. Ibid., p. 131.
35. Ibid., p. 130.
36. F. Scott Fitzgerald, *The Great Gatsby*, p. 154.
37. Ibid., p. 120.
38. Ibid., pp. 174-75.
39. Ibid., p. 99.
40. Ibid., p. 111.
41. Ibid., pp. 180-81.
42. Ibid., p. 182.
43. Maxwell Geismar, *The Last of the Provincials*, p. 72.
44. Sinclair Lewis, *Arrowsmith*, p. 291.
45. Sinclair Lewis, *Babbitt*, p. 155.
46. Ibid., p. 234.
47. Michael Millgate, *American Social Fiction: James to Cozzens*, p. 129.
48. Sinclair Lewis, "Mr. Lorimer and Me," *Nation*, CXXVII (July 25, 1928), 81.
49. Sinclair Lewis, *Dodsworth*, p. 32.

2 / Dream or Fantasy: The Depression Widens the Gap Between Popular Myth and Reality

In the twenties the widespread devotion to the cult of success was often incredibly naïve and crass. But it was understandable, in part at least, in terms of the prosperity of the period. It was a time when the myth of success seemed to be supported by economic realities, or at least when disparities between myth and reality were not superficially obvious to the ordinary citizen. In the thirties, the grim realities touched personally large numbers of people from all classes. Within a year after the crash, every fourth factory worker in Muncie, Indiana (the Lynds' Middletown), was jobless, and throughout the decade the number of unemployed in the nation ranged, according to estimates, somewhere between 8 and 20 million. Millions of investors lost their savings, businessmen went bankrupt by the thousands, and farmers, having fared poorly even in the twenties, lost their land as mortgages were foreclosed. For millions, the real struggle was not to "get ahead" and climb the ladder of success, but to find some kind of job and ward off starvation. With the stock-market crash and the collapse of businesses and banks, the spectacle of riches-to-rags failure was much more dramatically apparent than rags-to-riches success. In fact, events seemed almost calculated to destroy the very faiths that were most fundamental to the traditional myth of success. Industry didn't do any good if one couldn't get work. Thrift didn't do any good if one's savings were lost in a bank failure. Scraping together the capital and the nerve to launch a business in the best enterprising American tradition didn't do any good if small businesses were the first to succumb to the Depression. In general, Depression conditions seemed to negate the assumption that young men of ambition and industry were sure to succeed, that poverty was a result of laziness or incompetence and could best be relieved by private charities, that America's business leaders were the great benefactors of mankind, and that the American economic system was on a steady course of inspiring growth.

Given such a dramatic clash between an established myth and a contradictory reality, one might anticipate several possible reactions: (1) attempts to change external conditions so that they are in harmony with the myth; (2) rationalizations of external conditions so that they *appear* to be in harmony with the myth; (3) modification of the myth—including questioning, rethinking, or perhaps rejection of the values clustered around it—so that it is less at variance with realistic possibilities; (4) persistent efforts to reaffirm and perpetuate the myth despite the pressure of a contradictory reality. As myth and reality collided in the Depression years, all four of these responses played their part. There were countless schemes designed to improve existing conditions and reestablish America as a promised land. Huey Long's Share Our Wealth plan, Howard Scott's pseudo-scientific technocracy, Father Coughlin's Christian Front, and Dr. Townsend's Old Age Revolving Pension Plan were schemes that attracted numerous adherents by promising direct and immediate solutions to the discrepancy between the expectations of ordinary Americans and the reality they were living under in the Depression years. There were also many efforts, especially early in the Depression, to rationalize reality away by the insistence that the Depression was not serious and that prosperity was just around the corner. On the other side, the reality of the Depression certainly had its effects on the myth of success. As later chapters will show, the economic crisis led to significant disillusionment with many of the ideals associated with the dream of success and to modifications, adjustments, and new emphases of various sorts. If for several years the bitter realities of Depression conditions could be neither significantly changed nor rationalized away, then eventually there had to be some tarnishing of the image of success, some compensations for the loss of material success as a viable goal, or at least some scaling down of the goals in order to mitigate the discrepancy between expectation and fulfillment.

One of the predominant themes of the period, however, (and the subject of this chapter) was the persistent attempt to perpetuate the old myths and reaffirm the old values in the face of contradictory realities. Business publicists, political figures, movie makers, writers of how-to-succeed guidebooks, writers of popular fiction, and those who endlessly discussed economic conditions in the mass-circulation magazines often seemed, consciously or unconsciously, intent on preventing any erosion of faith in the standard American dream. The result was a widening of the gap between myth and reality. As popular writers tell and retell the old rags-to-riches story in the pages of magazines, which also have accounts of coal miners starving in Pennsylvania or ruined businessmen committing suicide, one gets the impression that the dream of success has become a fantasy, a fairy-tale escape mechanism, a secular ritual serving as a shield against hopelessness.

In a book titled *The Image, or What Happened to the American Dream,* Daniel Boorstin expresses the fear that America—the land of dreams where people have considered themselves free to aspire toward whatever their energies and abilities would allow—is becoming a land of illusions. The unprecedented opportunities of America have tempted us to confuse the visionary with the real, he says, and now we are threatened by a distinctly American menace, the menace of unreality: "We risk being the first people in history to have been able to make their illusions so vivid, so persuasive, so 'realistic' that they can live in them. We are the most illusioned people on earth."[1] Boorstin illustrates his generalizations primarily by reference to such contemporary phenomena as political image making, our preoccupation with projecting a favorable image of America among peoples abroad, and our worship of pseudo-heroes or "celebrities" who have been created by publicity men. However, his insights are also relevant to what happened in the thirties as the myth of success collided with the reality of an economic collapse. Rather than give up the extravagant expectations that had been nurtured in the prosperous twenties, many Americans respond to the Depression by escaping to a world of illusion. The American dream lost much of its solidity as a vision which could be compared to reality and took on the quality of an illusion which could be used to replace reality and protect one against it. Instead of serving as an inspiration for action, the image tended to become sufficient in itself. It is likely that the experience of the Depression, which created a conflict between dream and reality too severe for many Americans to accept realistically, did more than any other single event in recent history to develop the habit of thought that Boorstin refers to as "the menace of unreality."

This tendency to cling to old symbols regardless of their clash with reality was emphasized by Robert and Helen Lynd in *Middletown in Transition.* When they returned to Muncie, Indiana, for their 1935 follow-up study of "Middletown," they were, of course, deeply interested in what the Depression had done to Middletown values, or what they refer to as "the Middletown Spirit." The general conclusion they reached was that, despite some changes, the Middletown Spirit was essentially the same as in 1925: "Basically the texture of Middletown's culture has not changed. . . . Middletown is overwhelmingly living by the values by which it lived in 1925; and the chief additions are defensive, negative elaborations of already existing values," such as resistance to social legislation and fear of labor unions.[2] Discussing the dream of success specifically, they conclude that though the Depression had increased the "helpless commitment of a growing share of the population to the state of working for others with a diminished chance to 'get ahead,'" the myth of success had lost little of its potency in Middletown. "As symbol and reality draw thus apart," they observe, the situation would seem to be ripe for some deep questioning of the symbol. "But dreams, when they express urgent hopes and are heavily supported by the agencies of public opinion, have a habit of living on in long diminuendo into an era bristling with palpably contradictory realities. . . . So [Middletown] tends to be oblivious of the apparently fundamental alteration in the American ladder of opportunity."[3]

It is probable that, in their summary generalizations, the Lynds under-estimated the degree of change that the Depression had wrought in the Middletown outlook.[4] Yet it is difficult not to be impressed by the extent to which the myth of success was vitally alive in the popular mind during the years of relentless Depression. The dream may have slipped so out of tune with reality as to become mere fairy-tale wish fulfillment; it may have become perverted and distorted as popular writers grasped for any kind of success story they could find; but the strength of its endurance indicates that many Americans were not yet ready to give up their image of America as a land of opportunity or their faith in the established values associated with the myth of success. On a darker and more realistic note, serious writers of the thirties, very much aware of the discrepancy between the promise and the fulfillment of the American dream, portray the tragedy of characters who are victims of delusory and unrealizable dreams. This motif plays an important part in works by J. T. Farrell, John Steinbeck, Nathanael West, Eugene O'Neill, and other writers of the period. Their visions of the American dream as delusion will be the subject of Chapter 3.

Defense of the Dream

In the popular-magazine nonfiction of the thirties, there is an almost obsessive concern with questions involving success in the Depression.

Articles ask, Does opportunity still exist in the Depression for men of initiative and ability? Is a college education crucial to success? How can one profit from the bad times? Are New Deal policies destroying initiative and otherwise queering the chances for rags-to-riches success? Occupying much of the space in the popular magazines are biographical articles outlining the means by which successful people achieved their prominence. *The American Magazine,* furthermore, printed a monthly feature entitled "Interesting People" and, in some issues, a cartoon story called "How They Got That Way," both of which consisted of thumbnail biographies of people who had achieved distinction in some profession or occupation.

The biographical articles and sketches, for the most part, fit a very simple formula—that of the classic American myth of success. The successful man is one who started to work at a very early age, probably had little formal education, and got to the top by virtue of initiative, honest hard work, and perhaps a degree of luck. One comes to expect such details as these: At the age of thirteen Colonel Matt Winn began as a Louisville grocery boy. At the age of nine L. G. Treadway "had started to earn his own living by working as an office boy. . . ." At an early age Henry Sanders, fell heir to a pair of guinea pigs and now, by hard work and shrewd dealings, has a large menagerie and is known as the youngest zoo director in America. Some kind of lowly origin is essential to the formula. In a *Collier's* article titled "Strive and Succeed," Grantland Rice claims that practically all current sports stars began with the odds against them and became "honor graduates of the Horatio Alger school." Furthermore, there is a preference in the success stories for rural origins, as an article about Secretary of State Cordell Hull illustrates. His success surprises many people, says the author, but not those "who know the romance of his backwoods Tennessee beginnings, who know the slow toil of the forty years which have gone into preparation for the very position he now holds." A half-century ago he was "a tall, lean, quiet hill-boy who used to raft logs down the Cumberland River."[6] Through some obscure process, this experience in rafting helped him in his career as a diplomat.

During the 1936 Presidential campaign, Alfred Landon was an appealing figure for the popular writers because he could be fitted so neatly into the formula. A typical article on Landon draws on the poor-boy-to-President myth to magnify Landon's appeal. In Kansas, the author says, "they are beginning to believe again what all good Americans used to believe—that every boy has a change to become President of the United States by practicing in a small way the homely virtues of his country." What these "homely virtues" are is suggested by the title of the article, "Frugal Alf." He is described as honest and thrifty, "a cash and carry governor . . . who counts his change . . . remembers to turn out the lights . . . keeps himself and his state out of debt."[7]

Writers of success stories juggled facts which did not readily fit the standard formula and also resorted to other expedients in order to demonstrate that the American dream could still become a reality. One of these expedients was the story of the self-made woman. Accounts of self-made women are numerous in the thirties and considerably more numerous in the latter years of the decade than in the earlier years. Few of them follow the old Cinderella legend of the poor girl who marries well; the real interest is in the successful career rather than the successful marriage. Often the stories feature entertainers like Olivia De Havilland whose success proves "that the dreams of millions of high school girls and their mothers are not always as fantastic as they seem," or like Jeanette McDonald, "The Girl Who Sang in the Bathtub" and traveled the "rocky road" to success after her father died and left her on her own.[8] But many are stories of ordinary women who rose to prominence in less glamorous fields. An example is Anna Berry who began by serving cheap meals to students in order to work her way through school and was soon cooking for over three hundred men, owned her own car and home, and had a bank account in four figures. Another example appears under the title, "With Her Needle She Stitched a Fortune," and describes a woman who began with a tape measure and some needles and pins as capital and developed a business which grew into a large clothing factory.[9] These women, like many others featured in the popular magazines, succeeded because of their enterprising pioneer spirit.

A more drastic variation in the success-story pattern, one which illustrates the extent to which the myth of success separated from reality during the Depression and became wish-fulfilling fantasy, can be conveniently labeled the "cashing in" story. According to the standards of the traditional success story, which makes the assumption that success results from industry and virtue, many of these stories would have to be considered perversions of the dream. They retain the blind optimism present in most success stories, but they forget about industry, frugality, and even shrewd agressiveness and emphasize instead alertness, luck, and get-rich-quick opportunism. In some of the 1937 issues of *American Magazine* there is even a feature titled

"Cashing In" in which prize money is offered to people who send in "original or unusual" ideas for making a fast dollar. The blurb insists, "Dozens of original ideas are floating around in every community, waiting for some energetic persons to seize them and turn them into cash."[10] One such idea is illustrated by an article, titled "It Pays to Keep Your Eyes Open," in which a museum curator, claiming that "wherever you are, you can find treasures under your feet," explains how stones, bugs, shells, and old pieces of bone may be worth big money.[11] A similar article cautions in the title, "Don't Throw That Away," and explains that apparent trash may be valuable: old papers may contain valuable signatures; old pictures may be by great masters; old envelopes may have valuable stamps on them. The article provides several specific accounts of people who have stumbled across items worth a fortune in old attics and other unlikely spots.[12] While these articles ostensibly offer practical advice for taking advantage of hidden opportunities for wealth, their actual appeal is not to the reader's legitimate hopes for success in a realistic, adult world. Instead, they offer an escape to a child's world of fantasy in which striking it rich is described as if it were equivalent to the child's game of searching for hidden treasure.

A *Popular Mechanics* article panders to the hope of "cashing in" by encouraging daydreaming. Again there is a fairy-tale quality: "Do you 'Day Dream' on the job? Perhaps you can 'Live Your Dreams' in your hobbies and recreations—and cash in on them." Examples are narrated of people who have realized their dreams and "cashed in."[13] In a sense, what this article calls for is simply the use of old-fashioned Yankee inventiveness. The language used in the appeal, however (especially "daydreams" and "cash in"), has the effect of both cheapening the old tradition of Yankee ingenuity and transferring it from the world of reality to the world of fantasy. The author seems to assume that his audience (1934) would understand more fully and respond more sympathetically to vague images of daydreaming and cashing in than to concrete language which would force the reader to touch down to practical reality. That element of shrewd Yankee practicality which has traditionally helped to prevent the American dream from being too "soft" and visionary is missing from this article and others that it exemplifies.

The cashing-in story could, in a sense, be interpreted not only as a strange perversion of American optimism, but also as an unconscious, covert admission that opportunity in America had been reduced to the absurdity of stumbling over valuable old rocks and bones. Unintentionally

these articles convey an image of America as a land whose people have
had their legitimate hopes so completely shattered that they live on dreams
only slightly less bizarre and illusory than those of Erskine Caldwell's
Ty Ty Walden, who digs for gold futilely and relentlessly in the eroded
hills of his Georgia farm. Outwardly, however, the popular magazines
strive to project the opposite image of America. In fact, one of the predominant themes of articles dealing with success is that opportunity still
abounded in the America of the 1930s. It was the "land of opportunity"
ideal that was most obviously belied by the Depression, and not coinci-
dentally it was this indispensable foundation of the dream of success that
was defended most vigorously by the popular writers. In some of the
romanticized accounts of self-made men who started their careers in the
late nineteenth century, the writers merely imply that the same opportunity
exists at present. Frequently, however, faith in America as a land of
opportunity is specifically reaffirmed.

In many cases, articles on opportunity begin on a defensive note and
proceed to "prove" that the "current doctrine of defeat" is unwarranted.
A 1937 article in *Reader's Digest* titled "New Frontiers for Youth" comments that youth are told "that the American dream of enlarging opportunities . . . no longer corresponds with reality." The author admits that
the dream has been "disturbed during the past few years," but he argues
that "Though conditions have changed, opportunities have not lessened.
Our frontiers are no longer geographical, but exist wherever young people
apply trained imagination and resourcefulness." He goes on to mention
some of the frontier professions that were developing—retailing, industrial
design, movies, air conditioning, aviation—but he does not offer advice
on how to break in to one of these fields.[14] Another author describes
how his fears of unemployment and lack of opportunity were allayed by
a friend who convinced him that opportunities were "never as great as
now" *for logical thinkers.* The article mentions specific fields such as
electricity, atomic energy, gravitation, and radiation in which opportunities
exist.[15] These writers have no difficulty in establishing the fact that there
were "frontier professions" out there waiting to be developed. But they
do not really grapple with the problem of what happens to "opportunity"
when a breakdown in economic machinery cuts men off from the work
they would like to do.

In other cases, the opportunities are found in strange and unlikely places.
An example is an article that tries to revive interest in one of America's
most hallowed traditions—homesteading. Under the alluring title "Land

for the Taking," the author says that "There is still homestead land in
this man's country . . . and Americans are still homesteading right here
in the good year 1932." He goes on to tell the story of a man who foresaw
financial difficulty in 1929 and went west to become a "modern pioneer."[16]
Ignoring the fact that the frontier had long since ceased to function as a
safety valve which could take the economic pressure off the highly pop-
ulated regions of the country, the author paints an idyllic picture of a
rugged and rewarding life close to nature. His pioneer image represents
a romantic attempt to escape to a golden past and has little relation to
reality. This article and others urging a return to the farm are doubly ironic
in view of the fact that farmers, many of them already suffering in the
twenties, were hit hard by the Depression. Altogether farm income, esti-
mated at $7.7 billion in 1929, declined to nearly one third that figure in
1932.[17] And for many, worse years were to come as the ravages of drought
and dust compounded the problem of low farm prices. It is an ironic commentary on the "Land for the Taking" article that by the end of the decade
upward of 200,000 farm people had abandoned their homesites on the
Great Plains, where much of the homestead land was available, and migrated
further westward in search of a promised land which the vast majority of
them never found.[18]

   Another unlikely source of opportunity in the world of the popular
magazines is the Depression itself. A recurring argument, demonstrating
again the tendency to rationalize and avoid reality, is that the very conditions which were throwing some businesses into bankruptcy were opening
up new opportunities for the brave and the venturesome. Articles declare,
"Right Now [1930] is the Time to Begin to Get Rich" and ask, "Have
You the Courage to Make Money?" The latter title introduces a story of
a man who "turned lean years into fat ones" by putting new ideas into
production in 1931 when other companies were trying merely to stay
solvent. The man who did this says, "If ever there was a time for a man
with an idea to put it to work, *it is now.*"[19] Most profit-from-the-Depres-
sion articles seem to be a part of the propaganda campaign designed to
fight fear and stimulate business. They are considerably less in evidence
by the mid-decade than in the early Depression years before the professional
optimists were convinced that the Depression was going to be deep and
long-lasting.

   An informative check on how accurately these discussions of opportunity
reflect what the populace was thinking is provided by one of the *Fortune*

Magazine quarterly opinion surveys. Quarterly survey VII, published in
January, 1937, posed the question: "Do you think that today any young
man with thrift, ability, and ambition has the opportunity to rise in the
world, own his own home, and earn $5000 or more a year?" In their intro-
duction to the survey, the editors observe that the Depression, the growth
of corporations, "New Deal paternalism," and other influences had changed
the patterns of opportunity and success in America. The idea of the poll
was to discover, "How persistent, then, in the face of so much evidence
that an American should be accounted lucky if he gets along at all, is the
tradition that this is still a land of opportunity?" The results: 39.6 percent
said "yes"; 18.0 percent said "yes, if he's lucky"; 34.7 percent said "no";
and 7.7 percent didn't know. Though slightly more than one-third of
those interviewed thought that opportunity had diminished, substantially
more (57.6 percent if the equivocal "yes" answers are included with the
unequivocal ones) held to the image of America as a land of opportunity.
Fortune's breakdown of the data by economic levels shows that pessimism
about opportunity rises gradually as one moves down the economic scale.
More than half of even the very poor, however, expressed the belief that
it was still possible for an American to achieve prosperity through his own
abilities. Only the farmers of the northwest plains, where drought had
blighted crops, were profoundly pessimistic in their replies; almost 56
percent of them were convinced that America was no longer a land of
opportunity.[20] In general, the survey corroborates the impression left by
the popular magazines—that there was a very strong strain of at least
professed optimism about opportunity in the thirties despite the fact
that the Depression had wiped out opportunity for many.

Frequently, those who comment on opportunity in the popular magazines also strongly emphasize the importance of hard work. One writer
says, "To one who has learned the lesson of hard work nothing is really
impossible in America." Taken from an article appropriately titled "Grind,"
this is a characteristic statement of what was still an abiding faith for
many people of the thirties—a faith in the gospel of work. In keeping with
the traditional myth of success, the belief that opportunity existed was
accompanied by a strong belief that the only quality really essential
for success was a willingness to perform work, "hard, driving, continuous
work," "daily drudgery."[21] The value of work is exaggerated until talent,
ability, and economic circumstances are beside the point: "I say that
if one plows the field and sows the grain, the harvest will come as surely

as day follows night." The idea is to "Work a little harder; work a little longer; work! . . . Work should be one's life, not merely one's job."[22] The commitment to the gospel of work, in short, seemed to intensify as a result of conditions which deprived men of the opportunity to work.

Interestingly, this commitment was so strong that leisure and entertainment tended to become negative values. For a practical-minded people nurtured on a long tradition of hard work and worldly achievement, to be cut off from the opportunity to work was to be separated from a very important source of salvation. There was no consolation in the fact that shortened working hours, the scarcity of jobs, and the effects of the economic slowdown were creating more leisure time. Due to the strength of the old traditions of material achievement, industry, and productiveness, leisure has never ranked high as an American value; and it has been observed many times that their emphasis on doing and producing has rendered Americans unfit to appreciate leisure or use it intelligently. As the Depression produced more leisure, the writers of popular success stories tended to look more negatively than ever on leisure and entertainment, often renouncing them explicitly in such statements as these: "He works hard and doesn't go in for entertainment." "I don't like to do anything but work." "Opposed to vacations, he relaxes by inventing something for himself."[23] From a practical standpoint, of course, leisure was associated for some victims of the Depression with hardship or even hunger; but compounding this difficulty was the fact that in many minds idleness still carried overtones of sinfulness and moral failure. As we shall see in a later chapter, not everyone remained committed to the gospel of work; the Depression also produced efforts to adjust values to conditions by demeaning the gospel of work and affirming a new gospel of leisure. But such efforts were not conspicuous in the popular magazines.

A corollary of this professed love of work and suspicion of leisure was the widespread assumption that a willingness to work was the *only* requirement for success—a time-honored assumption among self-help propagandists. Inherent in this belief is a species of anti-intellectualism—the idea that higher education is unnecessary, indeed, in many cases, harmful. In his *Anti-Intellectualism in American Life,* Richard Hofstadter observes that the ideal of the self-made man, with its suspicion of genius or brilliance, its emphasis on starting at the bottom and on learning by experience, and its cult of practicality, has traditionally been a leading source of American anti-intellectualism. In the late nineteenth century, the golden age of

American business enterprise, there was almost no disagreement on two matters, Hofstadter says: "education should be more 'practical'; and higher education, at least as it was conceived in the old-time American classical college, was useless as a background for business."[24] A similar skepticism about the value of education is still remarkably prevalent in the popular literature of the thirties. It would be easy to jump to the conclusion that a well-learned lesson of the Depression was the importance of higher education to success. But this would minimize too much the strength of the older self-help tradition, with its persistent hostility to formal education and its compensating cult of experience. Well before the Depression, of course, the development of large, bureaucratic corpora- tions had made formal education in engineering, accounting, economics, law, or other fields a distinct asset, if not a necessity, for the aspiring business executive. And, as Mabel Newcomer's figures show, even in 1925, 51.4 percent of America's top business executives had some college education; by 1950 this figure had risen to 75.6 percent.[25] Miss Newcomer concludes that by 1950 it was "accepted that the college degree [was] the ticket of admission to a successful career with the large corporation."[26] Perhaps, but it was by no means fully accepted in the 1930s. The myth of the uneducated self-made man still persisted vigorously in those years.

The amazing ability of those who perpetuated the myth of the self- made man to close their eyes to increasing technology, complexity, and specialization (all, of course, requiring increased education) is perhaps best symbolized in the blacksmith, described in one of *American Magazine*'s "Interesting People" columns, who has ignored the industrial revolution and is "forging ahead to a fortune" by making suits of armor for museums and private collectors. Obviously, he does not need a formal education. Even advertisements for correspondence schools and extension universities are hesitant to claim too much for education. Lasalle Extension University, for example, says, "We do not deny that hard work and learning through day-to-day experience will eventually win you some measure of success." But success will come sooner, the advertisement rather modestly claims, to those who take the course.[27] Obviously, the copy writer felt the need to pay tribute to the still appealing self-help tradition. Thus, he makes no claim that education or even training is necessary for success; only that it might serve as a kind of catalyst to speed up the process.

The key objection to higher education found in such articles as "How Colleges Rob Men of Priceless Years," "Are College Men Preferred?" and

"Which College—If Any?" is that college is a waste of time because it does not teach young men how to work. The connection between the gospel of work and anti-intellectualism is obvious. Those who undercut higher education assert that on-the-job experience, preferably begun at an early age, is more valuable than a formal education. A *Saturday Evening Post* article of 1936, titled "Horatio Alger at the Bridge," illustrates well the anti-intellectual attitude. The article is a lengthy one in which the author, Boyden Sparkes, succeeds, by means of judicious questions posed to several important businessmen, in putting together a number of Horatio Alger stories in almost pure form. One interviewee claims that what he learned by work as a boy (he started as an office boy at the age of thirteen) has been the ruling benefit of his career. Another, who started as an office boy at the age of fourteen, airs his belief that "experience is still more valuable than half-baked education." On the basis of all his interviews, the author finds it possible to conclude that "The most successful manufacturers in the United States are men who did not go to college and who worked as boys." And he poses the telling question: if Mr. X were starting today, would he find the same opportunities to fashion a no-education, up-from-the-bottom success? The answer, of course, is "yes." But there is a hitch. The author grumbles that because of New Deal child-labor regulations anyone starting out now would have to wait until he was sixteen instead of starting work at the most desirable age— thirteen or fourteen.[28]

In this attack on child labor laws we have an explicit illustration of a theme that runs through many of the popular-magazine articles on the subject of success: the use of popular sympathy with the myth of success to attack New Deal policies. One of the most effective weapons used by conservative critics of the New Deal was the accusation that New Deal policies would destroy the self-help tradition. In the *Saturday Evening Post* article, the title "Horatio Alger at the Bridge" is intended to arouse the fear *not* that the Depression itself was undermining the Alger tradition, but that the New Deal was a dangerous threat to the ideal of success as expressed in the old rags-to-riches formula. New Deal labor regulations, it was argued, would destroy the traditional opportunity of potential self-made men to begin working as children. Welfare legislation would destroy initiative. In general, New Deal tampering would undermine the whole tradition of individualistic, highly competitive, laissez-faire capitalism, which the myth of success depended upon and supported. The enormous vitality of the myth of success in the face of Depression conditions can be understood, in part, as a backlash response to the New Deal threat. Thurman Arnold observed at the time (*The Folklore of Capitalism*, 1937) that the elaborate and still highly potent system of mythology surrounding American capitalism was one of the greatest obstacles to action at a time when effective action was desperately needed.

Pseudo-Science in How-to-Succeed Guidebooks

Many of the how-to-succeed guidebooks which appeared in the thirties responded to the Depression with essentially the same conservatism that characterized the popular magazines. They constituted a kind of sub-literature, which perpetuated the traditional myth of success in a remarkably insistent way even as the reality of the Depression became increasingly clear. The guidebooks will be discussed more fully later in another context, but a few observations are relevant here. One is that during the Depression there was no slackening in the output of advice on how to succeed. Among the multitudes of success books are such titles as *Through Failure to Success, Full Speed to Success, Will Power and Success, Practical Methods to Insure Success, Gold in Your Back Yard, What's Holding You Back?* and *Six Laws of Business Success*, none of which betray any doubt that they have the full answer on how to succeed. The fact that so many "how to" books were published in the thirties perhaps suggests that readers bewildered by the Depression desired the illusion that there were answers about success which could be capsulized in a how-to-succeed guidebook.

And, indeed, an emphasis shared by almost all the success guidebooks in my sampling is that there is a clear path to success which can be discovered and followed ("Six Laws," "Eight Rules," "Ten Sure Steps"). One author says that he likes the success stories in monthly magazines, but complains that the authors often fail to say *how* the great men of the success stories achieved their success: "I want to know the formula. I want to know the rules which governed the great man's life. . . . I want the machinery removed from his head so that I can see it tick."[29] There is a pseudo-scientific quality here which is typical of many of the guidebooks of the thirties. The author of a guidebook titled *The Super-Science of Success* (1933), for instance, declares that "there is a Science, a pre-ordered method of Success. . . ." He insists that "success comes only by effort, by action of certain kinds, in accordance with fixed and definite laws and principles."[30] Couching his argument in terms of absolute, fixed principles, the author, like many of his counterparts, treats success in a vacuum and manages to avoid entirely the problems of the Depression and its effects on the pursuit of success. This deliberate disregard of the specific social and economic context in which the struggle for success had to be made was an important part of the myth. By isolating their subject for "scientific" study, the writers of guidebooks attempted to create the illusion that there was a phenomenon called success which functioned according to its own universal laws and was not affected by the specific conditions of a specific time.

Related to the pseudo-scientific emphasis on the "fixed principles" of success was the tendency to exaggerate the individual's responsibility for his own success or failure. If external conditions were ignored or if it were merely assumed that America was still a land of opportunity, then the "laws of success" had to be discovered within the character, personality, and behavior of the individual. As we have seen, this emphasis on qualities within, rather than conditions without, has been a central doctrine of our best known philosophers of success, from Bruce Barton and Roger Babson in the twenties to Russell Conwell, Andrew Carnegie, and T. S. Arthur in the nineteenth century. It is true—and this will be developed in a later chapter—that by the thirties there was a shift away from an emphasis on character toward an emphasis on personality. But whether the emphasis fell on character or personality, broadly speaking the dominant ideology of the thirties still located the key to success within the individual and not outside him. In many of the guidebooks, this view of success is presented so emphatically and pointedly that, as in the popular magazines, specific political overtones become obvious. Generally the political overtones amount to attacks on the New Deal. One author, for instance, insists that men make their own success and failure and that the path that leads to failure is just as clearly marked as the one leading to success. "Let us keep this one fact in mind at all times [he says] : We cannot blame others or outside influences for our failure to achieve certain ends. Whatever we do or fail to do in this life will be the result of our own actions."[31] Implied in this attitude toward success and failure is a strong opposition to any welfare legislation that would make it too easy for the "lazy poor" to take advantage of the industrious. The Lynds report that in 1935 the belief that the leading cause of poverty was a lack of ambition and industry was still very much a part of "the Middletown Spirit," along with the belief that private charity was good but that government relief "undermines a man's character."[32]

Perpetuating the Myth in Popular Fiction

If how-to-succeed guidebooks as well as innumerable articles and features in the popular magazines seemed stubborn and insistent in their perpetuation of the traditional American myth of success, the popular-magazine fiction of the thirties was marked by much the same conservative defense of time-honored ideals. In countless popular stories, the business-oriented, go-getting values associated with the myth of success are reaffirmed through allegories, characterizations, carefully contrived plot situations, and other fictional devices. As later chapters will point out, the Depression did produce some disillusionment with the myth of success, including changes in the type of hero preferred, in the type of goal or reward offered by the happy endings, and in the definition of what constitutes the good life. Nevertheless, a substantial proportion of the popular fiction of the thirties simply provides more evidence of the tendency to reaffirm old values and live by old symbols.

In the process of reaffirming their faith in the myth of success, the popular stories propagandize on a wide range of subjects. They attempt to demonstrate that the evils of the time are attributable to a loss of commitment to the traditional values associated with the myth of success. They suggest that economic salvation would follow automatically from a renewed dedication to the proved ideal of individual aggressiveness and ambition. They caution against the stultifying effects of fear, shiftlessness, and lack of confidence. They defend the profit motive and other aspects of the commercial ethic with a frankness and conviction that sometimes surpasses the philistinism of the twenties. They lament the growing emphasis on security and call for a new expression of entrepreneurial courage.

One of the most prevalent themes in the stories is that recovery from the Depression has been hampered because people have lost sight of the importance of ambition, aggressiveness, entrepreneurial daring, industry, and other virtues prescribed by the myth of success. The solution to the Depression, the stories suggest, is simply to relearn the old virtues. A typical example is a story which uses a bridge-game allegory. Its hero is a young businessman who wants to use his initiative but finds that in the Depression people (including his wife) fear enthusiasm and initiative. Because he likes to take chances, his wife accuses him of being irresponsible in bridge and in business. The bridge allegory is simple-minded and contrived, but it affords the author an opportunity to proselytize without seeming too directly didactic. The hero, who needs money to realize his dream of starting a trucking business, takes a long chance in a bridge game and wins. A banker and bridge enthusiast, who has been watching, is impressed by the gamble and decides to lend the hero the money for his business venture.[33] Despite the fact that countless small businessmen with a shoestring of capital had been ruined by the Depression, the story calls for a new commitment to the old entrepreneurial spirit. It is representative of many stories which make the concession, either explicitly or implicitly, that the Depression posed a threat to the ideal of entrepreneurial daring. These stories make a rather obvious attempt to indoctrinate the reader with a renewed sense of the importance of not yielding to fear and timidity. Though the quest for security and peace of mind was dominant in much of the inspirational literature and some of the popular fiction of the Depression years, readers of magazine stories were also confronted repeatedly by efforts to mitigate the desire for security and encourage a spirit of daring and venturesomeness.

While in this story the young man has the ambition and his wife is fearful and cautious, frequently these roles are reversed so that the heroine possesses ample ambition and the hero suffers from a lack of it. A story titled "Homing," for example, portrays a former stunt flyer who has left the profession because his wife, who had also been a stunt pilot, was killed in a crash. His new venture is to try to support himself and his five-year-old daughter by operating a fruit farm in Florida.[34] The story implies that bravery in a business enterprise is both more difficult and more admirable than physical courage, for though the hero has been a courageous stunt pilot, he is weak and uncertain as a businessman. His lack of drive and profit-making aggression is symbolized by his refusal to charge visitors to see the peacocks which populate the farm, though he could make a handsome profit by doing so. His scruples bring him nothing but failure and, desperate, he soon leaves his daughter with the heroine of the story, a plucky kindergarten teacher, and returns to stunt flying. The heroine, a true entrepreneur with all the ambition and aggressiveness required by the cult of success, promptly begins charging people to view the peacocks while selling fruit on the side. When the hero returns to the farm, after a crash which has broken his leg, he finds that the farm has become a profitable business, and there is nothing for him to do but marry the heroine.[35] There is no mistaking the author's contempt for the false pride and lack of aggressiveness which are at the root of the hero's failure. On the other hand, the initiative and aggressiveness of the spirited heroine are celebrated as the potential salvation of all the timid and fearful victims of the Depression.

Along with its celebration of the entrepreneurial spirit, an important theme in this story is its frank and unequivocal affirmation of the commercial ethic; being too proud or too soft to make a profit is bad, and being shrewd and aggressive in taking advantage of business opportunities is good. It is significant that similar direct and pointed reassertions of the commercial ethic appear frequently in the stories of the thirties, as if the Depression's challenge to business values were being recognized and specifically answered. Characters who lack the courage to embark on commercial ventures or who have a distaste for making a profit from others are frequently portrayed as weak, soft-headed, immature, or even vaguely immoral people whose scruples prevent them from supporting their families adequately. As in "Homing," they generally come to the realization that the solution to their problems lies in a firm commitment to business values.

Sometimes, however, anticommercial characters are portrayed as thoroughgoing villains who are beyond salvation and worthy only of contempt or ridicule. An example is "The Genius," a story by Sophie Kerr which combines anti-intellectualism with an almost hysterical defense of commercialism in art. The protagonist is a young literary critic and poet who believes that he is intellectually superior to other people, a genius. He serves as the author's target for some very vicious satire. She ridicules his complex and difficult poetry, siding instead with the "happy-enders, optimists, uplifters, prettifiers and puritans." She criticizes his snobbery and the bohemian life he leads. But her most acid remarks attack him for not being a financial success. She scoffs at him because he lives off his family and, especially, because he sends poems to magazines and doesn't get paid for them.[36] The author implies, sincerely and unblushingly, that the goal of a writer should be to bring himself financial success by writing what the public wants to hear and can understand. Thus, she creates as her antihero a caricature of the sophisticated modern writer who is alienated from the commercial values which she considers self-evidently proper. The heretic who has rejected commercial success is shown to be totally despicable. The tone of angry hostility which pervades the characterization of the story's antihero illustrates the fervor with which some popular writers were prepared to defend the ideals of self-help, financial success, and commercialism.

Another story uses nineteenth-century material, including the familiar nature-versus-civilization conflict, in a very different approach to the defense of the commercial ethic. The hero is a young trapper who, valuing unspoiled nature, is hostile to a group of commercially minded westward migrants, but agrees to become their guide because he is interested in a girl in their group. By the end of the story, he is so "civilized" that he is eager to marry the girl and become a clerk in the group's store. He has taken on the commercial ethic and forgotten his wilderness ethic. As the title "Boy Grows Up" suggests, the author's theme is that the boy's initiation has been a good and profitable one. Implicitly the story teaches that to grow up is to accept not only civilization but also the commercial ethic which, the story implies, is the very foundation of civilization. Some stories of the thirties reflected a countertendency in which the retreat to nature was viewed as a welcome alternative to the struggle for success in the commercial world. Nevertheless, the fact that stories like "Boy Grows Up" specifically rejected the return to nature in favor of commercial success illustrates once again the persistence of the myth of success despite the ravages of the Depression.[37]

As in the popular stories of the twenties, the merit of the ambitious and aggressive self-made man is often dramatized through cautionary tales in which a girl chooses the ambitious self-made man and rejects the spoiled, shiftless, purposeless, complacent, or incapable alternative. A *Saturday Evening Post* story, for instance, portrays a girl's rejection of a charming track star because he does not take things seriously and has no real ambition or desire to work. She has "stern, disciplined pioneer stock in her," and, though she loves the young man, she fears that he will never amount to anything.[38] An *American Magazine* story, titled "Don't Call Me Darling," is based on a girl's choice between a cocky young salesman who has made it on his own in the highly competitive automobile business and a steady, sedate, and not very aggressive young banker who is accustom to leaning on his well-to-do father. The salesman wins the girl by means of an impressive demonstration of success in his job; he makes a sale to a tough prospect who turns out to be the banker's father.[39] In another story, the girl's choice is between a boy from a comfortable background and a poor service-station attendant who is trying to earn his way through law school. The difference in their status is symbolized by the fact that the former is a swaggering golfer from the country-club set, while the latter likes to hang around a driving range in his spare time. Their confrontation comes in a golf tournament, which the upstart wins while the rich boy reveals himself to be a spoiled brat. The girl, predictably, decides to marry the poor boy after he has made good as a lawyer.[40]

In all these examples the pattern is essentially the same. Like their counterparts in the twenties, the stories interrelate the themes of love and success in such a way that the young man's path to love and happiness is unmistakably clear. He must be deadly serious in his determination to succeed. He must not depend on help from others. He must not come from a well-to-do family and, in fact, preferably he should begin in absolute poverty. Frequently he must demonstrate through some dramatic triumph his ability to succeed. If anything, these cautionary tales are more ominous in their warnings against idleness, ineptitude, and lack of initiative than the corresponding stories of the twenties. Thus, without any apparent awareness of the fact, the stories confronted young men with a difficult dilemma. On the one hand the Depression seemed virtually to eliminate the chances for material success, but on the other hand the purveyors of the popular mythology of success continued to warn that there could be no love and personal happiness for those who lacked the ambition to achieve success in the traditional American way.

Innumerable stories of the thirties illustrate the fact that the value of initiative, ambition, aggressiveness, profit making, starting from the bottom, competition, entrepreneurial chance taking, and hard work had certainly not been lost sight of by the popular writers. Many of the stories of the thirties reflect an awareness that the Depression was calling into question some of the traditional faiths that Americans were accustomed to living by. Thus, frequently the stories are highly transparent vehicles of propaganda designed to buttress the old values. Just as prevalent in the thirties, however, were fanciful success stories which betrayed little awareness that the Depression even existed. These stories created a fairy-tale world where everything was possible and no one suffered. As in the "cashing in" stories which they resemble, myth and reality have completely separated; the dream has become pure illusion, not a means of interpreting and responding to reality but a means of escaping it.

Ironically a popular format for the fairy-tale success story is one in which a character strikes it rich playing the stock market. In the light of actual circumstances, it would be difficult to conceive of a more unlikely

source for success stories. But despite the crash of 1929 and the financial
chaos that followed, popular writers continued to tantalize their readers
with tales of fabulous stock-market coups. There is a story, for instance,
of an attractive young lady who makes a fortune by using her charms to
manipulate brokers and big businessmen. As a bogus concession to morality
the author carefully arranges for the heavy losers to be the lechers who try
to collect on the "favors" they have understood the heroine to promise;
but the main effect of the story is to pander to the dream of sudden wealth
Another stock-market story portrays an unemployed, happy-go-lucky Irish-
man who has lost in stock-market speculation all of his own money except
enough to buy his fiancée a ring. Once he has "sacrificed" by buying the
ring instead of gambling the money away on the stock market, his reward
is sudden and splendid; his fiancée accidentally finds some old stocks left
by her father which, the hero discovers, have split and accumulated a value
of over $20,000.[42] Unlike the didactic tales which attempt to reconsecrate
all the solid, middle-class, Protestant virtues associated with the myth of
success, these stories make no pretense of celebrating ambition, industry,
and aggressiveness. In their fairy-tale world, nothing so strenuous as work
is required; it is sheer good fortune that brings success.

Essentially the same pattern is illustrated by a story titled "Push Your
Luck," except that in this case the Depression is not ignored; it contributes
to the conflict. The hero is a dancer who is out of work and on the bum
because of the Depression. He begins to get lucky, but thinks: "No such
thing as luck. Ability and practice, and mostly practice . . . Hard work
and knowing your trade—that was all there was to it." But ability and
hard work bring him no success, and luck does. He finds a dollar bill, and
every time he tries to spend it, it comes back doubled. This goes on at
some length until he finally loses the money he has accumulated; but out
of the whole affair comes an offer of a fabulous dancing job in the movies.[4]
This story illustrates the paradox that underlies many of the wish-fulfillment fantasies. In one sense it is cynical; it denies the assumption that
the individual can assure his success by following the proper rules and
cultivating the proper personal qualities. But in another sense it is romantic
and fanciful. Instead of giving up on the ideal of success, it creates a totally
implausible situation in which blind chance brings about the success that
ability and perseverance cannot. Covertly this story and other fantasies of
unexpected success concede that the Depression had shattered the realistic
hope of self-made success. Instead of responding with disillusionment,

however, they simply blot out objective reality and replace it with a comfortable vision of things as they might be. In the process they free the individual from any responsibility for his own success or failure.

If nothing can be done, one can simply have faith, as a story about a poverty-stricken Mexican-American family recommends. Pedro and Lucito, having eight children and no money for food, decide to leave the latest baby on the church steps. But when Pedro delivers it, he finds another baby already there in a basket. With an abiding faith that somehow the family will be provided for, he takes both babies back home with him. The reward for his faith and compassion is that in the basket of the abandoned baby he finds more money than he has ever seen before or dreamed of.[44] Unlike most of the wish-fulfillment fantasies, this story portrays honestly the desperate poverty of its characters. It is quite representative, however, in the fact that its resolution encourages not a courageous confrontation of reality, but an escape to a world of miracles. Any social relevance inherent in its portrayal of poverty and desperation is blunted by the fact that it advocates passive acceptance, blind faith, and the comfortable assumption that problems will be solved by a deus ex machina. Like most of the popular stories, it suggests no need for change in the status quo. Illusion and escape are a substitute for action or even indignation.

Understandably, this impulse to escape reality was strong in the Depression years. Readers for whom the five-cent purchase price of *Liberty* was a sacrifice did not want to be reminded too often of the unpleasant reality of unemployment, hunger, and shattered dreams. They preferred light reading that would take them momentarily out of reality. Popular tastes in other forms of literature and entertainment reflected the same preference. As James Hart points out in *The Popular Book,* works which provided some means of escaping the grim realities of the Depression were among the most popular books throughout the thirties. Detective stories such as the Erle Stanley Gardner series and Dashiell Hammett's *The Thin Man,* historical novels such as *Anthony Adverse* and *Gone with the Wind* and even nonfiction dealing with happier times in our past (Allen's *Only Yesterday,* Clarence Day's *Life With Father,* and Carl Van Doren's *Benjamin Franklin,* for instance) were all big sellers during the thirties. The desire to escape to the magical world of childhood was reflected in the fact that Munro Leaf's *Ferdinand,* a children's book about a flower-loving bull, was very popular even among adults.[45]

It is worth adding in passing that the desire for escape as well as the enormous discrepancy between Depression realities and the myths which fed the popular mind is nowhere better illustrated than in the typical movies of the decade. Frederick Lewis Allen has said that "the America which the movies portrayed—like the America of popular magazine fiction and especially of the magazine advertisement—was devoid of real poverty or discontent, of any real conflict of interests between owners and workers, of any real ferment of ideas. More than that, it was a country in which almost everybody was rich or about to be rich."[46] Others who have commented on the movies of the thirties have found few exceptions to Allen's generalization that most films so successfully dodged the unpleasant realities of the day that they would not convey to later viewers the faintest indication that the nation experienced a crisis in the thirties.[47]

To anyone who is accustomed to thinking of the thirties as preeminently a decade of social consciousness, disillusionment with American business values, leftist class-consciousness, and intellectual ferment, an exposure to such sources as popular magazines, how-to-succeed guidebooks, and movies should serve as an effective reminder that *The Nation* and *New Republic,* Steinbeck, Farrell, Dos Passos, and Caldwell reveal only one side of the America of the thirties. Clearly, a large number of people were not yet ready to give up their image of America as a Horatio Alger paradise where anyone willing to make the effort could find success and happiness. On the popular level, the bitter experience of the Depression did not deal the death blow to the capacity for dreaming, the idealistic faith in the future, the extravagant expectations that Americans have been noted for. To judge from the popular literature of the period, the capacity to dream suffered much less than the capacity to face reality and to distinguish legitimate hopes from puerile illusions. More than ever the dream of success and happiness became an end in itself, a fantasy which freed the individual from reality instead of infusing him with the energy and ambition needed to cope with it.

If the myth of success offered escape to victims of the Depression, it also had another, more important, function. During the Depression it became more inescapably clear than ever before that the rags-to-riches tradition was no longer valid as an interpretation of American social and economic reality. But the myth continued to function as an ideological support for long-standing social, economic, and political policies. Broadly speaking, the dream of individual success motivated individuals to work

within the existing capitalist system rather than to become totally disillusioned with it. In terms of partisan politics, the myth was used by
many conservatives as an ideological answer to the New Deal. The Depression itself, as well as the New Deal efforts to combat it, threatened to
erode such venerable ideals as individualism, self-help, and entrepreneurial
daring. And, of course, these ideals did lose some of their appeal during
the Depression years. But the myth of success was tirelessly invoked to
buttress the conventional faiths. Whereas the New Deal offered welfare
programs, the apostles of success preached self-help. Whereas the New
Deal passed child-labor laws, the apostles of success glorified the self-made
men who began work at the age of thirteen or fourteen. While the Depression, the New Deal, and other developments contributed to an increasing
emphasis on security, the old-line advocates of success strove to revitalize
the waning entrepreneurial spirit. While New Deal agencies imposed regulations on business and industry, the cult of success advocated rugged individualism and laissez-faire.

One of the most striking characteristics of the popular-magazine fiction
of the Depression decade is the self-consciousness with which so much of it
attempts to influence public opinion. Though stories of pure escape make
up a considerable proportion of the popular fiction, a surprisingly large
number of stories obviously have as their primary aim not entertainment
but instruction. Transparently didactic stories expound the importance
of ambition, industry, and self-help, while sounding ominous warnings
against the loss of these ideals. In many cases the writers seem sharply
aware of the fact that in the conventional success story lay the perfect
ideological weapon with which to defend America's traditional ideals.
Though most of their stories are superficial and stereotyped, they are often
anything but pointless entertainments. Many of them drive home their
themes with a deadly seriousness worthy of the most propagandistic proletarian novel.

The endless reassertions of the faiths clustered around the myth of
success must be given careful consideration when one asks what the
Depression did to the values of the ordinary American. For many, the
Depression had not destroyed the belief that the pursuit of money was
the key to happiness, that business values were American values and true
values, that individual aggressiveness and ambition were the proper personal
traits, and even that formal education might be less valuable than experience as a preparation for success. Deprivation may have created some

doubt in the validity of the dream of success, but it also created a need for secure faiths to cling to; and probably nothing was more firmly established as a faith worth holding to than the traditional ideology of success.

Notes

1. Daniel Boorstin, *The Image, or What Happened to the American Dream,* p. 240.

2. Robert and Helen Lynd, *Middletown in Transition,* p. 489.

3. Ibid., pp. 71-72.

4. As Malcolm Cowley pointed out in a review, Middletown did give Roosevelt 59 percent of its vote in the 1936 Presidential election. This represented, essentially, a 6-4 majority *against* "The Middletown Spirit." See "Still Middletown," in *Think Back on Us . . . A Contemporary Chronicle of the 1930's by Malcolm Cowley,* edited by Henry Dan Piper, pp. 142-43.

5. *American Magazine,* May 1937, p. 97; July, 1930, p. 98; July, 1937, p. 87.

6. *Collier's,* July 11, 1931, p. 23; *American Magazine,* February, 1937, p. 22.

7. *American Magazine,* March, 1936, p. 51.

8. Ibid., September, 1937, p. 59.

9. Ibid., May, 1937, p. 98; August, 1930, p. 80.

10. Ibid., May 1937, p. 61.

11. Ibid., p. 62.

12. Ibid., October, 1930, p. 54.

13. *Popular Mechanics,* February, 1934, pp. 196-97.

14. *Reader's Digest,* June, 1937, pp. 24-28.

15. H. V. Roff, "Opportunity," *Christian Science Monitor Magazine Section,* June 10, 1936, p. 7.

16. *American Magazine,* March, 1932, p. 54.

17. Harvey Wish, *Society and Thought in Modern America,* p. 506.

18. Frederick Lewis Allen, *Since Yesterday,* p. 161.

19. *American Magazine,* June, 1932, pp. 24-25.

20. "Is There Still a Land of Opportunity?" *Fortune* Quarterly Survey VII, *Fortune Magazine,* January, 1937, pp. 86-87.

21. *American Magazine,* July, 1930, p. 24.

22. Ibid., July, 1935, p. 11.

23. Ibid., May, 1937, p. 26; September, 1937, p. 35; September, 1937, p. 86.

24. Richard Hofstadter, *Anti-Intellectualism in American Life,* p. 257.

25. Mabel Newcomer, *The Big Business Executive: The Factors That Made Him,* p. 69.

26. Ibid., p. 77.

27. *American Magazine,* October, 1937, p. 87; May, 1937, p. 167.

28. *Saturday Evening Post,* May 2, 1936, pp. 20-21.

29. Julian Scott Bryan, *From Father to Son,* p. 5.

30. Ernest Raymond, *The Super-Science of Success*, pp. 2, 25.

31. Robert A. Gebler, *Full Speed to Success*, p. 81.

32. Lynd and Lynd, p. 415.

33. Bruce Gould, "Four Hearts," *Saturday Evening Post*, July 9, 1932, pp. 17, 67.

34. Eustace Adams, "Homing," *American Magazine*, October, 1937, pp. 20-21, 114.

35. Ibid.

36. Sophie Kerr, "The Genius," *Saturday Evening Post*, January 30, 1936, pp. 40-42.

37. John Reed Byers, "Boy Grows Up," *American Magazine*, August, 1939, pp. 47-49.

38. Paul O'Neill, "The Melody Lingers On," *Saturday Evening Post*, August 28, 1937, pp. 14-15, 69.

39. Fannie Kilbourne, "Don't Call Me Darling," *American Magazine*, September, 1935, pp. 18-21, 136.

40. Ben Ames Williams, "Skyrocket," *Saturday Evening Post*, May 18, 1935, pp. 22-23, 116-20.

41. Robert Winsmore, "A Kiss for Miss Simpson," *Saturday Evening Post*, January 27, 1934.

42. Thomas McMorrow, "Lady with Lamp," *Saturday Evening Post*, January 20, 1934.

43. Richard Normser, "Push Your Luck," *Saturday Evening Post*, May 20, 1939, pp. 10-11.

44. Harold C. Wire, "Faith," *Liberty*, November 4, 1939, p. 61.

45. James Hart, *The Popular Book*, pp. 257-63.

46. Frederick Lewis Allen, *Since Yesterday*, pp. 223-24.

47. See, for instance, Margaret Farrand Thorpe, *America at the Movies*; Arthur Knight, "The Movies," in *The Thirties, A Time to Remember*, edited by Don Congdon; and Merle Curti, *The Growth of American Thought*.

3 / Dream or Delusion: The American Dream as Fantasy and Ritual in Serious Literature

Most of the popular literature which perpetuated the myth of success in the Depression years shows little awareness of how wide the chasm between myth and reality was becoming, except indirectly through a vague defensiveness of tone. Serious writers, like John Steinbeck, Nathanael West, and J. T. Farrell, however, tended to be very much aware of the chasm; many had come to view America as a land of broken promise and the American dream as a fantasy that people clung to because they had nothing else. In the twenties, writers who treated the dream of success as a theme in their fiction were frequently critical of American culture for its philistinism, its narrowness, its encouragement of a thoughtless and mechanical pursuit of shallow material goals—in short, for its inability to satisfy the needs of the spirit. Dreiser, Fitzgerald, Lewis, Cather, Anderson, and many others questioned the shallow values inspired by the dream of material success. In the thirties, a different kind of emphasis was required by the fact that American capitalism seemed incapable of satisfying even the nation's physical needs, much less its spiritual needs. The crucial problem was no longer that the American dream had become materialistic and corrupting, but that the promises of the dream had been so utterly broken as to cast millions into poverty and desperation. In their pre-Depression works, such writers as Dreiser, Fitzgerald, and Lewis frequently portray characters who realize their dreams of material success, but find them empty, corrupt, or otherwise unsatisfying. Reflecting a new set of conditions, the writers of the thirties portray characters for whom the dream is completely illusory and unrealizable. It may also be shallow and puerile, but it is above all a delusion.

This image of the American dream as delusion or fantasy is one of the major motifs running through the literature of the thirties, linking works which are otherwise diverse in subject and treatment. In Steinbeck's *Of Mice and Men,* the major theme is the dream Lennie and George have of buying a farm and living "on the fatta the lan'." In O'Neill's *The Iceman Cometh* the dominant theme is the illusions or "pipe dreams" which sustain the down-and-out characters who inhabit Harry Hope's bar. In Farrell's *Studs Lonigan* trilogy a major theme is the discrepancy between Studs's dreams of glory and the failure and frustration of his life in reality. In numerous other works of the decade—works by Nathanael West, Erskine Caldwell, Clifford Odets, and William Saroyan, for example— characters dream and talk endlessly of the things they are going to do, the success they will achieve, in the future. Generally it is understood, clearly by the reader and vaguely by the characters themselves, that there can be no actual fulfillment of the dreams. The expectations expressed by the dreams are often absurdly out of harmony with the reality in which the characters exist. The dreams function, then, not as a stimulus for effectual action but as a substitute for it. In a world too frustrating for the characters to face squarely and cope with successfully, dreams become an end in themselves. They are repeated mechanically as if, through some occult process, they might serve to stave off despair and justify the dreamer's devotion to them. In a context where real action and achievement have been totally thwarted, the words and format of the dreams take on great importance. Thus, the language expressing the hopes and delusions of the characters is often patterned and repetitious, like the incantations of primitive rituals designed to bring rain or insure success in battle.

Writers who treat the subject assume varying attitudes toward their characters and toward the illusions from which they draw life. To Caldwell the dreams are pathetically humorous; to Steinbeck they are compelling but distracting; to Farrell they are shallow, pernicious, and enervating; to O'Neill they are the last safeguard against despair; to Saroyan they are therapeutic and beautiful; and to West they are grotesque and potentially sources of violence. But whatever the specific attitudes toward the dreams and the dreamers, the central fact that these works of the Depression years repeatedly come back to is that the dreams are illusory, far removed from the reality which the characters are thrust into.

The Agrarian Dream as Delusion

As our writers of the thirties turned their eyes on the broken promises of American life, one of their focal points was the poor farm people who, excluded for the most part from the prosperity of the twenties, were in an even worse position in the Depression years. In popular literature, as we have seen, the agrarian myth was by no means dead. Popular writers still invoked the image of an idyllic life of independent and self-reliant success close to nature. Less superficial writers, however, portrayed rural settings in which the agrarian dream had turned into nostalgic fantasies, absurd illusions, and a nightmare reality. The most complete and suggestive treatment of this theme is in Steinbeck's *Of Mice and Men.* But illusions of a rural paradise where the fruit is lush and no one is hungry serve as an important motif also in *The Grapes of Wrath.* And Erskine Caldwell portray even more groundless and absurd illusions in the poor Georgia clay farmers of *God's Little Acre.*

In a commentary on the origins of his novel, *Tobacco Road,* Erskine Caldwell recalls walking in the midsummer heat among the eroded clay ridges of Georgia, surrounded by stunted cotton plants trying to survive in the depleted soil. Across the fields people in tenant shacks were waiting for the cotton to mature.

> They believed in cotton. They believed in it as some men believe in God. They had faith in the earth and in the plants that grew in the earth. Even though they had been fooled the year before, and for many years before that, they were certain the fields would soon be showered with tumbling, bursting bolls of glistening white cotton.[1]

Caldwell goes on to report how in midwinter he had seen people in rags, searching for food and warmth, hoping to stay alive until spring so they could put out the next year's cotton crop. What most impressed him was that the people still had faith in nature and still could not understand how the earth could fail them. "But it had failed them, and there they were waiting in another summer for an autumn harvest that would never come."

In most of Caldwell's novels and stories a vague and indefinite hope is about all the characters have left, if they even have that. Their losing struggle to wrest a living from the desolate land has sapped them of their ambi-

tion, and few of them are capable of realistic and constructive efforts
toward self-improvement. The absurdity to which the American dream
has been reduced for them is best symbolized by the ludicrous spectacle
of Ty Ty Walden and his family digging up their farm in search of gold in
God's Little Acre. Unlike many of Caldwell's characters, Ty Ty is a man
who is capable of pursuing his dreams and desires with considerable energy
and intensity. He has the industry and perseverance required by the mythology of success, refusing to let minor setbacks like dirt slides discourage
him: " 'I've been digging in this land close on to fifteen years now, and
I'm aiming to dig here fifteen more, if need be. . . . We've just got to keep
plugging away like nothing ever happened. That's the only way to do.
You boys are too impatient about little things."[3] In such proclamations
one can detect vestiges of the traditional teachings that have been passed
down from the Puritans, to Franklin, to the McGuffey reader, and on into
the present.

But despite his stoic perseverance Ty Ty has long since lost any hope
of making a decent living by devoting his energies to the practical task of
farming his barren land. Caldwell suggests that the only way Ty Ty can
avoid succumbing to frustration and despair is by the delusion that all
his efforts will be rewarded when he strikes gold. His dream of striking
gold thus has become an all-consuming passion, and his repeated expres-
sions of faith that gold will be found take the form of a ritual that keeps
the boys working and the whole family hoping for a better future. Any
questioning of whether there is really gold there or any suggestion that
Ty Ty should be farming instead of digging always draws a similar response:
"The lode is there, sure as God made little green apples," or "the gold is
there, if I could only locate it. I've got an albino now, though, and I'm
aiming to strike the lode any day now."[4]

At the end of the novel, when Ty Ty feels the desolation brought on
by watching one of his sons kill another, he looks at his scarred and pitted
land and has some realization of the irony in the situation: he has added
to the desolation of the land that he feels so tied to. "He wished then that
he had the strength to spread out his arms and smooth the land as far as
he could see. . . . He realized how impotent he was by his knowledge that
he would never be able to do that. He felt heavy at heart."[5] And soon he
is back in the latest crater, which is under a corner of the house threatening to topple it. He feels a "consuming desire" to dig, not so much because
he has any real hope of striking gold, but because he does not know any-

thing else to do. Delusion or not, the dream of locating the lode is all he has, and he must keep digging.

Caldwell exploits the comedy inherent in the outlandish behavior of his characters, but it is a wry humor deriving from the matter-of-fact, deadpan style with which he describes the characters and situations. His parody of the agrarian dream of an idyllic life close to the soil is bitterly comic, but it is not frivolous or condescending. It is based on a dark vision of the discrepancy between dream and reality in America and on a deep sympathy for the poor Georgia farm people for whom the American dream has become a farce.

While Caldwell portrays the deterioration of the American dream into the absurdity of Ty Ty's gold delusion, Steinbeck's *The Grapes of Wrath* dramatizes the bankruptcy of the old American hope of finding opportunit and fulfillment by going west. Though the dream of the Joads would appea at first to be more realistic than that of the Waldens, it soon becomes clear that the Joad family has about as much chance of partaking in the bounty of California as the Walden family has of discovering gold in the eroded hills of Georgia. In both cases the dream is a delusion which can postpone the necessity of facing reality, but cannot itself become a reality.

Just as immigrants and migrants have historically viewed America itself as a promised land and the western frontier as a land of opportunity where a man could get a fresh start, Steinbeck's Okies head for California worried only about getting there and convinced that if they make it their troubles are over. The handbills advertising jobs in the fruit country, combined with the hopeful visions of the migrants, have created an image of California as a lush, green paradise where the fruit is succulent and the work pleasant and full of rewards. The parallelism between California as the Joads envision it and the biblical land of Canaan is clear and appropriate.[6]

The Joads' dream of a California paradise, like the gold delusion of Ty T and his family, is repeated ritualistically and sustains the characters when they have good reason to despair. The pattern is established when, on the eve of their departure, a nervous uneasiness about the magnitude of what they are doing sets in. Tom advises Ma to stop worrying and adjust to their uncertain future by facing each day as it comes. " 'Yes, that's a good way,' she answers. " 'But I like to think how nice it's gonna be, maybe, in California. Never cold. An' fruit ever place, an' people just being in the nicest places, little white houses in among the orange trees.' "[7] A little later, Pa recites the same essential formula to Al. Needing some reassurance Al asks,

" 'You glad to be going, Pa?' " " 'Huh? [Pa says] Well sure. Leastwise—
yeah. We had hard times here. 'Course it'll be all different out there—
plenty work, an' everything nice an' green, an' little white houses an'
oranges growin' around.' "[8] Frequently, the dream-vision of paradise in
California is expressed through the symbolism of grapes. Grandpa Joad
says, for example, " 'An', by God, they's grapes out there, just a-hangin'
over inta the road. Know what I'm a-gonna do? I'm gonna pick me a wash
tub full a grapes, an' I'm gonna set down in 'em an' scrooge around, an'
let the juice run down my pants.' "[9] Through their repeated invocations
of these images of juicy grapes, green fields, and white houses among the
orange groves, Steinbeck's characters express a profound need for a shared
vision, a ritual, to support them in their struggle with an unpredictable
reality. As Ma Joad implies when she politely rejects Tom's suggestion
that they take each day as it comes, the family needs something which
transcends the existential, day-by-day acceptance of reality.

When the Joads set out, then, they are still, despite their junked lives,
able to bolster their spirits by dreaming the American dream, though
rather uneasily and with a vague inkling that it is illusory. As they proceed,
one of the main sources of dramatic tension is the ironic contrast between
their dreams of a California paradise and the brutal reality they actually
find. It is a contrast that conveys starkly Steinbeck's vision of the bankruptcy of the American dream in Depression America. The most obvious
line of development in the novel is a negative one, the opposite of a success
story. The Okies sink irreversibly into a deeper destitution and a deeper
disillusionment. When the bitter facts first begin to intrude themselves,
the Joads are able to delay facing reality by invoking a part of their
promised-land ritual. To the ragged man who gives them grim reports of
the wage swindle and of the starvation of his wife and children, their
response is: " 'What the hell you talkin' about? I got a han' bill says they
got good wages, an' little while ago I seen a thing in the paper says they
need folks to pick fruit.' "[10] But the delusory quality of their hopes soon
becomes painfully apparent as they encounter frustration after frustration,
until at the end of the novel those who remain have no food, no shelter,
no possessions (having abandoned their truck in the mud), no jobs, and
no immediate prospects of providing themselves with any of these things.
Worse, perhaps, they continue to lose each other. Granpa has died early
in their journey and Granma a little later; Connie, who had fed on the
daydream of "studying up" at night and "getting someplace," instead

deserts his pregnant wife; Noah wanders off; Casy is murdered; Rosasharn's baby is born dead; Tom becomes a fugitive; and Al wants to get away on his own as soon as possible. If there is any of the old ability to hope and dream left in the Joad family, it seems destined for extinction by the events which end the novel.

The dream of the Okies, then, turns out to be a pathetic illusion. Ironically, it is an illusion not in the sense that the real California lacks the lush, green beauty of their dreams, but in the sense that they are barred from sharing in the bounty. When they enter into California, they find the scene spellbinding:

> They drove through Tehachapi in the morning glow, and the sun came up behind them, and then—suddenly they saw the great valley below them. Al jammed on the brake and stopped in the middle of the road, and, "Jesus Christ! Look!" he said. The vineyards, the orchards, the great flat valley, green and beautiful, the trees set in rows, and the farm houses.[11]

But the American dream that lowly people like the Joads can acquire their share of the plentiful land through desire and individual effort is a monumental fraud, Steinbeck suggests. Only through a strong communal unity and class solidarity can the dispossessed hope to grasp their share. There is hope in the fact that bitter disillusionment helps to develop this sense of unity. When the dream of the grapes of plenty is shattered, the grapes of wrath grow. As Steinbeck says repeatedly in the novel's interchapters, "In the souls of the people the grapes of wrath are filling and growing heavy, heavy for the vintage." The implication is that the dream of individual success in a land of plenty, comforting though it may seem to people like the Joads, is actually a relic of the past which will have to be recognized as such before there can be any effective communal action to redress social wrongs.

If Steinbeck's treatment of the American dream as illusion in *The Grapes of Wrath* suggests that the dream's destruction might be a necessary preliminary to social improvement, the conclusion in *Of Mice and Men* seems to be that the dream of George and Lennie, though also pathetically illusory, is itself the only hope they have of happiness.

Steinbeck presents the dream as attractive and compelling, but leaves little doubt that it is an illusion which can never be fulfilled. It is like a religious ritual which they perform periodically when Lennie feels insecure.

The ceremony has become so familiar that even the half-wit Lennie knows it by memory and anticipates each part as George recites it. When George repeats the dream, his words come "rhythmically as though he had said them many times before":

> "Guys like us, that work on ranches, are the loneliest guys in the world. They got no family. They don't belong no place. . . . They ain't got nothing to look ahead to."
>
> Lennie was delighted. "That's it—that's it. Now tell how it is with us."
>
> George went on, "With us it ain't like that. We got a future."[12]

And George goes on to fill out their picture of an idyllic life on a picturesque little farm with a little house, an orchard, a cow and some pigs, a garden and a hutch of rabbits for Lennie. It is a childishly simple version of one of the dreams that have always touched Americans most deeply—the dream of achieving the dignity, security, and self-reliance that comes from owning and working one's own land.

In the world of popular fiction, such a beautiful dream would be almost certain to come true. But according to Steinbeck's vision of America, even so modest a dream can be nothing but a delusion for men like Lennie and George. From the beginning, the book moves with tragic inevitability toward the final scene in which Lennie is dead and the dream is shattered. Steinbeck creates a countermovement in which the dream, briefly, seems *almost* possible of realization. It is revealed that George has a specific farm in mind that they could buy for six hundred dollars. The old man, Candy, has three hundred dollars and would like to go into partnership with them. Adding the fifty dollars apiece that will be due them at the end of the month, they calculate that they will have most of the necessary money and could pay off the rest easily after they have the farm. But the effect of the countermovement is merely to intensify the sense of tragedy and loss which comes when the dream is destroyed. Steinbeck makes the reader believe in the dream momentarily, then shatters this belief, as if to illustrate the pathetic falsity of all the fairy tales and happy endings which assume that the nice dreams of nice people come true.

During the upsurge of hope midway in the novel, the power of the dream is so strong that the stable buck, Crooks, is easily converted from cold cynicism (" 'I seen hundreds of men come by . . . an' every damn one of 'em's got a little piece of land in his head. An' never a God damn one of 'em ever gets it.' "[13]) to a belief in the dream which is complete enough that he offers to work as a hand on the farm. But it is at this point that the threatening reality of the outside world enters the scene in the form of Curley's wife. After her appearance, the movement toward the catastrophic conclusion is precipitous. The dream recedes into the realm of fantasy again when Candy, sensing that the girl's presence is going to upset their plans, begins to speak of the farm in the present tense as if they already have it: "You don't know that we got our own ranch to go to, an' our own house. We ain't got to stay here."[14] Soon Lennie kills the girl the way he has always crushed his pet animals, and there is no longer any hope. When George learns of what has happened, he admits that deep inside he knew all along that they would never realize their dream: " 'I think I knowed from the very first. I think I knowed we'd never do her. He usta like to hear about it so much I got to thinking maybe we would.' "[15] The ending implies that for the Georges and Lennies of the world the dream cannot be realized in life—only in death. As George prepares to kill Lennie, they repeat once more the ritual of their dream-vision. Lennie begs " 'Le's do it now. Le's get that place now.' " George answers, " 'Sure, right now. I gotta. We gotta,' " and puts the bullet in Lennie's head.[16]

Steinbeck's attitude toward the content of Lennie and George's dream is one of considerable imaginative sympathy, and in certain respects, this positive attitude amounts to an affirmation of traditional American faiths. There is strong emphasis, for instance, on independence, self-reliance, and personal freedom. George says at one point, " 'S'pose they was a carnival or a circus come to town, or a ball game, or any damn thing. . . . We'd just go to her. . . . We wouldn't ask nobody if we could.' "[17] Also, the dream affirms the value of honest work and a close relationship to the land. All these ideals, of course, are deeply rooted in the American past and are fundamental, in particular, to the tradition of Jeffersonian agrarianism.

On the other hand, many of the values inherent in the dream-vision of the farm reflect the new temper of the thirties and constitute a marked departure from the ideals associated with the classic American dream of personal advancement. Most notably, the dream of Lennie and George rejects personal ambition and individual self-aggrandizement in favor of companionship and cooperation.

The characters need each other and realize it. They are different from the ordinary lonely and isolated ranch workers, their ritual says, "because

I got you to look after me and you got me to look after you." It is obvious
enough that George makes the dream possible for Lennie, who is incapable
of conceiving or planning such a thing. But it is also true that Lennie makes
the dream possible for George. When George, in the part of their ritual
game that Lennie refers to as "giving me hell," tells what he could do *if*
(another dream) he did not have Lennie to worry about, he always describes
a life of aimless dissipation with no future: " 'I could get a job and have
no mess. . . . An' when the end of the month come I could take my fifty
bucks an' go to a . . . cat house,' " and when the fifty bucks was gone,
he would find another job on another ranch and start the cycle again.[18]
As he tells Candy, this is exactly the kind of life he envisages for himself
after Lennie's death. Without Lennie, there can be no dream. Any hope
of fulfilling the dream depends on a cooperative effort, but more importantly the very capacity to dream the dream grows out of the shared
experience of two people and cannot be sustained by one man alone.
This marks an important departure from the highly individualistic standard
version of the American dream.

It should also be pointed out that, unlike many American dreamers,
George and Lennie have no desire to be financially well off. Their goals
are extremely modest: they simply want to be independent, comfortably
settled, and *secure*. More than anything else, their illusory farm represents
a safe place, a retreat from the vain strivings of the outside world. Like
the caves Lennie mentions several times and the thicket by the river, where
the action begins and ends, the farm represents a haven of protection and
security. It is a place where Lennie, the primitive, will no longer come
into conflict with the civilized world and where George will be freed from
the struggle to earn a living in the outside world. The farm, in short, is an
archetypal symbol of the return to the safety and serenity of nature. It
belongs to a tradition that goes at least as far back in American literature
as Washington Irving's "Rip Van Winkle." Thoreau's retreat to Walden
Pond and Mark Twain's portrayal of the river as a place of freedom and
escape from civilization in *Huckleberry Finn* are a part of the same tradition, as are Faulkner's description of Ike McCaslin's initiation into the
wilderness in "The Bear" and Hemingway's idyllic portraits (in *The Sun
Also Rises*, "Big Two-Hearted River," and other works) of fishing in cool
mountain streams far removed from the violence and confusion of civilized
life. In symbolically identifying George and Lennie's dream-farm with
this deeply rooted tradition, Steinbeck implicitly rejects the equally deeply
rooted dream of material success, for the desire to escape civilization is

fundamentally antagonistic to the American dream of striving and succeeding in a competitive system. Lennie and George want to disengage themselves from society, not move up in it. To attempt the latter is to run the risk of being plowed up like field mice.

Judging from the public reception of the novel, Steinbeck struck a responsive chord among readers of the thirties with his story of the tragic dream of Lennie and George. The book made some of the best-seller lists and was soon bought by a Hollywood movie producer, while the dramatization won both popular and critical acclaim, including the Drama Critics' Circle Award for 1937. A public which had seen dreams shattered by the Depression could identify on a deep emotional basis with ordinary men like Lennie and George whose modest dreams turned out to be so illusory. Though the story challenged the comforting myths propounded by the popular magazines and the movies, offering no hope that the simple dreams of men like Lennie and George could be realized, it nevertheless did not renounce the dream itself. It demonstrated with sympathy and compassion a truth that many people discovered for themselves in the Depression years—that impossible, illusory dreams were sometimes the only form of happiness one could expect.

The Power of Illusions

Another writer who had a profound understanding of the power—and, in some cases, the value—of illusions was Eugene O'Neill. Not merely in his plays of the thirties, but throughout his career, O'Neill kept working and reworking the theme of man and his dreams or illusions. In some works he portrayed illusions as dangerous and destructive; in others he presented them ambiguously as both destructive and life-giving; and in several plays he viewed them unequivocally as man's only source of happiness. Whatever the attitude toward the dreams, they enter significantly into the lives of O'Neill's characters in play after play. In "Bound East for Cardiff" (1914) Yank's dream is essentially the same one that Lennie and George live on in *Of Mice and Men*. He longs to escape the drudgery of his life as a sailor by settling with Driscoll on a farm in Canada or Argentina. Like the dream farm of Lennie and George, Yank's dream has made his life bearable even though he has never made an active effort to realize it. In "Diff'rent" (1920), on the other hand, Emma's illusion that she and Caleb are different from and better than other people eventually leads to tragedy—the suicides of both her and Caleb. In *Beyond the Horizon* (1918) and *Anna Christie* (1920) illusion leads to defeat, but also provides the courage to triumph over it. In the former, Robert's illusion that he can provide an idyllic life for himself and Ruth on the family farm leads to failure, physical decline, and an early death; yet he dies happily because of another illusion—that his suffering has been spiritually beneficial and that death will free him to pursue future dreams "beyond the horizon." In the latter, Anna's illusion that she is the victim of a bad background allows her to rationalize becoming a prostitute instead of taking a job as a governess; at the same time, her own illusions and those of her father and her future husband make it possible for the three to fashion a life in which they can accept themselves and each other. Clearly O'Neill had difficulty making up his own mind whether dreams should be regarded as a curse or a blessing.

However, without trying to prove that the period of hardship and broken dreams that America experienced in the Depression years was *the* cause, it can be pointed out that in the plays written during and after the thirties, O'Neill seems finally settled on the conclusion that illusions are necessary if life is to be worth living. In three of the last four plays he wrote on the subject of illusion (the exception being *Long Day's Journey into Night*), he takes a dim view of man's ability to find peace and fulfillment in the world of reality and treats illusion, consistently, as man's only hope for happiness. *A Touch of the Poet* (1935-41) is a whimsical but penetrating treatment of the tendency to prefer dreams over reality. It concerns a man's illusion that he is a cultured, well-to-do gentleman living among rabble. His daughter, a practical girl, tries to nag him out of his foolish fantasy. But when the old man does unexpectedly give up his pose, his daughter realizes that she has also depended upon the illusion and begs him to be "himself" again. In one of O'Neill's finest short plays, *Hughie* (1941-42), a Broadway sport named "Erie" Smith relates how the gullible and naïve Hughie, now dead, used to give Erie faith in himself by listening to and believing his fantasies and self-delusions. The play ends when the character who has replaced Hughie as night clerk also replaces Hughie as the sounding board for Erie's fantasies. But O'Neill's fullest and most powerful treatment of man's need for illusions is in *The Iceman Cometh* (written in 1939, first published in 1946), a play which reaches the unequivocal conclusion that men cannot live without their illusions.

Though *Iceman* is set in the early years of the twentieth century rather than in the Depression years, it portrays the kind of down-and-out characters who are so familiar in the literature of the thirties. They are characters, like so many of the characters of Steinbeck, Caldwell, Farrell, or Saroyan, for whom the American dream can be nothing more than a fantasy. It is a necessary fantasy however. As Larry Slade puts it, "To hell with the truth! . . . The lie of a pipe dream is what gives life to the whole misbegotten mad lot of us, drunk or sober."[19] O'Neill dramatizes this point with an excursion into a world rife with illusions, Harry Hope's Bar. For the circle of dreamers at Hope's, appropriately named since this is the one place where they can hope undisturbed by reality, the bar is a haven from the world of harsh reality. Here, each may be cynically tolerant of the others' illusions and, at the same time, maintain a surface faith in his own. Here, the whores can call themselves "tarts," the pimp can call himself a bartender with an extra income, and the others can believe that, if they wished to return to life, they would be instant successes in the endeavors they failed at before.

O'Neill portrays these dreamers as weak, wasted, and even grotesque in their self-deception. They represent an extremely decadent and ineffectual variety of American idealism. Yet they are harmless, they are surviving, and they are even reasonably content. There is no real dramatic conflict until O'Neill introduces Hickey into the scene to challenge the comfortable illusions of the other characters. Hickey is the archetypal American salesman, bearing some resemblances to Arthur Miller's Willie Loman; in the past he has been content to play the role of the affable, other-directed, boozing prankster, always good for a joke and a free drink and posing no threat to the alcoholic pipe dreams of the derelicts in the bar. This time, however, he comes into Hope's bar as an emissary from the world of reality, forcing a confrontation between illusion and reality. With evangelical zeal, he preaches that the dreamers must free themselves from their illusions. His contention is that once they know and face reality, they will be at peace with themselves. In this new role Hickey is not only unpleasant, but dangerous. He has become a fanatical, presumptuous peddler of salvation, representing the threat posed by all the salvationists and messiahs who disrupt other people's lives by their unsolicited meddling.

The havoc caused by his program of "salvation" is immediate and predictable. He goads the derelicts into venturing from the saloon to test their dreams against the reality of the outside world. Without exception they come back beaten, humiliated, and, worse, no longer able to find peace through dreams and drunkenness. They have lost the last reason they had for living—their pipe dreams or illusions—and are like the dead.

The implication is that it is false and pernicious to assume that the world is sufficiently hospitable and human character sufficiently strong for man to live in reality without protective illusions. Paradoxically, the worst pipe dream is Hickey's illusion that it is possible to live without illusions.

In order for the inhabitants of Hope's back room to be restored to their previous state of equilibrium, they must discover that Hickey represents not the voice of reason and wisdom, but the voice of insanity. They make this discovery, to their satisfaction, when they force Hickey to explain why he has changed and why he has not mentioned his usual joke about leaving his wife "in the hay with the iceman." Hickey explains that his wife is dead and that he has killed her "for her own sake." At this point the significance of the title's paraphrase of the biblical phrase "the bridegroom cometh" becomes clear. In Christian symbolism, the bridegroom is Christ, giver of life eternal. Hickey comes, also, he claims, as a giver of life.[20] But he has misunderstood the needs of his friends and has brought them not salvation but death. The iceman which finally came to Hickey's house was death and was brought by Hickey himself. Now he is bringing the iceman, death, to the bums in Hope's Bar.

The depth of Hickey's own illusions becomes clear in the course of his lengthy soliloquy explaining why he has killed his wife. He relates to the bums how his wife was ever-patient with him and forgave anything he did, and how because he loved her so much, he felt continually guilty until he killed her to avoid disappointing her anymore. But, strangely, as he relates the logic behind his actions, he realizes that all this, too, is illusion— that he really hated her because of her intolerable, overwhelming love. He blurts out, "Well, you know what you can do with your pipe dream now, you damned bitch!"[21] Then, horrified at the ugly truth about his sentiments, he bursts into frantic denial and retreats into another protective illusion: "No! That's a lie! I never said—! Good God, I couldn't have said that! If I did, I'd gone insane!"[22] When he appeals to his listeners, they welcome the chance to attribute his campaign against pipe dreams to insanity, for this explanation of his strange behavior, in a sense, restores them to life. Immediately they pick up their old roles and sink back into their comfortable illusions. Only Larry Slade, who has deluded himself that he was a grandstand philosopher waiting for death, is a convert to Hickey's "religion" of looking at reality. After giving Parritt permission to commit suicide, he finally realizes that he is not a detached philosopher, but just another down-and-out-bum, afraid of life but even more afraid of death.

He has also finally realized the crucial fact that death is all there is left: "Be God, I'm the only real convert to death Hickey made here. From the bottom of my coward's heart I mean that now."[23]

Although the pipe dreams of these characters make it possible for them to go on living, the dilemma O'Neill presents is cast in a darkness of tone that is as remote as it could possibly be from the easy optimism that we associate with the American dream of success and self-realization. With their dreams the characters survive, but they are inert, alcoholic bums; without their dreams, they are as good as dead. Among O'Neill's derelicts there is no youthful idealism, no feverish questing, no sensitivity to the promises of life. All they want is peace, and this they find only in their illusions. When O'Neill wrote *The Iceman*, at a time when the most miserable Depression in our history had still not lifted its pall and the most destructive war in our history was looming in the future, his vision of the possibilities for happiness in the real world was utterly bleak. In an interview concerning the play, he expressed a deep pessimism about the success of the American experiment:

> I'm going on the theory that the United States, instead of being the most successful country in the world, is the greatest failure. . . . It's the greatest failure because it was given everything, more than any other country. Through moving as rapidly as it has, it hasn't acquired any real roots. Its main idea is that everlasting game of trying to possess your own soul by the possession of something outside of it, thereby losing your own soul and the thing outside of it, too.[24]

Here, O'Neill is emphasizing the selfish and materialistic betrayal of the American dream, the failure to profit spiritually from the enormous possibilities represented by America. But his pessimism encompassed much more than the United States; it extended to humanity itself. He added in the same interview:

> If the human race is so damned stupid that in 2,000 years it hasn't had brains enough to appreciate that the secret of happiness is contained in one sentence which you'd think any grammar school kid could understand and apply, then it's time we dumped it down the nearest drain and let the ants have a chance. That simple sentence is: "What shall it profit a man?"[25]

In *The Iceman* O'Neill explores the broad implications of this simple question: What shall it profit a man? He asks, What shall it profit a man to venture from the protective sanctuary of his illusions into a fruitless struggle for happiness in the real world? More broadly, he dramatizes the ambiguity of "truth" or "reality" and asks whether there exists a reality or a meaning in the universe beyond man's illusions. If life itself is like a dream and if faith in life's meaning is merely one of man's illusions, then that other dream—the American dream of success and fulfillment—can have no meaning. Life can be endured by the aid of pipe dreams and liquor, but beyond these there is nothing else but death. As one critic summarizes O'Neill's philosophy, "dreams, drunkenness, and death" are the ends of life.[26]

Another play of 1939, William Saroyan's *The Time of Your Life,* though lighter in tone, is similar to *The Iceman Cometh* in its substitution of a world of fantasy for any real pursuit of the American dream. It also uses a barroom setting and strange, unfortunate characters who compensate for their failure by living in a childlike world of fantasy more rewarding than material success. The characters have no ambition to conquer the real world; the best they can hope for is to escape its harsh realities. The dream motif is most fully developed in the characterization of Kitty Duval, a prostitute who, very much in the manner of O'Neill's whore-tarts, deceives herself with dreams. She dreams that she was once a great burlesque star who had flowers sent to her by "European royalty." She dreams of home: "I've no *home*. I've no place. But I always dream of all of us together again."[27] And she dreams of wealth and fame, the splendor of big houses and big lawns with flowers, and the romance of being a famous actress courted by a young doctor who would see her at the theater and fall in love with her. Her dreams are banal imitations of the familiar magazine stories of success and romance, but Saroyan treats her with indulgent sympathy and never laughs at her.

Saroyan's attitude is that if the characters stay in their make-believe world, their dreams are a blessing. Joe, who represents the voice of wisdom in the play, would "believe dreams sooner than statistics" because dreams "correct the errors of the world."[28] But Saroyan suggests that *really* believing in the American dream of success is foolish and destructive. He says about Dudley Bostwick: "He is a young man who has been taught that he has a chance, as a person, and believes it. As a matter of fact, he hasn't a chance in the world, and should have been told by somebody."[29] Dudley's literal belief in the dream of success has trapped him in a life of overwork, dullness, routine middle-class virtue, and monotony. He is somewhat pretentious and ordinary (as his name suggests), saved from being a complete nothing only by the fact that he has a simple and basic desire for a woman—an urgent and violent need which brings him into contact with a natural and spontaneous force within himself. It is this natural spontaneity which has almost been subverted by his belief in conventional success.

Despite Saroyan's antagonism toward American bourgeois culture—its worship of money, its cult of success, its code of respectability—he was temperamentally incapable of the deep pessimism which pervades O'Neill's *The Iceman Cometh*. His Depression works depicted with sometimes bitter indignation the poverty, the squalor, and the absurdly delusive dreams of his humble characters. Yet, while O'Neill portrays illusions as a pitifully thin protection against despair and death, Saroyan sees his characters' dreams as truly symbolic of the resiliency of the human spirit. Despite the condition of the characters, a sense of life and youth is conveyed by the undisciplined and spontaneous structure of *The Time of Your Life,* whereas death is an overriding presence in *The Iceman Cometh*. Even Saroyan's bitter awareness of the suffering caused by the Depression could not quell his essential optimism. It was a naïve and sometimes sentimental bitterness, arising not from cynicism and despair, but from a deep need to believe in the American dream of unlimited possibilities and in the innate goodness of man. Because of the affirmation of America which shows through his antimaterialism and his hostility to the myth of success, Saroyan has sometimes been compared to Thoreau or Whitman. But another, less flattering, comparison suggests itself also. In many ways Saroyan's optimism resembles the sentimental idealism of the popular-magazine fiction of the Depression years. In that fiction, when the existence of the Depression is recognized at all, there is almost always some kind of affirmation, whether warranted by the circumstances or not. Saroyan's dreamy, vague, sometimes sentiment: optimism is similar—based on nothing more substantial than the use of illusions as an escape device to "correct the errors of the world."

Self-Delusion in the Chicago Slums

Of the many works of the thirties that portray the American dream as delusion, probably none is more relentlessly dark than James T. Farrell's *Studs Lonigan* trilogy. In that cycle there is a deep and heavy irony implicit in the contrast between dream and reality, between the exalted promises of American life and the bitter actuality. In Studs Lonigan's case there is no suggestion that his dreams are harmless fantasies that help to make life bearable; instead his dreams are not only pitiful self-delusions, but also pernicious destructive forces, contributing to his eventual ruin.

In his preface to the first novel in the trilogy, *Young Lonigan*, Farrell explains that he conceived the novel as a study of how boys were growing up in 1916: "What were their dreams of themselves and of their future? How were young Americans being 'made' by American society?" The answer for Studs, as a product of Southside Chicago, is that the dreams instilled in him by his environment are extremely shallow and potentially destructive. Studs's parents have relatively benign dreams for him: his mother wants him to become a priest and his father anticipates his taking over the family paint business. But Studs himself, more influenced by the ethic of the Chicago streets, dreams of being "strong and tough and the real stuff." He daydreams, for example, of impressing Lucy by beating up some hard guy to protect her character. Ironically, as *Young Lonigan* develops, Studs succeeds in realizing this tough-guy dream; he becomes increasingly tougher, meaner, and more brutal. The tragedy at this point is not that his dreams are impossible but that they are shoddy and do not represent the kind of aspiration that could lead to a decent future.

The early chapters of *The Young Manhood of Studs Lonigan* develop some of the consequences of Studs's tough-guy mystique. His "iron man" ideology of aggressive individualism, a perversion of the traditional American belief in self-reliance, is destructive because it spoils his personal relationships and his ability to adjust to the social world. He cannot communicate with Lucy, though he loves her, because he tries so hard to be tough, not soft. He has no desire to get an education or to work, and by the age of fifteen is already trapped in the pattern of dissipation and street-corner idleness that will continue until his early death. When he tries to use his tough-guy approach in a context outside the world of street-corner juvenile gangs, he finds that he is a miserable failure. He begins to dream of pulling a stickup, for instance, but when he tries it, he gets laughed at and runs. With respect to his tough-guy ethic, what he can dream and what he can do are no longer in harmony. Worse, his efforts to settle down to a job and rise above the life of degeneracy he is headed for are equally feeble and ineffectual. Increasingly, he merely dreams idly about reforming and making something of himself, incapable of any sustained action to save himself.

The quality of the idle dreams and fantasies that Studs dwells on at this point in his young manhood is barely a cut above that of his boyhood tough-guy aspirations. He begins to feel the emptiness of these early dreams and to want more. But his stunted imagination can conceive of nothing more exalted than the aspirations typified by the dream he slips into after seeing a movie about Alaska. He becomes "Yukon Lonigan in the gold fields. . . . Shooting his way out to keep the gold he's won. The picture made him want things like that, big dough, travel, broads as gorgeous as Gloria."[30] At this point in his life (he is twenty-one years old and the time is 1922) Studs's poverty is more spiritual than physical. Though his background is culturally squalid and stultifying, his father's paint business supports the family on a lower-middle-class level, and they have the means to move out of the Fifty-eighth Street neighborhood when the "niggers" move in. Studs's environment has simply not provided him with models and values of sufficient substance to give his life a direction. When he is not dreaming fairy-tale dreams like the one inspired by the Yukon movie, his conception of the "something else" that is missing in his life is very nebulous—a vague desire for a woman and a decent life. And he has moments of realization that even this is an illusory dream. In the midst of a dream of being reformed by a girl he sees at Mass, he thinks, "He wasn't just a hood. . . ." But then, "It was all a goddamn pipe-dream. He was just filling himself full of stuff. Only if the thing had turned out different. He'd missed his chance. . . . All a goddamn pipe-dream!"[31] And in two minutes he is drinking with the Fifty-eighth Street gang again. *The Young Manhood of Studs Lonigan* ends powerfully with Studs lying in a gutter dead drunk after a wild and sordid New Year's Eve party ushering in 1929. Farrell concludes with another reference to Studs's early dreams: "It was Studs Lonigan, who had once, as a boy, stood before Charlie Bathcellar's poolroom thinking that someday he would be strong, and tough, and the real stuff."[32]

In *Judgment Day* the pattern of failure and degeneration is brought to its conclusion, and the sense of social as well as individual dissolution is accentuated by the projection of Studs's final decline against the background of the terrible economic Depression. In beginning this last novel of the trilogy, Farrell was faced with a structural problem. Since the essence of life in Southside Chicago as Farrell viewed it was unrelieved sameness, the opposite of mobility, the inevitable subject of *Judgment Day* was more of the same sordidness and degeneration that had already been brought to a powerful climax in *The Young Manhood of Studs*

Lonigan. Farrell needed relief from the monotony of this steady degeneration. Thus, he begins *Judgment Day,* after an initial chapter which sets
the dominant mood of degeneration and death, on a note of rising hope
based on the prospect that Studs's new girl, Catherine, might be the incentive
he needs to straighten out his life. But Studs has always been incapable of
acting on his hopes, and when the paralyzing economic Depression hits,
effective action is even more out of the question for him. Increasingly, he
moves like one in a dream, with the dream life becoming more and more
active as his real life becomes more hopeless. He becomes a Walter Mitty,
living almost exclusively on dreams of sexual conquest, financial mastery,
and heroic adventure. Walking down Michigan Boulevard with Catherine,
he is inspired by the tall buildings. Inside were men with money and power.
"And he could be like them. A man could have anything in this life that
he wanted if he had the guts to go after it, and the faith and belief that he
could succeed. Some day he was going to do it for both himself and for
Catherine. . . ."[33] That Studs can think these thoughts despite his past
and the fact that already, because of the Depression, his father's business
is suffering underscores the extent of the gap between his dreams and
reality.

Studs's fantasies contribute to his plight by serving as a substitute for
action, but they are harmful in other ways also. His dream of making a
killing on the stock market, in the manner of the popular-magazine success
stories, results in the loss of the money he has saved. He believes the enticing
promises of Ike Dugan, who sells him the stocks, and adds his own fantasies
about how fast he will make a fortune through speculation: "Other guys
had cleaned up doing it, and he had been just too dumb to know it. Well,
it still wasn't too late, and he'd be worth a hell of a lot more than Red
Kelly ever would be, and it wouldn't be long, either." Even after he has
lost his savings, he dreams:

> But suppose . . . that he still had his two thousand bucks.
> Suppose he had even cleaned up on the market a little, two
> hundred, five hundred, two thousand, five thousand, fifteen
> thousand. . . . Bank accounts, checking accounts, buying any-
> thing he wanted to. Thinking of himself like this, too, it gave
> him a pleasant, sleepy, lulling feeling. His eyes grew heavy. A
> drowsing, dozeful sense of animal comfort caressed his limbs,
> his nerves, his muscles, his brain. Studs Lonigan, the big shot.
> He fell asleep.[34]

Farrell's vision of what the dream of success can do for someone like Studs Lonigan is cogently summed up by this passage: the dream has ended in disaster and now it lulls Studs to sleep.

In his moments of contact with reality, however, Studs realizes the desperateness of his situation; he knows that "things had gone too far for him to be kidding himself with such dreams."[35] As he approaches marriage to Catherine, who is pregnant, he is a pauper. He is jobless and has no skill or education, and his health is failing, though he has not yet reached the age of thirty. His state of mind alternates between delusions of success and bitter regrets about what he has done with his life. The regrets are as fruitless as the dreams, however, and, at the end, all is failure and ruin. As Studs is dying, his father is being finally ruined by the Depression, bewildered by the way in which the faiths he has believed in have failed: "Hadn't he earned his place in the world by hard work? Hadn't he always provided for his family to the best of his abilities, tried to be a good husband and a good father, a true Catholic, and a real American?"[36]

With Studs dead, his father broken and headed for alcoholism, and the Depression worsening, Farrell ends a monumental story of frustration and failure. The American dream has been present as a false image, a delusion, and a promise which could only be broken. The tragedy is partly that Studs's dreams, like those of Ty Ty Walden, Lennie and George, and the alcoholic bums who inhabit Harry Hope's bar, are the desperate self-delusion of a frustrated man who feels cheated by life. But just as pathetic is the fact that his dreams, from the early tough-guy visions to the Hollywood-inspired success fantasies, are shabby products of an imagination stunted by the thin banality of the mass culture which has provided him with his goals and images. Practically all of Studs's experiences are studies in starved values, delusions, false appearances, and disastrous miscalculations of life. He joins the Order of Christopher, listens to Father Moylan, the radio priest, goes to escapist movies, hears insipid popular songs, and watches dance marathons—all of which immerse him in shallowness and falsity. Thus, reality for Studs Lonigan is made up of failure and defeat, while the dream world which compensates for reality is cheap, drab, and shallow. The American dream has failed Studs completely.

Dream, Frustration, and Violence

In his treatment of the American dream as a foolish, shallow, and ultimately destructive delusion, Farrell shares an attitude with another important writer of the thirties—Nathanael West. Though West uses a surrealistic technique which is vastly different from Farrell's documentary naturalism, both convey a vivid impression of the frustration, the dissolution, and the waste that accompany the shoddy and illusory dreams of their characters. West will be discussed more fully in another context, but his works (especially *The Day of the Locust*) contain viewpoints and insights which are relevant and important to the present discussion. A recurring theme in all four of West's novels is man's self-delusion in a world of frustration and failure. West had worked as manager of a hotel in New York after the 1929 crash and had observed the lost and broken people who would fill the lobby, building elaborate daydreams out of the magazines and cheap tabloids they read.[37] He understood well the function of such dreams and their special importance in a time like the Depression. He observes through Miss Lonelyhearts that "Men have always fought their misery with dreams." The problem in the modern world, Miss Lonelyhearts goes on, is that "Although dreams were once powerful, they have been made puerile by the movies, radio, and newspapers. Among many betrayals, this one is the worst."[38] In the nightmare world that West creates, full of grotesque and disappointed people, dreams create longings that are seldom fulfilled, and frustration yields violence and destruction.

It is not surprising that, for his most ambitious novel, *The Day of the Locust* (1939), West turned to America's dream capital, Hollywood, where dreams "were sealed in cans and marketed to the world." With its false fronts, pretensions, and excesses Hollywood could provide West with a ready-made symbolism for the illusions and lies of American life. The dreamers and searchers who come to Hollywood seeking paradise find that, like life itself, the dream capital promises wonders, but delivers only frustration. As James Light points out in a study of West, the two elements that dominate the novel are search and frustration. The searchers are always cheated, as is suggested by the constantly recurring images of falsity. The centrality of this theme in the novel is suggested by the fact that West had originally planned to title the work *The Cheated*.[39]

West uses a magnificently apt and powerful image to suggest the cheap ephemerality of the dreams manufactured by Hollywood. As Tod Hackett is walking across the studio lots, he leaves the road and comes across a ten-acre field grown up in cockleburs and a few sunflowers and wild gum. In the middle of the field is a huge pile of discarded sets, props, and flats which West refers to as a history of civilization in the form of a dream dump. Dreams are conceived, photographed, and junked, West says, "but no dream ever entirely disappears. Somewhere it troubles some unfortunate person and some day, when that person has been sufficiently troubled, it will be reproduced on the lot."[40] The falseness and flimsiness of the Hollywood dreams, as well as man's inability to escape the dreams that torment him, are suggested by this image of the "dumping ground for dreams." The dream dump and Hollywood itself are symbolic of the futility and barrenness of modern life and of the attempt to disguise this barrenness by the creation of cheap and fraudulent dreams. From the beginning, Hollywood is characterized as an "Unreal City," echoing Eliot's description of the unreal cities in *The Waste Land*. West's description of the wasteland of discarded movie sets also recalls Fitzgerald's eerie description of the valley of ashes in *The Great Gatsby,* another symbol of the modern spiritual wasteland. In turn, West's image of discarded and reappearing dreams is echoed in Fitzgerald's *The Last Tycoon,* when Monroe Stahr sits in his projection room caught in the unreal atmosphere created by the flickering screen images. Fitzgerald writes, "Dreams hung in fragments at the far end of the room, suffered analysis, passed—to be dreamed in crowds, or else discarded."[41] Both Fitzgerald and West had a sharp awareness of the function of dreams, and both envisioned Hollywood as a symbol of the shallowness and falsity of the dreams of modern man.

Of West's set of grotesque characters, the most suggestive in relation to the dream motif is Faye Greener, the bit-part actress and part-time prostitute who is irresistible to both Tod Hackett and Homer Simpson. She is a caricature of the American dreamer, feeding on blatantly artificial and childish dreams with never an inkling of their falsity. Like O'Neill's tarts and Saroyan's prostitute, Faye's central dream is to become a Hollywood star, and she admits spending whole days making up stereotyped fantasies of success as an actress. West says, "She had a large assortment of stories to choose from. After getting herself in the right mood, she would go over them in her mind, as though they were a pack of cards, discarding one after another until she found the one that suited."[42] She believes implicitly in the myth of success and talks endlessly about how successful careers are made in Hollywood and how she intends to make hers, mixing "bits of badly understood advice from the trade papers with other bits out of the fan magazines and compar[ing] these with the legends that surround the activities of screen stars and executives. Without any noticeable transition, possibilities became probabilities and wound up as inevitabilities."[43] Through Faye, West dramatizes the process by which dreams become sufficient in themselves, regardless of their conflict with reality. Faye is herself so completely a product of Hollywood, the dream factory, and so totally absorbed in her dream life that she is protected against reality. It does not matter that her dreams of fame and fortune are sheer fantasy, for reality does not touch her anyway. Dreams are an escape for her just as sleep is an escape for Homer Simpson.

The fascination that Faye holds for Tod and Homer is rooted largely in the fantastic vitality of her dream life. But if she represents the appeal of Hollywood dreams, she also represents the falsity and frustration. Like Hollywood, from which she has learned her affected mannerisms and artificial voice, she is a tease and a cheat, no more a real woman, as one critic phrases it, "than are the shadows on the screen."[44] She is capable of being openly promiscuous and even of working as a prostitute, but she refuses to satisfy Tod's lust. To Homer, who is symbolic of all the frustrated and cheated people who come to Hollywood seeking life, Faye brings a new vitality for a while. But it does not last. She persecutes and torments him and eventually sleeps with another man, leaving Homer in frustration and misery. It is a frustration which can never be purged or escaped. After Homer's brief return to the womb, it explodes into violence in the nightmarish final scene of the novel. In his fury, he attempts to stamp out another of the Hollywood cheaters—the child performer, Adore. His violence then merges with that of the mass of people collected for a movie premiere. Just as Homer has been driven beyond endurance by the false promises and frustrations which have made up his life, the mob of moviegoers are unconsciously aware of having been duped and cheated by the false dreams of Hollywood and of life itself. Their frustration finds an outlet in mob violence.

The mob is made up of "The people who come to California to die; the cultists of all sorts, economic as well as religious, the wave, airplane, funeral and preview watchers—all those poor devils who can be stirred only by the promise of miracles and then only to violence." They have become savage and bitter, anything but harmless curiosity seekers:

> They realize that they've been tricked and burn with resentment. . . . The sun is a joke. . . . Nothing can ever be violent enough to make taut their slack minds and bodies. They have been cheated and betrayed. They have slaved and saved for nothing.[45]

West suggests, then, that the dreams mass-produced by Hollywood and other vehicles of popular culture are pernicious and productive of violence because they are shallow and puerile, because they create glorious expectations that cannot be fulfilled, and because eventually they saturate the mind to the point that nothing can stir the feelings and relieve the boredom. Perhaps better than any other writer of his time, West understood the relationship between the false and meretricious dreams created and merchandised by American culture, and the violence which sporadically bubble up from the seething frustrations of those who found themselves deluded.

The recurring tragedy in these works of the thirties is not merely the spiritual poverty which grows out of the pursuit of a shabby and materialistic dream (a familiar theme in the twenties). It is something more fundamental: the physical as well as spiritual suffering, the destitution and despair, of those who are taught to dream of wonders, but find themselves trapped in a struggle merely to survive. In place of the Gatsbys, the Dexter Greens, the Babbitts, and the Dodsworths, one finds hungry farm people dreaming absurdly of gold or pathetically of lush fields; one finds the degenerate and floundering city boy dreaming idly of financial mastery; and one finds, recurringly, a figure who serves as an appropriate symbol of the whole milieu—the prostitute who lives on the fantasies of Hollywood stardom.

For these characters of the Depression years, the American dream of personal advancement and material success is remote and delusory, but not forgotten. Events had destroyed much of the dream's basis in reality, but they had not destroyed the extravagant expectations and the habit of dreaming which lay behind the quest for material success; these found an outlet in pure fantasy. The tendency to turn dream into fantasy is clearly illustrated by the popular literature of the thirties and perceptively analyzed by serious writers like West, Farrell, O'Neill, and Steinbeck who make direct or indirect commentaries on the myths and falsities of American popular culture. The Depression experience threw into clear relief the tendency of American optimism to become stubborn in a time of crisis and harden into the kind of self-deceptive idealism that creates its own brand of "reality" and rejects or ignores any other reality, and it is appropriate that illusion-and-self-deception is a major recurring theme in the literature of the period.

Among the writers who are considered most representative of the thirties, the American dream of success had come to be viewed as a junk heap of delusions and broken dreams. By the same token, it was not the great

American success who was the center of attention among major writers of the Depression years, but the dispossessed, the losers, and the outsiders of American society. To a certain extent, despite the efforts to perpetuate the myth of success, little men and losers emerged as heroes in popular fiction also. This ascendancy of the little-man hero in popular fiction and in the fiction and drama of major writers will be the subject of the next chapter.

Notes

1. Erskine Caldwell, *The Caldwell Caravan: Novels and Stories by Erskine Caldwell*, p. 11.

2. Ibid., p. 12.

3. *God's Little Acre*, in *The Caldwell Caravan*, p. 135.

4. Ibid., pp. 203, 211.

5. Ibid., p. 276.

6. In *The Wide World of John Steinbeck*, Peter Lisca analyzes the biblical parallels at some length.

7. John Steinbeck, *The Grapes of Wrath*, p. 79.

8. Ibid., p. 96.

9. Ibid., pp. 81, 91.

10. Ibid., pp. 167-68.

11. Ibid., p. 202.

12. John Steinbeck, *Of Mice and Men*, pp. 28-29.

13. Ibid., p. 129.

14. Ibid., p. 138.

15. Ibid., p. 164.

16. Ibid., p. 184.

17. Ibid., p. 107.

18. Ibid., p. 170.

19. Eugene O'Neill, *The Iceman Cometh*, Act I, pp. 9-10.

20. Cyrus Day, "The Iceman and the Bridegroom," *Modern Drama*, I (May, 1958), 5.

21. *Iceman*, Act IV, p. 241.

22. Ibid., p. 243.

23. Ibid., p. 258.

24. Interview with O'Neill by J. S. Wilson, in *Twentieth Century Interpretations of The Iceman Cometh*, p. 22.

25. Ibid., p. 23.

26. Edwin A. Engel, *The Haunted Heroes of Eugene O'Neill*, p. 280.

27. William Saroyan, *The Time of Your Life*, in *Famous American Plays of the 1930's*, edited by Harold Clurman, Act I, p. 403.

28. Ibid., Act II, p. 429; Act II, p. 443.

29. Ibid., Act I, p. 399.

30. James T. Farrell, *The Young Manhood of Studs Lonigan,* in *Studs Lonigan: A Trilogy,* p. 146.

31. Ibid., p. 253.

32. Ibid., p. 411.

33. Farrell, *Judgment Day,* in *Studs Lonigan: A Trilogy,* p. 45.

34. Ibid., pp. 304-05.

35. Ibid., p. 361.

36. Ibid., p. 424.

37. D. D. Galloway, "Nathanael West's Dream Dump," *Critique,* VI (Winter, 1963-64), 46.

38. Nathanael West, *Miss Lonelyhearts,* in *The Complete Works of Nathanael West,* p. 115.

39. James F. Light, *Nathanael West: An Interpretative Study,* pp. 156, 163.

40. West, *The Day of the Locust,* in *Complete Works,* p. 353.

41. Quoted in Galloway, p. 61. Galloway points out the friendship and mutual influence of Fitzgerald and West.

42. West, *Day,* p. 316.

43. Ibid., p. 386.

44. Light, p. 161.

45. West, *Day,* pp. 411-12.

4 / *Little Men,*
Losers, and Outsiders

As Chapter 2 makes abundantly clear, one important strain in the popular literature of the Depression years was a dogged perpetuation of the rags-to-riches myth of success despite the bleakness of actual conditions. While novelists and dramatists like John Steinbeck, J. T. Farrell, Nathanael West, and Eugene O'Neill portrayed the dream of success as a groundless delusion, writers for the popular magazines vigorously reaffirmed the values traditionally associated with the American dream of material success in an open, competitive society. Nevertheless, certain adjustments, compensations, and new emphases, often clearly reflecting the influence of the Depression, did appear in the success stories of the thirties. One important phenomenon of the Depression decade, which is clearly evident in both the popular fiction and the works of major writers, was an increased interest in and sympathy for the ordinary little men, the losers, and the outsiders of American society.

The ascendancy of little men and losers is manifested in various ways in the literature of the thirties. In popular fiction the professional and the little man clearly displaced the big business tycoon as the typical hero. Assuming that the type of hero who appears frequently in mass fiction is a reliable index to popular values, those who have observed a disenchantment in the thirties with the businessman are clearly supported by popular fiction. The inner-directed and aggressive "titan" hero whose accomplishments in the business or financial world set him apart from the ordinary people below loses ground in favor of the more prosaic "little man" who achieves a more modest success or perhaps is not successful at all.[1] The popularity of Hans Fallada's *Little Man, What Now?*, a best seller of 1933, illustrates the fact that even as a total failure, a victim hero, the little man was engrossing to readers of the Depression era.

Indicative of the fascination with the loners and outsiders of American society was the development of the gangster-tough guy tradition during the Depression. Hard-boiled private detectives, outright gangsters and racketeers, and losers like Hemingway's Harry Morgan of *To Have and Have Not*, who responded in a "tough" way to a tough era, were all familiar figures in the literature of the thirties. Their cynical, sometimes brutal, and often self-destructive struggles to survive and succeed in a jungle world represent a dark contrast to the tradition of the idealistic, ambitious, and fabulously successful self-made man.

The little man was celebrated in yet another way in the proletarian novel which appeared in such profusion in the 1930s. In the proletarian formula the typical heroes were the simple workingmen and the fighters for the workingman's cause. Though the proletarian novels tend to be stereotyped and propagandistic, some of them (Albert Halper's *Union Square*, for instance) are valuable for their insights into the dreams, frustrations, and day-to-day struggles of the ordinary workingman of the Depression years. It is not within the scope of this chapter to do a comprehensive analysis of the tough-guy or the proletarian genre. But in both cases a discussion of selected, representative works will help to illuminate the emergence of little men and outsiders as literary heroes in the thirties.

Aside from the minor works of popular-magazine writers, tough-guy writers, and proletarian novelists, the ascendancy of the little man hero is also clearly apparent in the representative works of major novelists and dramatists of the thirties. The poor, the dispossessed, the grotesque, the farmer, the worker, the prostitute, the loser, the misfit, and the outsider are all familiar types in the fiction and drama of Steinbeck, Dos Passos, Saroyan, West, and other important writers of the period. The losers and the down-and-outers seem to hold something of the same fascination for writers of the thirties as Frank Cowperwood, the titan, held for Dreiser or as Gatsby held for Fitzgerald, or as the Horatio Alger hero held for millions of Americans. In fact, in some works of the thirties, including a good many popular-magazine stories, one detects what is essentially a "cult of failure" in which all the virtue and dignity of the world are portrayed as residing in the failures and losers while all the viciousness and cruel exploitation are the province of the "successes." In many novels,

of course (*Studs Lonigan* is a good example), the unfortunate characters
are portrayed as neither fascinating, nor particularly admirable, nor virtuous,
but simply as ordinary human beings who are victims of the failure of the
American dream during the Depression. But regardless of the attitude
taken toward the little men, the failures, and the victims, their stories were
told repeatedly in the literature of the thirties.

The Little Man as Popular Hero

In my sampling of popular stories of the twenties and thirties, the shift
from businessmen heroes to professionals and little men is clear. Over one-
third of the protagonists in the stories of the twenties are men in the business
world who are successful already or are on their way up. The typical heroes
are bankers, manufacturers, stock brokers, and simply "businessmen" who
have an aura of success and wealth about them. Immediately below the
financiers and business leaders is a large group of office workers and salesmen who are usually ambitious and aggressive and well on their way to
outstanding business success. Only approximately 16 percent of the
protagonists are professionals—doctors, lawyers, teachers, writers, entertainers, and sports heroes—and the professionals who appear most often
are successful and often well-to-do doctors and lawyers. There are a few
farmers and rural people, but not many blue-collar workers and virtually
no bums or even temporarily unemployed. The world of business and
finance, then, more than any other arena, provided the heroes that readers
of the twenties apparently identified with and aspired to imitate.

In my sampling from the thirties, approximately 20 percent of the
protagonists are classifiable as businessmen. But, more importantly, over
half of these are satiric or otherwise negative characterizations. In comparison, more than one-third of the heroes are professionals and another
one-third are little men of various types. Of the professionals, there are
writers, artists, professors, and some doctors and lawyers, though not as
many as in the twenties. The detective (especially the FBI agent) is a
favorite type, and there are students and newspaper reporters. But by far
the largest group of professionals are from the world of entertainment
and sports. This preponderance would appear to reflect the objective fact
that entertainment was one area in which rags-to-riches success was still
possible in the Depression years. If it seemed absurd, in view of the economic

collapse, to aspire to fabulous success in business, readers of popular fiction could compensate to an extent by identifying with the glamorous success of actors, singers, baseball players, and boxers. Among the little men who appear as heroes, there are farmers, trolley-car conductors, train engine men, cooks, mechanics, and unemployed down-and-outers. While very few blue-collar workers are portrayed in the stories of the twenties, the industrial worker clearly comes into his own in the stories of the thirties. There are as many blue-collar workers in my sampling, in fact, as there are favorably portrayed businessmen. Appearing particularly frequently is the simple steelworker, generally of foreign extraction, who represents the strength and dignity of the ordinary laborer. The popular magazines did not, of course, print "proletarian" stories comparable in political attitude to the proletarian novels which were a staple of the Depression years. But the fact that the steelworker type appeared as a hero at all in popular stories marked a significant change from the twenties.

The biographical articles in the popular magazines, and particularly the "Interesting People" feature in *American Magazine,* reflect something of the same shift in popular heroes. While the successful businessman by no means dropped out as a subject of biographical sketches in the thirties, other types of "interesting people" received a larger proportion of space as the decade progressed. Increasingly, the "interesting people" were figures who had achieved distinction in government, the arts, education, science, sports, and entertainment. A representative sampling of "interesting people" includes an author of western novels, a former child prodigy now part of Roosevelt's "brain trust," Lou Gehrig, the Assistant Secretary of Agriculture, the only female in the world with an aeronautical engineering degree, Sherwood Anderson, a husband-and-wife anthropology team, a female sculptor, a mountain librarian, a Broadway actress, the director of the Federal Soil Conservation Bureau, a football coach, an Olympic runner, and Albert Einstein. Entertainment and sports figures dominate the list, while businessmen are conspicuously absent from it. Particularly noteworthy is the extent to which intellectual and artistic pursuits were given recognition. Even the expanded Washington bureaucracy provided heroes for a publication that was generally hostile to that bureaucracy.

The decline of the business titan as a popular hero reflected a disaffection with those who, many felt, were chiefly to blame for the Depression; but it also reflected the objective fact that the nineteenth-century captain of industry was passing out of existence. The corporation was fast replacing the individually owned business enterprise. As Mabel Newcomer points out in a study of the big-business executive in the twentieth century, the trend in business even before the thirties was "management control." In this system of organization, ownership is widely dispersed among stock-holders, and the chief executives are professional managers, not daring entrepreneurs.[2] Obviously, a relatively obscure and prosaic professional manager could not attract the popular interest that the aggressive and colorful robber-baron figure had attracted. That the business tycoon continued to exist at all as a hero in the popular fiction of the thirties gives testimony to the staying power of the myths surrounding success and business in America. Thurman Arnold points out in *The Folklore of Capitalism* that the mythology embracing the American businessman continued to operate long after the business tycoon had disappeared as an independent individual. This persistence was possible because, as a part of the mythology, the corporation was personified and endowed with the attributes, rights, and prerogatives of a free individual.[3]

The elevation of the "little man" over the titan hero in popular-magazine stories of the thirties is apparent in various ways, but a favorite formula is one in which an ordinary, undistinctive man achieves recognition through an act of heroism or some other dramatic event. Implicitly these stories concede that the ordinary workingman, trapped by the Depression, had little opportunity to become wealthy, powerful, and famous. To compensate for the common man's decreased mobility, however, the stories dramatize the "truth" that the little man could remain economically and socially inferior and still rise to heroic stature. In a sense they are tales of resignation, implicitly accepting the fact that it was no longer possible for most ordinary men to distinguish themselves by rising rapidly to the top in an occupation. Thus, frequently the stories glorify not the dream of upward mobility, but the acceptance of social and occupational mediocrity and immobility. At the same time, they set about contriving situations in which heroic stature can be achieved by the little man without any change in his economic or social status.

A classic illustration of this celebration of the little man is a story titled "A Chance to Be Somebody." Its hero is James Martin, an unnoteworthy trolley-car conductor who, as a birthday treat, gives his eight-year-old son a conductor's uniform and takes him along on the trolley job. The first crisis comes when a rich woman, portrayed with dripping contempt, launches into a tirade in front of the son about the lowliness of streetcar conductors. This destroys the boy's pride in his father and the father's pride in himself. Then comes an emergency, a wreck, and James Martin becomes a full-fledged hero, rescuing passengers and trying to preserve some order in the chaos. Among the passengers rescued is the disagreeable rich lady, who in gratitude offers to finance the boy's education so that he will be able to "actually amount to something." But the boy is so impressed by the events he has witnessed that he refuses the offer, explaining that he would rather be a conductor like his father.

Thus, the little man has risen to heroism, and the author even philosophizes about the superiority of commonplace, mediocre men: "Now James Martin was not brilliant; he was not quick. But in an emergency, your plodder is apt to be of far more value than a more brilliant man."[4] This story is representative of many which replace the myth of success with a myth of mediocrity. Not only is upward mobility rejected, but there is a suspicion of qualities ordinarily considered valuable, if not indispensable—including intelligence and ambition. It is the good heart that matters, not the quick mind or the impressive personality. There seems to be an effort in this and similar stories to dignify and elevate all the ordinary people of the world who, confined by limited chances for fame and fortune, were likely to remain obscure. The son's role in the story is no less revealing than his father's. His decision represents a clear inversion of the values supported by the conventional success story. In a Horatio Alger rendering of the same materials, the boy himself would have performed the heroic act, and certainly his ambition and sense of duty would have prevented him from refusing the reward. The emphasis would have been on the young man's upward mobility. In this version, the focus is on the father, and the boy's decision to emulate his father rather than accept the opportunity to rise above him affirms the importance of family loyalty, tradition, and contentment with one's present status.

Similar stories are "Hero Enough," in which an outwardly obscure and unsuccessful man is revealed to be a secret FBI agent, and "Sutter's Crystal," in which an apparent loser is discovered to be a public benefactor who has quietly helped to found a school for the blind.[5] These characters represent virtually an exact inversion of the bright, ambitious, dynamic young hero who is predominant in the popular stories of the twenties. The sober virtues of the obscure and altruistic man were viewed with fresh appreciation in the thirties, and the flashy young man on his way up lost some of his glamour.

The elevation of the industrial worker to heroic stature can be illustrated by two stories which have steelworkers as leading characters. One, titled "Unknown Hunky," is a rhapsodic eulogy of a millworker of

Croatian descent named Nate Haugerty who goes down in legend after performing a heroic act which saves several lives.[6] The author waxes poetic in his description of the Croatian contribution to the steel industry, showing deep respect, even reverence, for the simple workingmen who are portrayed in the story. An Eastern European immigrant is again the hero in another story set in a Pennsylvania steel mill. Jack Kovatch, a young man from a poor family of Russian immigrants, is in competition with Ashley Drayer, who has breeding, money, and social position. The stakes are a girl and a superintendent's job in the mill. The girl's father objects to Jack because he is descended from a long line of manual laborers. But at the climax of the story Jack proves himself by acting to prevent a hysterical worker from attacking Drayer, who has pushed the men beyond endurance. Predictably, Jack wins both the job and the girl as a reward for his heroic action.[7]

These stories and others like them, which celebrate the industrial worker, are as near an equivalent as one finds in the popular magazines to the "proletarian" fiction which developed as a distinct genre in the thirties. Accompanying the deeply sympathetic portrayal of the simple worker is a certain amount of hostility toward the men of wealth and social standing who are frequently in positions of power despite their obvious inferiority to the laborers beneath them in the industrial hierarchy. Yet in the popular stories, there is seldom a hint of left-wing political protest. Rarely does a worker-hero in a popular story involve himself in a strike or become a vocal critic of the capitalist system. The celebration of the worker is not Marxian but Whitmanesque or Jacksonian in its emphasis on the common man's contribution to the building of America. The illustrations that accompany the stories resemble John Neagle's "Pat Lyon at the Forge" more than a Ben Shahn or William Gropper depiction of oppressed workers. The workers in the illustrations look muscular, rosy-cheeked, and contented; they are the very embodiment of health, strength, simplicity, and dignity. The protest painters who portrayed oppressive settings, anguished faces, and stunted human forms revealed a dimension of America which the popular magazines rarely seemed cognizant of.

The Cult of Failure: Romanticizing Ruin

It is an easy step from stories like the above, which commemorate the plodding, ordinary, prosaic little man, to those in which the heroes are, by the usual standards, failures and losers. Romanticized "riches-to-rags"

articles—accounts of once-wealthy men who have lost their money but
found happiness—are recurring features in the popular magazines, though
certainly not as commonplace as the conventional success story. The creation of a sentimental myth of failure was one of the ways in which the
popular magazines avoided responding realistically to the Depression.
Apparently assuming that honest reports of failure and bankruptcy were
unfit for public consumption, the popular magazines attempted to glamorize failure and ruin, stripping away any sense of unpleasant, firsthand
reality and casting the whole subject into the realm of myth. To take one
example, in *American Magazine* a man named Everett Hill, once Oklahoma
City's leading citizen, is described as having lost his entire fortune of $2
million in the Depression. But far from being despondent, "he is broke
and solitary, living the life of Riley on not more than fifty dollars a month."
This is the myth of success in reverse, and the affirmation that bankruptcy
is beautiful is no closer to reality than the myth of rags-to-riches success.
More commonly the "reverse" stories are double reverses, momentarily
confronting the reader with failure but ending on a note of renewed success. Once-successful people who have lost everything in the Depression
but later regained their success in a new career are favorite subjects for
biographical articles because they illustrate the inescapable fact of failure
but also the hope of recovery. Countless articles and biographical sketches
follow the pattern illustrated by *American Magazine*'s account of a woman
named Mary Whitmore, who was born wealthy, lost her fortune during
the Depression, turned to a career in architecture to earn a living, and
finally became the famous landscape architect who designed New Shawnee-
town, Illinois, after the 1937 flood.[8] As represented in these tales of lost
and regained fortune, the Depression experience is not a cause for despair
or even dismay; instead it provides the material for a fascinating new
twist to the old success story.

Many of the fictional portrayals of failure and bankruptcy reveal a
similar fascination with failure and also a similar tendency to romanticize
and glamorize it. The typical "failure" story dramatizes the virtues of
poverty and the disadvantages of wealth and success, but at the same
time contrives gimmicks to avoid confronting the reader with the authentic
reality of poverty and failure. The loss of a fortune can free a man from
pressures and responsibilities; it can bring leisure and privacy; and it can
give one a new perspective on what is really important in life, the stories
suggest. Typically, however, one gets the impression that there is more

rationalization than commitment behind these comforting thoughts. A
representative example is a story titled, not very originally, "Riches to
Rags." The blurb introduces it as a tale about a rich man who "clambers
down from the lap of luxury and finds the priceless gift of true friendship." As the title and the introduction imply, there is some tarnishing
of the image of success. The hero, a self-made millionaire, hates the fact
that he has no privacy and independence. Demands and responsibilities
weigh heavily on him, and he longs to escape them. The situation seems
designed to discourage the aspiration toward wealth and to soothe readers
who might have been touched by the Depression. But the riches-to-rags
theme is falsified by the fact that, despite the title, the hero does not
actually lose his wealth or give it up voluntarily. Instead, he periodically
dons old clothing and visits a college friend who does not know of his
wealth and with whom he can be himself.[9] It is a have-your-cake-and-eat-
it-too solution which is typical of popular-magazine fiction. The story
makes a half-hearted rejection of the myth of success and a half-hearted
affirmation of the joys of poverty. But it does not ask its readers to con-
front the problem of failure face to face or to give up an image of success
for an image of failure.

Not all of the "failure" stories, however, rely on gimmicks to avoid
portraying an actual riches-to-rags situation. A few make true reversals
of the conventional success-story formula that was virtually never departed
from in the popular fiction of the twenties. In these stories the fact of
economic failure is allowed to stand without the complication of trick
endings. But generally there is an implied redefinition of "success" and
"failure" so that what outwardly looks like failure becomes success when
viewed from the perspective established by the story. A story titled "The
Shamrock Waistcoat," for instance, concerns a man who was once wealthy
but has been ruined by the Depression. He is a horse lover whose situation
is so desperate that he gives his horse away to a stranger who appears to
be a stable boy. The happy ending of the story involves the revelation
that the stranger is a rich man who is in a position to offer the hero a job
as stable manager on his estate.[10] Implicit in this "happy" ending is a
drastic reduction of the hero's goals as well as his outward stature; he was
once a big man capable of desiring and earning a fortune, but now he is a
little man happy with a job in a stable. The story implies that as a little
man he is as worthy of respect as he had been before the loss of his fortune.
Like many of the stories that treat failures and little men, it is essentially

a story of consolation. In effect, it offers the reader a model for adjusting to the reality of the Depression. Instead of encouraging far-fetched dreams of success or urging a revival of ambition and individual aggressiveness, the story implies that the key to happiness lies in not expecting too much.

Some of the stories that focus on failures and losers establish a clear-cut and reasonably honest conflict between "failure" and "success," and resolve the conflict in favor of "failure." A story titled "The Failure" contrasts "a plug country doctor," who guiltily considers himself a failure, with his nephew, an aggressive young man who becomes a famous surgeon. The theme of the story is that the true "success" is the self-sacrificing country doctor; the young surgeon is seen as hard, grasping, and devoid of human compassion—in short, a moral failure.[11] The story is emphatic in its ironic reversal of our traditional assumptions about success and failure. Contrary to the conventional myth of success, it equates virtue and "failure," not virtue and worldly success. It teaches that ambition can be morally destructive and that refusing opportunities may be preferable to accepting them. It is highly critical of a society that indoctrinates a good man to feel guilty because he has not achieved wealth and fame. These attitudes are commonplace, of course, among major writers who have treated the myth of success. They are rare, however, in popular fiction written prior to the Depression.

A similar defense of "failure" is portrayed in a story, titled "As Big a Fool," about an unprincipled and brilliantly successful young businessman who continues to prosper even when others are being ruined by the Depression. His problem is that his girlfriend refuses to marry him because she doubts his integrity. Only after he gives up his own fortune to save his father from bankruptcy does she decide to marry him.[12] Like William Dean Howells' Silas Lapham, he is suspect as a success, but as an honest bankrupt he is a worthy and admirable man.

Such stories appear frequently enough in the thirties to suggest the emergence in popular literature of a "cult of failure" which could make some headway against the "cult of success." Disillusionment with the businessman is extended in some of the stories to include a suspicion of success itself. Conversely, the little men and the failures, certainly not among the most respected types in the popular stories of the twenties, are not only treated with sympathy, but invested with the kind of dignity and stature that John Steinbeck and William Saroyan attributed to their losers and misfits. Many of the "failure" stories are transparent attempts to rationalize and make palatable the dispiriting conditions under which many people were living. Failure was a pervasive fact in the Depression years, and it looked as if the little men were destined to remain little. Popular stories by the dozens offered escape through fantasies of success, but a few stories told their readers that success had its disadvantages and that failure had its own dignity, its own rewards, and its own mystique.

It should be emphasized, however, that even the stories that portray little men and failures are generally "success" stories in the broadest sense of the term. Since the popular-magazine formula required a happy ending, the stories usually progress toward some kind of accomplishment or reward for the hero. In the stories in which material success is not the goal sought after, the accomplishment is frequently a heroic or unselfish action which increases the moral stature of the hero. Many of the little men are heroes not merely in the sense that they are protagonists, but also in the sense that they perform some heroic deed which brings them recognition. Thus, readers were shown that "success" did not have to mean economic success and that little people like themselves could be admired and respected heroes. Few popular stories portray the little man as a complete victim of life, with no stature, no hope of economic success, and no compensatory rewards.

The Little Man as Victim-Hero

However, the fact that readers of the thirties could respond to a portrayal of the little man as victim is revealed by the appearance on the best-seller lists of novels like Steinbeck's *The Grapes of Wrath* and Hans Fallada's *Little Man, What Now?*, both of which portray characters who are utterly defeated in their struggle against strangling economic conditions. Since *The Grapes of Wrath* was the work of an already well-known author, it is difficult to judge how much the subject matter itself contributed to making it a best seller. But *Little Man, What Now?* was the work of a German writer who had not previously established a reputation in the United States. The English translation appeared in 1933, when millions of Americans were engaged in the same kind of struggle which Fallada (pseudonym for Rudolf Ditzen) describes in his story of a young couple trapped by the economic chaos of post-World War I Germany. Simple and readable in style, the novel offered no more intellectual difficulty to the ordinary reader than the typical popular-magazine story. However, it put the reader through a dark and difficult emotional experience, unrelieved by the hopeful and consolatory tone that the reader of magazine fiction could generally expect.

The little man who serves as the victim-hero of the novel is an ordinary, unassuming white-collar worker named Johannes Pinneberg. The almost four hundred pages of the novel consist primarily of a highly detailed day-to-day account of the downhill battle of Pinneberg and his wife, Bunny, to survive the ravages of low wages, scarce and expensive housing, high taxes, unemployment, and stifling bureaucracy. The texture of everyday life in postwar Germany is captured by the elaborate detail lavished on the most trifling matters, from the price of potatoes to the red tape involved in collecting relief money. It was a pattern of life that no doubt seemed authentic to victims of the Depression in America. But if American readers could identify with Pinneberg's plight, they could not look to his character or his career for inspiration. His struggle to provide a subsistence for himself and his family is weak and ineffectual—not heroic, but pathetic. There is no suggestion that the little man can rise to glory and no implication that failure has its own mystique. Pinneberg has little courage, no sense of his own significance, and virtually no aggressiveness. He is trapped in a narrow existence in which things happen to him instead of being initiated by him. He undertakes the perils of trying to support a family only because he gets Bunny pregnant and is forced to take some kind of action. Once they are married, he approaches all their problems with a sense of hesitation and dread. Fallada dwells on the anguish they go through even when Pinneberg has a job. They must count every penny in their effort to live on his salary, and still they find that there is not enough money for all the necessities. They eat poorly, rarely have money for entertainment, and live in a small, virtually inaccessible space over a garage.

Throughout his description of Pinneberg's monotonous and fruitless struggle, Fallada uses the motif of the little man as a unifying device. He refers to him as "the little man Pinneberg" or "the lad" and puts him in "a world of respectable and blundering captains of industry and little, degraded, downtrodden people always trying to do their best."[13] In the competitive business world that he is thrust into, Pinneberg lacks the opportunity or the aggressiveness to be one of the winners. As one of the losers, he is exploited, condescended to, and maltreated until he even thinks of himself as a worthless little man, an outsider, and a victim.

Fallada's analysis of the destructive psychological effects of Pinneberg's failure and frustration bears an interesting relationship to the popular-magazine stories which celebrate and dignify the little man as a respected hero. These stories, which create a myth of the little man that endows him with all the stature and significance denied him in the world of reality, seem specifically calculated to prevent the kind of shattered pride that Pinneberg suffers from.

Pinneberg has no support for his ego, real or mythological, and his battle to survive and maintain a shred of dignity is a losing one from the beginning. The climax in his deterioration comes in a chapter titled "The Jig Is Up" when, all of the fight and most of the hope gone out of him, he finally loses the struggle to keep his job as a salesman in a clothing store. The circumstances of his final downfall emphasize the anguish of false hopes. Pinneberg has one day left and five hundred marks to go to reach the monthly sales quota that he must maintain. There appears to be no hope for him. Then a famous actor comes in looking for a wardrobe for a movie. Pinneberg anticipates a big sale, and it begins to look as if the novel is going to have the same kind of bogus fairy-tale ending so familiar in popular fiction. But Fallada introduces the possibility of a happy ending deliberately in order to smash it. After looking at everything Pinneberg has to show him, the actor reveals that he has no intention of buying anything. This is too much for Pinneberg; he breaks down and begs: "You see I've a wife and a child, too. . . . Please, please buy something. You—you must know what we feel like!"[14] The actor complains to Pinneberg's superior about being "assaulted" by a clerk, and the end has arrived for the little man. His superior says simply, "We will dismiss him, he is quite useless."[15] The reader's last view of Pinneberg shows his condition fourteen months later. Ragged and unkempt, he has just been beaten and humiliated by the police, who have found him looking longingly into a shop window. The reader sees him shrinking in the bushes near the Pinneberg hut, too defeated to look anyone in the face. He has nothing left but Bunny, whose love is the one source of stability in an otherwise chaotic and hopeless existence.

This dark novel did not offer readers the opportunity to escape reality, nor did it elevate the little man to any kind of grandeur; but it did provide the opportunity to feel sympathy for a defeated man and indignation against the circumstances that destroy him. Perhaps there was some comfort for the American public in reading of the struggles of someone in a distant country possibly worse off than themselves. The author's own

attitude is one of tender sympathy for his downtrodden hero and hatred
of those who have the upper hand in a viciously competitive capitalist
system. But the book resembles a Dickensian melodrama more than a
"proletarian" novel. Like the popular magazine stories of the thirties, it
avoids any commitment to left-wing political ideas, a fact which no doubt
contributed to its acceptance by a large reading public in the United States.

Loners, Gangsters, and Tough Guys

Also prominent in the Depression years was a species of outsider or
loser very different from the little man of magazine fiction or the victim-
hero of *Little Man, What Now?*—namely, the gangster-tough guy. The
gangster-tough guy represents yet another response to the failure of the
American dream in a crisis period; that is, a hard-boiled, tough, violent,
antisocial, lawless response. The reading and moviegoing public of the
Depression years welcomed the opportunity to escape to a fantasy world
and responded warmly to such novels as *Little Man, What Now?* and *Of
Mice and Men,* which portray essentially "soft" reactions to hardship and
failure. But it was also fascinated by the hard-boiled response to a tough
era. It identified with the "tough" private detectives who seemed to thrive
on danger, with the hard-boiled loner who refused to give up easily in his
battle with the world, and even with the gangster who resorted to violent
and lawless methods of grasping what he wanted.

Many of the most memorable and popular movies of the thirties, of
course, were gangster movies. As Arthur Knight has pointed out, such
films as *Little Caesar* (1930), *The Public Enemy* (1931), and *Scarface*
(1932) portrayed a world of poverty inhabited by the disinherited and
the outsiders of American society for whom the dream of success could
be realized only outside the law.[16] Daniel Bell makes a related point in
an essay, "Crime as an American Way of Life." He observes that the
jungle quality of American business was caricatured in the underworld,
where coarse gangsters, many of them immigrants, "were 'getting ahead,'
just as Horatio Alger had urged."[17] In the thirties the stereotyped American
gangster became a legendary, mythological figure, symbolic of his environment and his era. His violent rebellion against society's laws represented
a perversion of the conventional myth of success, and yet in his career
the raw ingredients of the rags-to-riches success story could be observed.

His individualism was brutal and antisocial, but appropriate to a cruel and corrupt world, where attempts to succeed were of necessity aggressive acts. Readers and moviegoers could simultaneously identify with and keep their distance from the gangster, responding to his attractiveness as a rebel and yet dissociating themselves from his corruption and from the violent destruction that was the normal culmination of his career.[18]

The gangster films of the thirties perhaps contributed more than any other source toward establishing the tough guy as a folk hero. The tough guy was also a literary hero, however, who appeared in numerous gangster novels, detective novels, and other varieties of "hard-boiled" fiction. In his various forms, the tough guy was one of the mainstays of the fiction of the thirties. Prominent among the writers of gangster novels were Donald Henderson Clark (*Louis Beretti*), W. R. Burnett (*Little Caesar*), and Benjamin Appel (*Brain Guy*). The tough-private-detective novel was practiced most successfully by Dashiell Hammett (*The Maltese Falcon, The Thin Man*) and Raymond Chandler (*The Big Sleep, Farewell, My Lovely*) both of whom broke with the genteel mystery story in the British mode and created peculiarly American detective stories reflecting the hostile world of the Depression. Chandler said about Hammett that he "gave murder back to the kind of people that commit it for reasons, not just to provide a corpse; and with means at hand, not with hand-wrought duelling pistols, curare, and tropical fish."[19] In another class are the tough-guy novels of James M. Cain (*The Postman Always Rings Twice*) and Horace McCoy (*They Shoot Horses, Don't They?*). These works do not follow the formula of the gangster or private-eye novels and, in fact, have nothing to do with criminals or detectives. They are "tough" novels in the sense that they are written in a Hemingway-influenced hard-boiled style and in the sense that they respond with an attitude of hardness and cynicism to man's precarious condition in a hostile world. McCoy's *They Shoot Horses, Don't They?*, for example, is a brutally realistic account of the exploitation of desperate people in a marathon dance contest. It is based on a killing, but it is obviously not a murder mystery. Its power lies in McCoy's unflinching and objective portrayal of the hard-boiled heroine.

In his introduction to *Tough Guy Writers of the Thirties,* a collection of essays which treats all of these forms of hard-boiled writing as variations of the same genre, David Madden comments on the relation of the tough-guy genre to the Depression: "An unusually tough era turns out the hard-

boiled hero. . . . Those hardest hit become the down-and-out, the disinherited, and soon develop a hard-boiled attitude that enables them to
maintain a granite-like dignity against forces that chisel erratically at it."[20]
This is a rather pat and oversimple explanation of how those who become
the outsiders and the disinherited react to a crisis like the Depression,
which shatters the American dream. Judging from my study of the popular
literature of the thirties, various kinds of "soft" reactions such as fantasiz-
ing, sentimentalizing, and rationalizing were more common than the hard-
boiled pose. Nevertheless, the tough response was clearly one way of reflecting the times as well as living with them.

The essence of the tough-guy genre can be illustrated by the work of a
major writer—Ernest Hemingway's *To Have and Have Not* (1937). Though
critics agree that it is one of the least successful of Hemingway's novels,
David Madden and other students of tough-guy writings place it among the
best of the tough-guy novels of the thirties. Certainly its characterization
of Harry Morgan ranks as a vivid and memorable study of the "tough"
reaction of one of the outsiders of American society to the failure of the
American dream in the Depression years. Though the style of Hemingway's
early novels and both the style and subject matter of "The Killers" influenced gangster and tough-guy fiction, Philip Young is right in arguing that
To Have and Have Not is Hemingway's only hard-boiled book.[21] The
protagonists of his most important works—Nick Adams, Jake Barnes,
Frederick Henry, Robert Jordan, Richard Cantwell—are certainly not
tough-guy heroes, though they may put up a facade of toughness; and
there are relatively few tough guys among his minor characters.

Harry Morgan of *To Have and Have Not* is the tough-guy hero par
excellence. He is an outsider and a loser who, victimized by the Depression
and other circumstances, refuses to succumb passively to a world which
seems bent on destroying him. Instead, he scratches out a living for himself and his family by putting into practice an extreme version of American
self-reliance and rugged individualism. As in the gangster movies of the
decade, Harry's story represents the nightmare version of the American
dream. Instead of finding freedom and opportunity in America, he finds
a jungle world in which toughness is a necessity and only ruthless individual
action, sometimes at the expense of others, can make survival possible.
It is a world so rife with poverty, exploitation, and injustice that law and
morality are meaningless. Harry simply does what he must to support his
family, and it is an unfortunate fact of life in his world that survival re-

quires going outside the law to become involved in smuggling and killing. After being victimized by one of the "haves" of the novel, the rich tourist named Johnson who flees without paying for the charter of Harry's boat or for the loss of some expensive fishing equipment, Harry is destitute and resorts to smuggling because it is a way to make a living. When he must later kill, he performs with ruthless skill, but without gratuitous bloodlust. Killing simply becomes a part of his plan for survival. When Cuban revolutionaries attempt to hijack his boat, he has no choice but to kill them before they kill him; and he manages to do the job with cold and methodical dispatch, though he is mortally wounded in doing so.

In many ways, then, Harry is the prototypal tough hero. His milieu is the typical jungle world of the tough novels; his struggle to survive is essentially amoral, and he is a man of cold ruthlessness rather than senti-ment. He is the very essence of masculinity, having a rugged sexuality that stirs adoration in his wife and admiration in other women. In his strength and ability to withstand physical punishment, he is almost a superman. He grits his teeth and says nothing when, in the whiskey-smuggling episode, one arm is so badly mutilated that it has to be amputated. At the end when he is shot in the stomach by the Cuban, he musters the strength and courage not only to kill the man who shot him, but to stay alive for almost two days. But though he puts up a tougher fight than most men do, he is destined to suffer and die in the end. He comes to a realization of his own ultimate frailty and states it in what is now a famous passage: "No matter how a man alone ain't got no bloody f___ing chance."[22] He adds that it has taken him all his life to learn this truth. Understandably, this "moral" has been the focus of adverse criticism by practically every com-mentator who has discussed the novel. Harry Morgan is believable when he behaves as the tough protagonist, but after his rugged and sometimes ruthlessly individualistic battle with life, his statement of the social mes-sage that people need people rings false. The validity of the ideal of coopera-tion and brotherhood as an alternative to individual toughness is in no way dramatized in the novel. The "no man is an island" theme would be developed in *For Whom the Bell Tolls,* but the vision of *To Have and Have Not* is much darker and more hopeless.

Yet, gratuitous social message aside, the bulk of the novel stands as a powerful, negative study of the viability of individualism in modern America. Hemingway himself commented to his publisher that the theme of the novel was intended to be "the decline of the individual."[23] And, certainly, the novel suggests that the day was gone when the aggressive, self-reliant, rugged individualist could realize the American dream of carving out his own destiny amidst the rich materials of America. Harry Morgan has the independence and strength of the rugged individualist, but in a cramped world of brutal competition and limited possibilities his individualism is perverted and destructive, not dynamic and productive. Despite Hemingway's imposed moral, the novel's manifest theme is that loners and losers like Harry Morgan are destined to fight a brutal battle which they have no possibility of winning.

It is interesting to note that the tough guys in the popular private-detective school, unlike Harry Morgan, do prevail in the end. For instance, the heroes of Dashiell Hammett, who has been called a poor man's Hemingway are loners and outsiders, but not losers. The Hammett hero, particularly as represented by Sam Spade of *The Maltese Falcon,* is a tough man—free of sentiment, amoral, self-reliant, powerful, and invulnerable. Hemingway puts characters into a world where they have no ultimate control, while Hammett tough hero has a kind of absolute control over his destiny. He is a super-man—the epitome of cold efficiency, shrewdness, and skill—and he never puts himself into a position to lose. As Robert Edenbaum points out, the price he pays for his toughness is not death, but isolation.[24]

Paradoxically, the detective fiction of writers like Hammett and Raymond Chandler offered readers of the thirties simultaneously a hard-boiled and a "soft" or sentimental way of reacting to the hard times. It created a tough and coldly realistic world where only superior power and ruthlessness could win out, but that world was also a mythological one in which the tough hero was a larger-than-life (even demonic) figure who always achieved his desired ends. Depression-weary readers or movie audiences could, thus, once again enter a fantasy world in which the hero was always in control and never failed.

Another novel which deserves at least brief mention in the context of little men, losers, and outsiders is Richard Wright's *Native Son* (1940). The novel offers some sharp insights into the psychology of those who stand on the fringes of American society, totally barred from sharing in the American dream. Because he is a black man as well as a slum product, Bigger Thomas is an even more desperate outsider than Harry Morgan of *To Have and Have Not* or the gangster hero. His story is set in the Depression years, but the Depression has little impact because, for his race, oppression has long since become a way of life. Whether the rest of the

nation is living in prosperity or Depression makes little difference. To the
Biggers of America the myth of success is a constant mockery because in
the midst of images of success and splendor they are completely thwarted.
As Bigger's lawyer says, "These bright colors [the promises and allure-
ments of advertisements, movies, and the like] may fill our hearts with
elation, but to many they are daily taunts."[25]

Bigger's response to the taunts and the frustration provides a chilling
insight into the mentality of the outsider who becomes tough. Bigger is
not a full-fledged tough-guy hero in the same sense that Harry Morgan is.
But he adopts a pose of toughness in an effort to camouflage his fear and
vulnerability, and certainly his actions are an extreme expression of toughness. He commits two brutal murders, and only after becoming a killer
does he begin to feel that he has some significance as a person, some freedom,
and some responsibility for his own destiny. He feels that for the first
time he is living, making choices, incurring consequences, performing
actions that carry weight. In short, the most terrible irony of the novel is
that after he kills he is less an outsider than before. He is doomed, of
course, but he goes to his death feeling that he has become a real man for
a short time and convinced that he has expressed himself in the only way
that was open to him.

The Worker as Hero—Proletarian Novels

The many radical or so-called "proletarian" novels of the thirties are
another symptom of the increasing interest in the little men, losers, and
outsiders of American society. Most of these novels were stereotyped and
of little interest as works of art. But a few did succeed in capturing in a
simple, authentic, and unsophisticated way the texture of life in the Depression years among the workers and other little men of America. Jack Conroy's
The Disinherited, for instance, is a detailed rendering of day-to-day existence
among coal miners, automobile workers, and high-iron workers of the Depression era. Similarly, Robert Cantwell's *Land of Plenty* is impressive for the
authenticity and accuracy with which it portrays life among the workers
in a veneer factory in the Northwest.

One of the most informative of the now obscure leftist novelists of the
thirties is Albert Halper. As a novelist of the little people of the thirties,
he chronicles in elaborate, firsthand detail their external environment as

well as their inner thoughts, dreams, and frustrations. *Union Square* (1933) centers around the tenement in which he was living at the time he wrote the novel.[26] Its characters are based on the people he observed, and its mood grew out of his own privation, loneliness, and desperation.

Among the assorted failures and losers who people the novel are a half-starving ex-poet, a jobless factory worker, a demented printer, and a wide-eyed idealist in love with communism and with a comrade named Helen. Jason, the ex-poet, is cynical and despairing; he has no dreams and no energies. " 'I live in filth [he says], I'm lazy and unambitious, I have no urge to grab the jack, to be one of the go-gettum, there's-big-opportunities-waiting boys. . . . I'll never amount to anything.' "[27] To Halper, he represents burnt-out youth and talent. He has rejected the American dream and has no faith with which to replace it.

Leon, the idealist, has a Communist dream, but he is stupidly naïve and ripe for the disillusionment which comes when he finds his comrade Helen, who is a promiscuous slob, in bed with another comrade. His disillusionment with Helen shatters his belief in Communism, because Helen and Communism have been so inseparably connected in his own mind (an association which resembles the interconnection of the Golden Girl and the dream of success in the works of Dreiser and Fitzgerald). The worker, Hank Austin, walks the streets aimlessly after losing his job; he is confused and hopeless, his eyes dead. At the end of the novel, he is caught in the melee of a Communist march and crippled for life, viciously beaten by the police and trampled in the spine by a horse. Ironically, Hank is a good conservative American worker who barely knows what Communism is; he cries as they beat him: " 'I'm no communist, I ain't a Red, I'm an Amerikin! Halper uses obvious but powerful images to convey his vision of American life in the grim Depression years. Images of iron hooves recur frequently and suggest, among other things, the trampling under of little people like Hank Austin. Yet, despite the dark images and the agonies of his characters, Halper ends the novel on a note of hope for eventual progress: "In this world things move on apace. Life must go on. There are children to be born, and some will cry out when their tender skin is cut. But progress overleaps all barriers. Time does not stop, it moves."[29] Though his hope is rather vague and wistful, Halper shared the millennial faith in the future which was characteristic of the proletarian novelists of the thirties.

In *Union Square,* Halper portrays his workers and other little men as victim-heroes, trapped by circumstances and powerless to do anything

more than hope for a better future. Though the novel has overtones of
that "revolutionary élan" which Michael Gold described as one indispensable
quality of proletarian fiction, the central characters are not actively and
effectively engaged in a struggle to improve their lives. Like Pinneberg in
Little Man, What Now? they are, generally speaking, passive and defeated
victims of their economic and social environment. In other proletarian
novels of the thirties, the worker-hero is endowed with more heroic qualities.[30]

Strike novels like Robert Cantwell's *Land of Plenty* and William Rollins'
The Shadow Before tend to idealize the simple, honest workingman and
to glamorize the strike leader and the martyr to the workingman's cause.
In their depiction of the workingman, these novels can be compared to
the popular-magazine stories which celebrate the heroic actions of ordinary,
obscure people. Though they reflect vastly different political attitudes,
both endow the workingman with significance and stature. They create
admirable, even legendary, figures intended to arouse respect and perhaps
hero worship on the part of the reader. Novels portraying a conversion to
radicalism dignify the little man by dwelling on the drama and significance
of an individual's transition from passive victim to class-conscious militant.
Like Jack Conroy's *The Disinherited* they generally conclude with the
protagonist's emergence as a leader in the battle to secure the workingman's
rights.[31] All varieties of proletarian fiction, of course, treat the little man
with profound sympathy. Whether the workingman is characterized as
victim or as leader and hero, the proletarian novels insist on his worth as
a human being and his significance as a literary subject.

Losers and Misfits in Major Writings

If the little men, the downtrodden, the outsiders, the misfits and failures
of American society were prominent in much of the subliterature of the
Depression years, they were also overwhelmingly the concern of writers
in the mainstream of American literature. The trend away from the titan
hero and toward the little man which is discernible in popular-magazine
fiction is magnified many times in the works of major writers. The businessman's image is so tainted that there are virtually no sympathetically or even
neutrally portrayed business successes in the serious fiction of the thirties.
In fact characterizations of successful men from any occupation or profession are rare. The interest is in failure; the authors' sympathies are with

the failures; and often their respect and admiration are lavished on the
failures or losers and conspicuously withheld from the "successes." Even
novels like Fitzgerald's *Tender Is the Night* and Marquand's *The Late
George Apley* which center on the world of the "haves" rather than that
of the "have nots" are essentially stories of failure and loss, having protagonists who in the end are defeated and broken. Dreiser had anticipated
this emphasis on failures and losers in *An American Tragedy* (1925), but
inversions of the American success story became much more common in
the literature of the thirties and the little man came into prominence as
never before in American literature.

The typical characters in the fiction and drama of the thirties make up
a wide spectrum of struggling little men, failures, and outsiders. There are
the poor Chicago Irish of Farrell's *Studs Lonigan* trilogy and other works.
There are the disinherited Georgia farm people of Caldwell's *Tobacco
Road, God's Little Acre, Journeyman,* and dozens of stories. There are
Clifford Odets' New York Jews struggling and dreaming and failing in
Awake and Sing and *Paradise Lost.* There are Eugene O'Neill's alcoholics,
bums, prostitutes, and pimps in *The Iceman Cometh.* And, of course, there
are the unforgettable and often grotesque losers and misfits of Nathanael
West's novels—the hapless Lemuel Pitkin of *A Cool Million;* the neurotic
Homer Simpson, who sleeps or cries much of the time; and the broken and
victimized people who write to Miss Lonelyhearts begging for help. Many
of West's characters have physical deformities and oddities which symbolize
the spiritual battering that life has dealt them. Homer Simpson, for instance,
has large, almost detached, hands that seem to lead a life of their own;
Abe Kusich, also in *The Day of the Locust,* is a dwarf; Peter Doyle in
Miss Lonelyhearts is a physical as well as a spiritual cripple. Through the
highlighting of physical deformity and the use of other types of exaggeration, West creates a surrealistic atmosphere that overstates and intensifies
the same qualities of wretchedness and loss which so many writers of the
thirties portrayed in their downtrodden characters. The unfortunates who
write to Miss Lonelyhearts for help—Desperate, who is miserable because
she does not have a nose; Harold S., whose thirteen-year-old deaf-and-
dumb sister was raped; and Broad Shoulders, who tells an interminable
story of abuse by her husband, near starvation, and general wretchedness—
all are in a sense hyperbolic symbols of all the losers and misfits of the
Depression years.

In the works of some writers of the thirties, the sympathetic portrayal
of the little man is similar in tone to the celebration of the little man hero

in magazine fiction or the idealization of the worker hero in proletarian novels. Saroyan and Steinbeck, for instance, betray a deep respect and admiration for the "failures" and losers of the world and heap a blanket of contempt upon the "successes." In other words, they replace the cult of success with a cult of failure. In their inversion of the traditional myth of success, evil is identified with "success" and a kind of grandeur is discovered in "failure."

In Saroyan the cult of failure which replaces the American dream takes the form of a sentimental admiration for the humble, the meek, the excluded, and the down-and-out. In his works of the thirties there are virtually no characters who are both successful and admirable. The sympathetic characters are those like the starving writer who appears in "The Daring Young Man on the Flying Trapeze" or the hungry Russian in "The Man with the French Post Cards" who, willing to degrade himself to help another man, is described as looking like Christ. In *The Time of Your Life* Saroyan's mystique of failure is apparent in various ways. Obviously the indigents who inhabit the bar are the good people. As Saroyan says about Kitty, the whore with the heart of gold, they have "that element of the immortal which is in the seed of good and common people."[32] Joe, the voice of wisdom who himself has an air of dignity and inner greatness, recognizes Kitty as a "great person" immediately. Dudley Bostwick, like the others, is "apparently nobody and nothing, but in reality a great personality."[33] The good characters live and let live, dream their dreams, and follow their impulses. Conventional success, respectability, moneymaking, and even being busy are suspect. Joe feels guilty because he has money, and he drinks, according to his own self-analysis, to avoid becoming a slave to such "unimportant" bourgeois values as industriousness and efficiency. Any kind of power or authority is suspect. The villain of the play is Blick, the head of the vice squad, who, amidst the good and happy failures, represents authority. He is evil because "he hurts little people" and because, opposite to the apparent failures who are actually great people, he is "a strong man without strength."[34] In his whimsical and sentimental way, Saroyan inverts all the basic doctrines of the "cult of success" and virtually deifies his failures and little people.

Similarly, Steinbeck's sympathy with the failures and misfits of the world is so strong that it sometimes takes the form of sentimental idealization. In his works of the thirties the "haves" are ignored or treated contemptuously while the poor, the oppressed, and the incomplete (primitives like Lennie and Tularecito) are invested with a plentitude of dignity or goodness. The attitude is expressed in *Of Mice and Men* when, speaking of Lennie, Slim says: " 'Guy don't need no sense to be a nice fella. Seems to me sometimes it jus' works the other way around. Take a real smart guy and he ain't hardly ever a nice fella.' "[35] Permeating *The Grapes of Wrath* is not only a deep admiration for the courage and dignity of the Okies—especially Ma Joad, Tom, and Casy—but also the implication that these qualities are not to be found among those who have wealth and power. The Okies learn early that the poor must turn to other poor people, and not to the "haves," if they are to find compassion, warmth, and assistance. The suggestion is that there is a kind of moral success which can be found only in failure.

In *U.S.A.* John Dos Passos establishes essentially the same dichotomy between the "good" little men and the "bad" owners and leaders of the system. In the Biographies of historical figures, the slanting is clear and effective. The heroes are men like Eugene Debs, Bill Haywood, and Robert La Follette who struggled for the little man. The villains are the aggressive and greedy business titans like Andrew Carnegie, Minor C. Keith, Henry Ford, Samuel Insull, and J. P. Morgan. Dos Passos uses his most hostile language in describing Morgan, the financial manipulator:

> War and panics on the stock exchange,
> machinegunfire and arson,
> bankruptcies, warloans,
> starvation, lice, cholera, and typhus:
> good growing weather for the House of Morgan.[36]

Other Biographies read like inversions of popular-magazine success stories. The story of Samuel Insull, for instance, begins with a characterization of Insull as the office boy who made good, but the details which follow emphasize Insull's unscrupulous grasping of power and money at the expense of those who had to be squeezed out.[37]

The use of the Biographies allowed Dos Passos to interpret actual historical figures and events according to his own biases. In the portrayal of his fictional characters, Dos Passos as author intrudes less obviously, but the same attitude toward the successful characters is present. J. Ward Moorhouse, for instance, is in a class with the businessmen of the Biographies—self-interested, pompous, and inhuman. Charlie Anderson, whose story is told in the latter part of *42nd Parallel* and throughout most of *The Big Money*, is an originally decent little man who is ruined by material success. He begins as a talented mechanic, but his pursuit of the dream of success becomes so obsessive that it isolates him from honest labor and destroys his humanity. The "moral" is the familiar idea that economic success and inner, personal success do not coincide. Most of the other outwardly successful characters in the novel—Eleanor Stoddard, Margo Dowling, Richard Savage, Eveline Hutchins—are no more admirable or successful as people than Charlie Anderson or J. Ward Moorhouse.

While Dos Passos has nothing but contempt for big business and a strong abstract sympathy for the little man, he does not portray him as always admirable and virtuous. Mac, the well-intentioned, incurably sensual drifter, is not idealized or made into a hero, nor are Joe Williams or "Vag." The Communist labor organizers, Mary French and Ben Compton, are dedicated, but their efforts are merely pathetic and futile. All of Mary's causes fail, and her personal life is marred by frustration and betrayal. Ben is a deadly serious, even fanatical, party worker who really does nothing to help the workingman and who, in fact, is guilty of callously using individuals to further the Party Cause.

Dos Passos' unfavorable characterization of Ben Compton, and particularly his criticism of Ben's willingness to sacrifice the individual to the cause, illustrates the distance between *U.S.A.* and the typical party-line proletarian novel. Dos Passos, like Steinbeck, was much too deeply committed to the American traditions of independence and individualism to look favorably upon anyone who was prepared to subordinate the needs of the individual systematically to the needs of the organization. While both Steinbeck and Dos Passos saw the need for the workers and little people to organize and cooperate against the inequities of the capitalist system, they feared the vast and powerful forces which submerged and strangled the individual, and in their minds these forces included big business, big government, and the Communist Party.

Steinbeck's strike novel, *In Dubious Battle,* strongly emphasizes the theme that the rabid devotion to the Party Cause resulted in a consistent sacrificing of individuals to an abstraction. Despite his sympathy with the goals of the organizers, Steinbeck does not hesitate to expose the fact that seasoned organizers like Mac are capable of using violence, bloodshed, and even the martyrdom of party workers to create class hatred. The same attitude appears in Dos Passos' *U.S.A.* and in *Adventures of a Young Man,* which was written at the end of the thirties. The sympathy of Steinbeck and Dos Passos for the individual little man clearly has less to do with twentieth-century radicalism than with the traditional American ideal of the common man. In one of the Camera Eye sequences in *The Big Money,* Dos Passos invokes not Marx, but Walt Whitman: "I go home after a drink and a hot meal and read . . . the epigrams of Martial and ponder the course of history and what leverage might pry the owners loose from power and bring back (I too Walt Whitman) our storybook democracy."[38] According to Dos Passos' vision of America, the solution to the little man's oppression was to be found, not in an imported ideology, but in the recovery of the true spirit of American liberty and democracy.

Many varieties of literature in the thirties contribute to the impression that the Depression years were preeminently the era of the little man, the loser, the tough hero, and the victim-hero. Americans have always loved a winner, particularly a winner who begins in obscurity and rises above his humble background. Men who have inherited a position of wealth and special privilege have rarely ranked high as popular heroes at least since the time of Washington and Jefferson.[39] But the underdog who becomes a winner has throughout our history attracted more than his share of interest and admiration. In the 1930s the underdog who remains a little man and, in conventional terms, a loser rose to a new prominence of his own, arousing more interest, more sympathy, and more admiration and respect than ever before. The great story of the Depression era was the story of failure, not the story of success, and a consistent pattern in the literature of the decade is a searching and many-angled anatomy of failure, hardship, and loss. Inversions of the conventional myth of success are a dominant pattern in the works of major writers and a relatively frequent occurrence in popular literature. Even the story of the period's outstanding political hero, Franklin Roosevelt, represented one kind of inversion of the conventional myth of success. Roosevelt represented not the poor boy who made good, but the aristocrat who overcame the handicap of hereditary wealth and status to become the friend and champion of the little man.

The anatomy of failure in the literature of the thirties can be understood, in part, as an objective response to the economic reality of the era. At the same time, however, the ascension of little men, losers, and outsiders as literary heroes illustrates the mythmaking function of literature. Many writers were not content merely to portray failure and loss as a phenomenon of their time. They went further and created a myth of failure and a cult of the little man which helped to make failure respectable by investing it with its own compensations and its own mystique. Contrary to the Protestant ethic, humility and failure rather than ambition and worldly success are the marks of godliness in much of the literature of the thirties.

It is paradoxical that not only *inversions* but *perversions* of the traditional success story appealed to the imagination of Americans during the Depression years. The rebels, the outsiders, and the outlaws who pursued their nightmare versions of the American dream with toughness, cynicism, and even violence represented a distinct aberration in the pattern of American hero worship. Rebels and outlaws (western heroes like Jesse James or Billy the Kid, for instance) had early become legendary figures for Americans. In general, however, as Dixon Wecter has observed, Americans have expected their heroes to be infused with a sense of fair play and certainly to be devoid of cynicism.[40] The fascination in the thirties with the coldly cynical tough-guy hero suggests that, even on the popular level, the Depression experience had undermined that sense of idealism which had in the past caused Americans to respond to the dreamer and reject or ignore the cynic. The proletarian hero in the fiction of the thirties is also an outsider, in revolt against American bourgeois society, and in that sense there is a kind of logic in the fact that the tough guy and the proletarian came to the front as literary heroes at roughly the same time. Both represent a profound disillusionment with the pursuit of the American dream of individual success within the capitalist system. Furthermore, implicit in many tough guy writings, including Hemingway's *To Have and Have Not*, McCoy's *They Shoot Horses, Don't They?*, and some of the works of James M. Cain and Raymond Chandler, is a sympathy with the underdogs and "have nots" of American society which resembles the "social consciousness" of the proletarian writers. The tough-guy hero himself, however, is a man with no creed, an individualist who uses violence in order to succeed or survive in a hostile world; the proletarian hero is a man with a creed who sometimes resorts to violence in order to translate his manifesto into action.[41] In the first case, the shattering of the conventional American dream has led to cynicism; in the latter, it has led to the espousal of an alien ideology.

In popular-magazine fiction, the little-man theme represents an obvious effort to adjust to the reality of the Depression by scaling down expectations and, in effect, redefining "success." The myth of the little man offered consolation to America's Depression victims by idealizing the average man and pointing to the value of mediocrity and "failure"; at the same time it reflected and promoted a very different set of values from those distilled and dramatized by the traditional myth of success. The Depression also produced other efforts to adjust the myth of success to the reality of the Depression, many of which reflect a similar search for new values to replace those that seemed challenged by the economic breakdown. It is to this subject that Chapter 5 will turn.

Notes

1. This shift is emphasized by Patricke Johns-Heine and Hans H. Gerth in their article, "Values in Mass Periodical Fiction, 1921-40," in *Mass Culture*, edited by Bernard Rosenberg and David M. White, p. 231.

2. Mabel Newcomer, *The Big Business Executive: The Factors that Made Him*, p. 6.

3. Thurman Arnold, *The Folklore of Capitalism*, pp. 185-90.

4. Louis F. McCabe, "A Chance to Be Somebody," *American Magazine*, April, 1931, pp. 64-66, 86.

5. Ann Morse, "Hero Enough," *Liberty*, October 13, 1934, pp. 26-27.

6. R. G. Kirk, "Unknown Hunky," *American Magazine*, December, 1935, pp. 104-07.

7. R. G. Kirk, "Ladies Go Last," *American Magazine*, June, 1938, pp. 45-47.

8. *American Magazine*, November, 1939, pp. 49, 95.

9. Gelett Burgess, "Riches to Rags," *American Magazine*, November, 1930, pp. 28-29, 141.

10. Gordon M. Hillman, "The Shamrock Waistcoat," *American Magazine*, January, 1933, pp. 14-17, 86.

11. Katherine Haviland Taylor, "The Failure," *American Magazine*, November, 1932, pp. 14-17, 66.

12. Ben Ames Williams, "As Big a Fool," *Liberty*, April 18, 1936, pp. 46-50.

13. Hans Fallada, *Little Man, What Now?*, p. 319.

14. Ibid., p. 333.

15. Ibid., p. 334.

16. Arthur Knight, "The Movies," in *The Thirties, A Time to Remember*, p. 370.

17. Daniel Bell, "Crime as an American Way of Life," *Antioch Review*, XIII (Summer, 1953), 131.

18. Robert Warshow makes a similar point in an essay titled "The Gangster as Tragic Hero," in *The Immediate Experience*.

19. Quoted in James Hart, *The Popular Book*, p. 258.

20. David Madden, "Introduction," *Tough Guy Writers of the Thirties*, p. xvii.

21. Philip Young, "To Have Not: Tough Luck," in *Tough Guy Writers of the Thirties*, p. 42.

22. Hemingway, *To Have and Have Not*, p. 225.

23. Quoted in Young, p. 45.

24. Robert Edenbaum, "The Novels of Dashiell Hammett," in *Tough Guy Writers of the Thirties*, p. 103.

25. Richard Wright, *Native Son*, p. 332.

26. John E. Hart, "Albert Halper's World of the 30's," *Twentieth-Century Literature*, IX (January, 1964), 185-95.

27. Albert Halper, *Union Square*, p. 171.

28. Ibid., p. 354.

29. Ibid., p. 378.

30. In *The Radical Novel in the United States, 1900-1954*, Walter Rideout describes four major types of proletarian novels: (1) those dealing with the "bottom dogs" (*Union Square* would fall into this category), (2) those describing the decay of the middle class, (3) those centered about strikes, and (4) those portraying a conversion to radicalism.

31. Ibid., p. 184.

32. William Saroyan, "The Time of Your Life," in *Famous American Plays of the Thirties*, p. 393.

33. Ibid., p. 398.

34. Ibid., p. 410.

35. John Steinbeck, *Of Mice and Men*, p. 73.

36. John Dos Passos, *1919*, in *U.S.A.*, p. 340.

37. *The Big Money*, in *U.S.A.*, p. 525.

38. Ibid., p. 150.

39. Dixon Wecter, *The Hero in America*, p. 484.

40. Ibid., p. 486.

41. David Madden touches on the relationship between the tough-guy hero and the proletarian hero in his introduction to *Proletarian Writers of the Thirties*, p. xxxii.

5 / Adjustments, Compensations, and the Search for New Values

If the 1930s saw the displacement of the successful business titan by little men and victim-heroes, it was also a period of general upheaval, adjustment, and ambivalence in American popular thinking about success. Despite the efforts of many popular writers about success to reaffirm the old values, realities of many sorts were making the traditional myth of success increasi untenable. The Depression itself added new insecurities to the already existi uncertainties caused by the experience of living in an age of increasing technology, industrialization, and corporate complexity. The economic collapse helped to dramatize the inapplicability of the older ideals of individualism and self-help, but of course many other factors came together in the thirties which contributed to a sense of ambivalence and confusion of values. The growth of big labor and the establishment of the welfare state as an accepte institution represented major, permanent social changes which were bound to affect the success myth and its associated values. Not only the specific problem of unemployment but the general trend from a production-oriente toward a consumer-oriented society had important implications concerning the gospel of work and the use of leisure. The whole concept of social planning and design—reflected in forms ranging from Howard Scott's Technocracy, to the new efforts toward industrial design, to New Deal planning itself—struck at the foundations of individualistic self-help and laissez-faire. The social sciences, which came into their own in the thirties, were looked to for a sense of rational order in society; and much of the emphasis—in the burgeoning field of counseling, in psychiatry, in the efforts of social scientists like Elton Mayo to improve the adaptation of workers to industrial operations—ran counter to traditional American concepts of individualism. The concern was with the *adjustment* of the individual to the social order, not with self-reliant personal accomplishment by the individual who stands apart from others. One cultural historian, searching for labels, has suggested that the period might be thought of as an Adlerian age of adjustment, in the sense that so much of what was happening seemed to parallel Alfred Adler's concern with feelings of inferiority or insecurity and the individual's need to compensate by finding a way to belong and identify within the human community.[1]

In their sometimes uncertain and ambivalent efforts to accommodate the myth of success to the economic and social realities of the times, inspirationalists and apostles of success altered some of the old formulas, rejected others, and proposed various new emphases indicating a search for new values. Belonging, security, acceptance, positive thinking, peace of mind, the wise use of leisure, and the adjustment to existing conditions were among the most important of the new emphases. In varying degrees, they are reflected in the period's best-selling works of moral, social, and economic instruction, including Dale Carnegie's *How to Win Friends and Influence People* (1936), Walter Pitkin's *Life Begins at Forty* (1932), Lin Yutang's *The Importance of Living* (1937), and Henry Link's *The Return to Religion* (1936). Carnegie's *How to Win Friends and Influence People* represents a clear shift away from the traditional emphasis on individual strength of character as the key to success toward an emphasis on personality and getting along. Carnegie and others who exploited popular interest in psychology created a cult of personality and positive thinking in which the goals are selling oneself and cultivating the proper mental outlook. Whereas earlier how-to-succeed guidebooks emphasized the control of the external world through strength of character, the exponents of positive thinking emphasize the control of one's own inner world through exercises in mental manipulation. Other best sellers— Pitkin's *Life Begins at Forty* and Lin Yutang's *The Importance of Living,* for example—cast doubt on the beauty of the rat race for success and reject the ideal of long and arduous industry in favor of a new gospel of leisure. Lin Yutang's work, along with other popularized works of religiophilosophy like Henry Link's *The Return to Religion,* reflected also a search for inner values which might replace material success as a source of direction. For Link contentment and the well-adjusted personality are the essence of happiness, regardless of outward accomplishment.

Even the popular-magazine fiction of the decade contains a strain of disillusionment with material success which, though far from being dominant, is nevertheless significant. It is particularly conspicuous in comparison with the popular fiction of the twenties, which is virtually unanimous in its worship of the gospel of success. Antisuccess themes are portrayed directly and unequivocally in a few stories of the thirties, and one notes an increasing emphasis on peace of mind, security, love, family life, and other nonmaterial values in the rewards offered by the happy endings of the stories.

Personality and Positive Thinking

Among the many how-to-succeed guidebooks which appeared in the thirties, the most consistently used approach was a pseudo-psychological emphasis on personality selling and positive thinking. The key to success, according to this philosophy, lies in the manipulation of others by means of an ingratiating personality and the manipulation of one's own behavior by means of a positive frame of mind. In *How to Win Friends and Influence People,* Dale Carnegie used this approach to put together one of the most popular how-to-succeed books ever written, a best seller which remained on *The New York Times'* list for ten years and which, still selling, has long since topped the 5 million mark. Numerous similar but less popular works also emphasized the cultivation of the proper personality traits and mental attitudes. The titles of many of them suggest the positive thinking approach. There are, for instance, Napoleon Hill's *Think and Grow Rich* (1937), Dorothea Brande's *Wake Up and Live* (1936), Frank Welsh and Frances Gordon's *Thinking Success into Business* (1932), and Allen Chalfant's *What's Holding You Back?* (1937).

In many respects the typical how-to-succeed guidebooks of the thirties conform to the pattern established by nineteenth-century philosophers of success like Russell Conwell and Orison Marden, and carried on by writers like Bruce Barton and Roger Babson in the twenties. The central assumptions of earlier proponents of success tend to be repeated as platitudes by their counterparts in the 1930s. The dream of success is assumed to be a goal which can be fulfilled for any individual in America. The key to success is considered to be within the individual and not in external circumstances. America itself is viewed as a land of extraordinary opportunity and freedom. And, almost always, success is viewed as operating according to certain magical laws which the writer of the guidebook proclaims himself capable of discovering and codifying. Yet, in certain of their tacit assumptions and special emphases, Dale Carnegie's best seller and other how-to-succeed books of the thirties are clearly products of their time. They reflect the specific impact of the economic Depression as well as certain broader-based developments, including the growth of the middle class, the impact of big government and big labor, and the ascendancy of the corporate system, which were changing the patterns of success in America.

The emphasis on adjusting and controlling one's mental outlook would seem to reflect a tacit recognition of the fact that by the 1930s it was no longer easy to exercise an actual physical control over external forces by virtue of individual character and will. By giving primary importance to mental exercises rather than to tangible achievement in the external world, writers like Dale Carnegie and Napoleon Hill could avoid making too many elaborate, and perhaps implausible, claims about the impact that a strong-willed individual could have on the world outside himself. Their theory of positive thinking offered readers a hope for success that seemed within grasp because it simply required control over one's own mind. Dale Carnegie states the principle in these words: "Everybody in the world is seeking happiness—and there is one sure way to find it. That is by controlling your thoughts. Happiness doesn't depend on outward conditions. It depends on inner conditions."[2] Carnegie goes on to quote from William James, Shakespeare, and Abe Lincoln in proving the point that people are as happy as they think they are. It is an approach to success that, followed to its logical conclusion, would make unnecessary the strain of dealing with the outside world. In these terms, positive thinking could be interpreted as offering readers yet another possibility of escaping from actual conditions in the real world.

Yet writers like Carnegie and Hill did not, in their concern with inner conditioning and mental transformation, forget about the problems of dealing with the practical world. Far from it. Despite the emphasis on "inner conditions" and "controlling your thoughts," the real purpose of personality cultivation and mental conditioning is to produce success in the business world. For all the insistence on inner happiness, material success is still held up as the primary goal, largely, it seems, because the writers of success books do not know how to conceive of happiness in any other terms. Besides using such titles as *Think and Grow Rich* and *Thinking Success into Business*, the advocates of positive thinking reveal their commitment to the pursuit of wealth in other ways. Napoleon Hill recommends that his readers use their mental powers to cultivate a desire for wealth. "You can never have riches in great quantities [he insists] unless you can work yourself into a white heat of *desire* for money."[3] He even suggests that it would be wise to fix the mind on the exact amount of wealth desired, repeating this amount "once just before retiring at night and once after arising in the morning."[4] Similarly, Dale Carnegie holds out material rewards as the main enticement to his readers to practice the principles outlined in his book. In suggesting how to get the most out of the book, he points to one "magic requirement"—a "deep, driving desire to learn." This desire can be developed, he says, by picturing how the mastery of positive thinking will aid you in your race for richer social and financial rewards. Say to yourself over and over: " 'My popularity, my happiness, and my income depend to no small extent upon my skill in dealing with people.' "[5] The vast majority of Carnegie's illustrations in *How to Win Friends and Influence People* have to do with men from the business world who have achieved financial success by applying the principles Carnegie recommends. Carnegie is particularly fond of quoting former students of his course who testify to the sheer cash value of his instruction. "Smiles are bringing me dollars, many dollars every day,"[6] reports one graduate; and similar testimonies are woven throughout the book.

In *Thinking Success into Business* by Frank Welsh and Frances Gordon, the emphasis is again on the relationship between mental attitude and business success. In the foreword the authors explain that the object of the book is to demonstrate the importance of mental discipline and to provide readers "practical ways in which they can successfully direct their mental efforts into the channels of success."[7] What follows is a simpleminded parable demonstrating the inevitable effectiveness of "Right Thinking," as the authors label their variety of positive thinking. A man whose business is failing is rescued from despair, and therefore failure, by the principle of "Right Thinking," a concept that makes him happy and confident. Magically his new attitude inspires good work by his employees, increased orders from clients, and in general a full recovery of his business. The automatic way in which the external facts of the situation right themselves once the proper mental outlook is mastered must have seemed comforting, if not particularly credible, to readers of the Depression years.

These Depression-era guides to positive thinking, as well as later works like Norman Vincent Peale's *The Power of Positive Thinking*, were clearly influenced by the New Thought movement which developed in the early years of the twentieth century. New Thought was, in A. Whitney Griswold's terms, "a system of high-powered mental telepathy" which held that matter could be spiritualized and brought under the complete domination of thought. Its motto, "Think Your Way to Wealth," states its frankly materialistic emphasis.[8] In *Thinking Success into Business*, Welsh and Gordon reflect a pure version of this "New Thought" position in their assumption of "the indisputable fact that all cause is mental." Since man can control and manipulate the material world through his mental powers, they argue, business success is merely a matter of having the right thoughts.

It is not surprising that the philosophy of success represented by the "New Thought" movement should become predominant in the Depression years. It was a philosophy which kept wealth as a goal, but which held that the goal was to be achieved not so much by activity in the real world as by mental manipulation. The connection between mental discipline and success was portrayed as a vague and mystical one, not as an objective one. Thus, there was no need to take into account the complexities, difficulties and frustrations of the outside world. When the New Thought mind-power movement developed around the turn of the century, it seemed to be, in part, a way of plausibly reaffirming the ideal of the autonomous individual despite the increasing submergence of the individual in the emerging urban-industrial society. In the thirties there was an even greater need to find a way of asserting the power of the will within a context which could ignore external reality.

Closely related to the positive-thinking theory was the growing emphasis among the best-known success books of the thirties on the cultivation of personality rather than the development of character as the real key to success. If the cultivation of a positive mental outlook implied the manipulation of self more than the manipulation of things, the cultivation of personality implied the delicate handling of people more than the direct attempt to control them by the use of superior power and strength of character. The other-directed character type, which David Riesman identifies as predominant in twentieth-century America, is clearly the ideal in *How to Win Friends and Influence People* and other how-to-succeed guidebooks of the thirties. In the twenties, novelists like Dreiser and Lewis had analyzed the other-directed type, and in some popular-success literature other direction and inner direction were both stressed in an ambiguous mixture. But the emphasis was still primarily on inner direction and strength of character. It was not until the thirties that personality cultivation was widely acclaimed as the key to success.[9]

In addition to such broad developments as the increasing influence of psychology and other social sciences and the growth of huge, bureaucratic business, labor, and government organizations in which getting along with hundreds of people was a necessity, the Great Depression itself undoubtedly contributed to this shift. The competition for jobs in the years of high unemployment made selling oneself a necessity. It was a buyer's market, and one way to improve the chances of marketing one's skills was to cultivate personality traits that would make one both well liked and skillful in handling people. The "selling yourself" motif appears frequently in books and articles which specifically refer to the fact that the Depression was making success more difficult and competitive. Loire Brophy's *Men Must Work* (1938), for example, has a whole section on selling oneself through personality. Similarly, Albert Fancher's *Getting a Job and Getting Ahead* (1931) warns that in bad times a good man might have outstanding beauty of character and still go begging unless he advertises "himself and his achievements with the aim of increasing his market value."[10] The fear of failure which the Depression created made the lonely success of the inner-directed man seem precarious and, thus, less attractive than the more secure, if unspectacular, type of success which emphasized getting along, being liked, and fitting in. As Dale Carnegie's title suggests, if one cannot influence people and gain what he wants, he can at least win friends through the cultivation of personality. Carnegie promises the security of belonging as well as the glamour of success. The inner-directed man's supreme disregard of public opinion has no place in his philosophy of success.

The shift of emphasis from character to personality can be easily documented by reference to the personal qualities most frequently recommended by how-to-succeed manuals. The traditional self-help book invariably listed industry, ambition, integrity, initiative, thrift, honesty, punctuality, dependability, and similar qualities of character as the most important requisites for success. This emphasis is still strongly apparent in the best-known success books of the 1920s. Roger Babson's *What Is Success?* (1923), for instance, identifies as the most important requisites integrity, hard work, intelligence, initiative, intensity, and interest in one's work.[11] Nothing is said about flashing a pleasant smile or performing other personality tricks.

Bruce Barton's Christ is an appealing personality man, but he is also an aggressive, assertive individualist who is capable of a lofty disregard of public opinion. In the more imitative success manuals of the thirties, lists of crucial character traits similar to the above are commonplace. But the trend among the best-known guidebooks was clearly toward a focus on personality traits rather than on character traits.

In *What's Holding You Back?* (1937), Allan Chalfant lists as the enemies of success such problems as fear of the boss, paranoia, dullness, and the lack of a healthy self-image; he says nothing of lack of initiative, lack of integrity, or lack of thrift. The number-one enemy, he says, is "self center," the kind of "brooding preoccupation with self" which destroys a person's ability to get along with others. Rejecting the self-sufficient individualism of the inner-directed man, he urges that the would-be success make friends by showing an interest in other people, that he circulate among important people and keep up contacts, and that he avoid being a bore in conversation.

It is obvious that Chalfant's magic secrets to success are very similar to those outlined in *How to Win Friends and Influence People,* and it is to Carnegie's enormously popular book that we should look for the best illustrations of the new emphasis on personality. In keeping with the penchant of how-to-succeed guidebook writers for lists of foolproof keys to success, Carnegie enumerates "Six Ways to Make People Like You," "Twelve Ways to Win People to Your Way of Thinking," and "Nine Ways to Change People Without Giving Offense or Arousing Resentment." In the details that fill out the lists, Carnegie's emphasis is always on the cultivation of personality, and the ultimate objective is to improve one's chances for material success. The cumulative list of things a person must do to be well liked and successful seems depressingly long. One must be genuinely interested in other people, smile, remember names, be a good listener, talk in terms of the other man's interests or let him do the talking, make the other person feel important, avoid arguments, show respect for the other man's opinions and sympathy with his desires, lavish praise and honest appreciation on others, and ask questions instead of giving direct orders.

The list could hardly be more other-directed. Everything is geared toward selling oneself by adjusting to others, getting along, being agreeable, and creating goodwill. The traditional emphasis on aggressive self-assertion is reversed. Any kind of self-assertion, Carnegie seems to assume, is bad because it creates resentment instead of goodwill. The man who wants to succeed must not assert himself by arguing for his opinions; it is agreeing and not arguing that creates goodwill. "Figure it out for yourself," Carnegie says. "Which would you rather have: an academic, theoretical victory or a man's good will? You can seldom have both."[12] In building up the ego of others, one should certainly avoid the self-assertion inherent in making known one's own accomplishments. "Let's minimize our achievements. Let's be modest,"[13] the advice goes, because people are interested in their own achievements and are only bored or threatened by hearing of someone else's. In denying self-assertion and insisting on modesty, Carnegie verges on a rejection of material success itself. As David Riesman has observed, the aggressive self-assertion of the inner-directed man can bring a lonely success. Carnegie is very sensitive to this pitfall, and he gives specific advice on how to avoid it. In leading up to his "let's minimize our achievements" stricture, he quotes from La Rochefoucauld, "If you want enemies, excel your friends; but if you want friends, let your friends excel you." The reason this aphorism is true, Carnegie explains, is that "when our friends excel us, that gives them a feeling of importance; but when we excel them, that gives them a feeling of inferiority and arouses envy and jealousy."[14] The moral could be, "Therefore, don't excel." But the one Carnegie states is "Therefore don't talk about excelling." Paradoxically, the near-rejection of success is not an actual rejection; it is rather a part of the strategy for assuring success.

The special emphases in Carnegie's discussion of success reveal some important assumptions about the source and nature of success in the America of the 1930s. His advice seems most appropriate for the salesman, the public-relations man, the middle-class white-collar worker, and the organization man interested in finessing his way upward in a complicated corporation hierarchy. All these types, of course, were becoming very important in the pattern of modern business. By his warnings against self-assertion and inner-direction, Carnegie seems to assume that the day of the old, individualistic captain of industry was over. Carnegie's doctrines also seem to assume an audience in whom the confusion, frustration, and uncertainty of the Depression have helped to create a fear of rising above others and a need for the security of belonging.

One of the most fundamental questions about the personality and positive-thinking guidebooks of the thirties has thus far been discussed from various angles but not posed directly: that is, to what extent do they reflec a loss of faith in the conventional American ideal of material success as the prime motive in life? The question cannot be answered easily and unequivocally because the books are complicated by ambivalence and paradoxes.

And yet the ambivalence itself is a partial answer to the question. That is, the ambiguities and seeming contradictions in Carnegie's book and others seem to imply considerable uncertainty about the soundness of material success as a value. On the other hand, however, there is an obvious lack of commitment to any other ideal that might replace material success. It is commonplace in these books for the author to state the most frankly materialistic attitude imaginable on one page and to reject it indignantly on another. Napoleon Hill's title, *Think and Grow Rich,* is blunt enough, and he insists upon the importance of working up a "white heat of desire for money." But he ends the book on a note of skepticism about the dependability of the material world: "If you must be careless with your possessions, let it be in connection with material things. *Your mind is your spiritual estate!* Protect and use it with the care to which divine royalty is entitled."[15] Carnegie refers to "the kind of smile that will bring a good price in the market place" and, in general, keeps the reader well informed of the cash value of his suggestions for manipulating people. Yet he feels called upon occasionally to attack the very ideology of success that permeates his own book. "If we are so contemptibly selfish," he says heatedly at one point, "that we can't radiate a little happiness and pass on a bit of honest appreciation without trying to screw something out of the other person in return . . . we shall meet with the failure we so richly deserve."[16] In this passage, Carnegie seems supremely unaware of any inconsistency in the fact that he combines advice on how to use people with homilies about the wickedness of doing so.

Other ambivalences and paradoxes abound in the treatises on positive thinking. At times, peace of mind or a positive mental outlook seems to be the end in itself, but most of the illustrations and other details of the books imply that positive thinking is only a means to the end of worldly success. Self-interest is taken for granted, but self-assertion is feared and rugged individualism is dead as an ideal. Copious detail is devoted to the discussion of skills in getting along with people; but the possibility of cooperation with others toward a common end is scarcely mentioned because so much attention is devoted to the competitive business of using others for self-aggrandizement. The central ambivalence of Carnegie's book is conveyed in his double-barreled title. Winning friends and influencing people are given equal billing; both are desirable, and since the two are not always compatible, it is no wonder that the book contains contradictions and paradoxes. The final irony of Carnegie's book is that he adopts a deterministic view of the world which virtually destroys the philosophical foundation of his own work, or any work in the self-help tradition. The ideal of the self-made man depends on the belief that each individual is free to make of himself what he can. But in a deterministic mood, Carnegie tells his readers, "You deserve very little credit for being what you are— and remember, the man who comes to you irritated, bigoted, unreasoning, deserves very little discredit for being what he is." The body, temperament, and mind that a person inherits, coupled with his environment and experiences, are the factors that make him what he is, Carnegie says. The individual will has nothing to do with it.[17] Carnegie has attempted to demonstrate his awareness of modern theories of hereditary and environmental determinism. But he has failed to reconcile these theories with his book's theme that unlimited possibilities are open to the individual who can master the principles of positive thinking and the skills of personality selling.

Peace of Mind, Spiritual Harmony, and Adjustment

Though the advocates of positive thinking were somewhat confused and uncertain in their worship of material success, they were not prepared to reject the ideal of success and replace it with another goal. However, the Depression decade also produced popular inspirational books which were much less equivocal in their questioning of the pursuit of success as the prime motive in life and more committed to the definition of other values which might replace, or at least balance, material success. Walter B. Pitkin's *Life Begins at Forty* (1932), Henry C. Link's *The Return to Religion* (1936), and Lin Yutang's *The Importance of Living* (1937), all best sellers in the thirties, are didactic works on the conduct of life which reflect a sincere skepticism about the value of the frantic pursuit of material success. The fact that these and similar works were popular with the general public suggests that Americans were becoming increasingly aware of the need for inner certitudes that might compensate for the loss of material success as a valid and satisfying ideal.

In turning a skeptical eye on the rat race for material success, Pitkin, Lin Yutang, and Link share a highly critical attitude toward what they consider to be a characteristically American failing—that is, a narrow, singleminded, even obsessive devotion to hard work and hustling for the purpose of achieving material success. The three differ, however, in the perspectives they bring to the problem and in the solutions they suggest. Pitkin's central theme is a severe indictment of the traditional American gospel of work. For many, the problem of unemployment during the Depression had the effect of making the gospel of work seem more sacred than ever, as countless articles and stories in the popular magazines indicate. But Pitkin argues that a new gospel of leisure would be more appropriate to the twentieth century than the old gospel of work. With an optimism characteristic of inspirational books, he emphasizes the positive effects of the Depression. Since one effect of the economic slowdown was increased leisure time, he attempts to invest leisure with value and to devaluate work.

It should be pointed out that, though they do not emphasize the point as Pitkin does, other writers of inspirational books were also looking skeptically at the doctrine of hard work. Even Dale Carnegie and Napoleon Hill, emphasizing mental transformation as they do, minimize the importance of hard work. Hill says that "riches begin with a state of mind, with definiteness of purpose, with little or no hard work."[18] Carnegie finds the idea of success through sheer hard work laughable. He reports: "I once interviewed Jim Farley and asked him the secret of his success. He said 'Hard work,' and I said, 'Don't be funny.' "[19] Carnegie's own explanation of the key to Farley's success is that he could call 50,000 people by their first names.

But Carnegie and Hill minimize the importance of hard work because they believe that other factors are more crucial in bringing about material success. Pitkin ridicules the American passion for work because he thinks that working for its own sake or for the sake of producing wealth is a foolish and unpleasant way to spend one's time. One of his central arguments in support of the proposition that life begins at forty is that the efficiency of the modern machine age has created the possibility of a life of ease. Rather than be worn out at forty, he argues, a man can be just arriving at the peak of his ability to enjoy life, if he is wise enough to put money and work in their proper perspective. The Depression has contributed to the new era, says Pitkin, by making it necessary for industry to institute the five-day week and the six-hour day. In attacking the gospel of work, which he refers to as "one of The Million American Myths," Pitkin argues that, in the age of technology and specialization, most jobs are routine drudgery, demanding only a small fraction of a man's abilities and certainly offering no chance of self-realization or self-expression. Thus work grows increasingly trivial as a way of life and becomes merely a way of making a living. He predicts that "A few more years, and the Gospel of Work will have joined astrology and palmistry; it will be no more than the after stench of rotten quackery."[20] Pitkin chides Americans for living by an outdated philosophy, clinging to the "faded shreds of a pioneer outlook in which harsh toil, ceaseless striving, overshrewdness, animal cunning, and crude piety blend badly."[21] Work and the constant striving for success must be put in their proper place.

In a sense, Pitkin merely replaces one myth with another when he assumes that it is possible for the average man to live a life of ease and enjoyment without paying for it by hard work. His answer to this objection is that the life of leisure does not have to be costly. He grants that the average man, the young man in particular, must devote a considerable amount of his time and energies to earning a living, but he rejects the pursuit of wealth as a goal in itself. He criticizes what he calls "our silly dollar chasing" and objects that "the regular trick of the big business organization is to fill young men with rosy dreams of swift promotion and wealth; to drive them to the limit as junior executives or as foremen; and then to trust to dull human nature to hold the pace as a matter of habit."[22] The result is that Americans die young, having never really started living. A sensible goal, he says, would be just enough money above the bald necessities to allow a person to make something of his life outside his job.

Implicit in this idea of having a life outside one's job are some of the values Pitkin affirms as a replacement for "dollar chasing" and the gospel of work. The reason for working, he says, is to create leisure, not money. The object is to live as full, many-sided, and versatile a life as possible, and to do this, to "master the art of living" as Pitkin puts it, one must emancipate himself from such narrow concerns as making money and succeeding in a job. In a chapter titled "Busy Leisure," Pitkin discusses some of the specific ways in which the person who has mastered the art of living might spend his leisure. He includes travel, reading, conversation, painting, and similar activities, all of which, as he interprets them, require little money and are particularly well suited for mature and intelligent men and women of over forty who have scaled down their desires and know the true art of living.

Thus, Pitkin emphasizes leisure over work, the full and balanced life over the narrow pursuit of success, the life of simple pleasures over the life of materialistic extravagance, and the life of mature contentment over the life of youthful dreams and desires. Essentially, his book offered those who were young, money-hungry, and extravagant in the twenties a set of guidelines for growing up to a more mature and genuinely satisfying life in the thirties. The fact that a good many readers of the Depression years responded to the message is indicated by the book's sales history. It was not only a substantial seller when first published in 1932 but found an

increasing number of readers as the Depression wore on; by 1938 it was
selling around 200,000 copies per year.[23] The fact that Pitkin reached so
large an audience with a book which ridiculed the gospel of work, attacked
the American tendency to equate material success with happiness, and
inverted a number of other values associated with the traditional myth of
success would seem to be a symptom of growing popular disaffection in
the thirties with values that were seldom questioned before the economic
crisis.

Similar in its rejection of the American philosophy of go-getting and
in its emphasis on easygoing leisure is *The Importance of Living,* a graceful
and readable book of reflections by the Chinese-American journalist and
philosopher, Lin Yutang. Lin views the American passion for practicality,
productiveness, efficiency, and material success from the perspective of
his native Chinese culture, which he views as diametrically opposite to
American culture in most ways. As a native Oriental, he places more
emphasis on the inner life of meditation and spiritual repose than does
Pitkin, and yet the two offer a critique of the American myth of success
which is more similar than different. Judging from sales figures Lin's work
was even more appealing to Depression-era readers than Pitkin's; it ranked
as the top nonfiction best seller for all of 1938. Lin's comparison of
American and Chinese culture can be seen as a popular expression of the
ethical and cultural relativism that dominated the social sciences in the
twenties and thirties. Anthropologists and others had studied diverse cultures
as a means of providing a nonethnocentric perspective on American and
Western culture, and it seems that the general public in the thirties was
increasingly prepared to question whether "the American way" represented
an absolute expression of "true" and appropriate values. It might be added
that *The Importance of Living* was only one of several best sellers that
exposed frustrated Americans to times, places, and value systems which
were attractively remote from the American present. The list of such best
sellers includes Willa Cather's *Shadows on the Rock* (1931), Lloyd Douglas'
Magnificent Obsession (1929); Pearl Buck's *The Good Earth* (1931);
Charles Morgan's *The Fountain* (1932), which portrays a hero who desires
to escape from the world and find inner peace, and James Hilton's *Lost
Horizon* (1933), which describes an idyllic land of eternal youth and
Eastern mysticism.[24]

In presenting his philosophy, which he calls a Chinese philosophy and
"an idle philosophy born of an idle life, evolved in a different age,"[25]
Lin offers American readers of the Depression a new approach to their

problems. Since the Chinese national mind has been historically so isolated from Western culture, he says, "we have the right to expect new answers to the problems of life, or what is better, new methods of approach, or, still better, a new posing of the problems themselves."[26] He speculates that despite the differences between American culture and Chinese culture, many harried Americans crave exactly the sort of easygoing idleness that he describes as basic to the Chinese way of life. He says:

> I am quite sure that amidst the hustle and bustle of American
> life, there is a great deal of wistfulness, of the divine desire
> to lie on a plot of grass under tall beautiful trees of an idle after-
> noon and *just do nothing.* The necessity for such common cries
> as "Wake up and live" is to me a good sign that a wise portion of
> American humanity prefer to dream the hours away.[27]

Judging from the success of the book, Lin was right in his speculation that Americans of the Depression era were capable of appreciating a philosophy of life that amounts to a complete rejection of the American dream of success.

And the philosophy Lin describes is certainly unequivocally hostile to the dream of success. As Lin sees it, the highest ideal of Chinese culture has always been a man with a sense of detachment and wise disenchantment, a man with no dreams, who is "seldom disillusioned because he has no illusions, and seldom disappointed because he never had extravagant hopes."[28] This ideal type is able, because of his detachment, to assume a high-mindedness that allows him to go through life with an attitude of tolerant irony toward fame, wealth, and material success. Lin's emphasis on the ideal of wise disenchantment is intended to place Chinese attitudes toward worldly success in glaring contrast with American attitudes. Implied in the contrast is an attack not only on the usual target, American materialism, but also on that capacity for dreaming, that idealistic belief in the future, which has been so often celebrated as the source of American greatness. In other words, Lin suggests that the American dream itself and not merely materialistic perversions of it should be questioned.

Lin's contrast between the American tendency to worship success and the Chinese tendency to scorn it is extended even further when he observes that some branches of Chinese thought—most notably Taoism—not only disapprove of the pursuit of material success, but give specific counsels against any kind of eminence. "Never be first in the world," goes one

Taoistic aphorism quoted by Lin. According to this view, one can never have both success and inner peace. The greater a man's success, the more he fears losing it. Thus, the obscure man is at a tremendous advantage. Lin does not sympathize fully with the kind of extreme cynicism regarding success that would result in a complete shrinking away from the world. But he feels that modern man is so overbalanced in the other direction, so obsessed with success and so dominated by deeply ingrained impulses toward action, that he needs this "refreshing wind of cynicism."

Accompanying the rejection of material success in Lin's book is an affirmation of such alternative values as leisure, humor, culture, and the easygoing enjoyment of simple pleasures, physical and spiritual. He writes about the enjoyment of lying in bed, of sitting in chairs, of food and drink, of nature, of travel, of art, knowledge, and contemplation. He emphasizes, and devotes an entire chapter to, "The Importance of Loafing," pointing out that ironically all nature loafs, while only man works for a living.[29] In a section titled "The Scamp as Ideal," he describes as one of his ideal types the opposite of the successful man. The curious, undisciplined, humorous waywardness of the scamp or vagabond, he says, is the hope of mankind. To be feared is the disciplined, efficient, aggressive achievement of the successful man and, even more, the qualities of the "lowest type," the obedient, disciplined, and regimented soldier.[30] The "three American vices"—efficiency, punctuality, and the pursuit of success—rob men of their time to enjoy life and of the inner peace and happiness that make life worth living.

Another widely read didactic book of the thirties, Henry Link's *The Return to Religion,* though it reaffirms many conventional American values, provides still more evidence of the public's warm reception of books which attempted to substitute other values for the pursuit of material success. Despite the misleading title, Link's book does not set out to show that the Depression created a revival of interest in religion. The author has something to say about why he personally returned to religion after a period of agnosticism. However, more than anything else, the book is a didactic treatise on how to live one's life; and like many of the how-to books of the thirties, it combines religion and popular psychology in a curious mixture. Link returned to religion, he explains, because he found that modern psychology confirmed many of the New Testament insights into human nature and because he came to realize that the people he counseled as a psychologist desperately needed some kind of spiritual faith in order to develop well-adjusted personalities.

If the period is to be seen as an age of Adlerian adjustment, then Link must be considered one of its important spokesmen, for with him adjustment becomes a mystique. As a practicing psychologist, Link considers himself "necessarily a student of happiness and its causes,"[31] and the key to happiness which he emphasizes throughout the book is the development of an extroverted, well-adjusted personality. In a chapter titled "The Abundant Life," he attacks those who define the abundant life in terms of money and possessions and offers a definition of his own in which he emphasizes the importance of a well-rounded personality. Material success, or even noteworthy accomplishment of other sorts, is conspicuously absent from his list of factors which contribute to happiness. At one point he describes the profile of one of his interviewees who, he suddenly realizes, "is the ideal type of well-balanced individual, the unsung hero in a world of mental and moral conflict."[32] The ideal man is unemployed, not handsome, not intellectually brilliant, and not college educated. But he is active in church work and various social activities, interested in sports, dancing, and card games, and well above average in extroversion, emotional stability, and social skills.[33] It is as if Link's ideal man has achieved the perfect adjustment to insecurity by means of his skills in belonging and fitting into society. Inherent in this description of the ideal man is a celebration of mediocrity. The essence of the description is that the ideal man is not outstanding in any way *except* in his averageness and his adjustment to what is expected of him. Significantly, it is not required that this ideal type even have a job, much less that he be an achiever in the mold of that older ideal type—the self-made man. Like some of the popular-magazine stories portraying little men and losers, Link's statements seem calculated to assure readers of the Depression years that they could be happy and admirable without being brilliant or successful.

Link's emphasis on personality and extroversion relates him, in a sense, to the Dale Carnegie school of popular psychologists. With Link, however, peace of mind, extroversion, and the well-adjusted personality are ends in themselves and not means to material success. If an individual has a pleasing, well-adjusted personality, he implies, nothing else matters very much. Essentially his approach is to carry to its logical conclusion Carnegie's theory of how to win friends and to omit his advice on how to influence people. While Carnegie's gospel of personality is inextricably interwoven with his gospel of success, Link was prepared to reject material success and turn to the cult of personality as the sole key to happiness.

Viewed in relation to each other and against the background of the Depression, the significance of these best-selling books of Pitkin, Lin Yutang, and Link is that they all represent an effort to tarnish the image of material success and substitute broader and more spiritually oriented goals. They had a great appeal to Depression readers, largely, no doubt, because they provided the comforting assurance that one could fail or simply drop out of the frustrating struggle for material success and still live the good life—the abundant, satisfying life of simple pleasures and inner content. The emphasis by Pitkin and Lin Yutang on leisure as opposed to hard work points up another of the many ambivalences in popular thinking about success during the Depression years. Judging from the popular success of *Life Begins at Forty* and *The Importance of Living,* their renunciation of the traditional gospel of work struck a responsive chord in many readers. Yet, as suggested earlier, the gospel of work was one of the tenets most emphasized by the popular-magazine articles and stories geared toward the preservation of the traditional gospel of success. Thus, on the one hand, the scarcity of work during the Depression seems to have created a renewed sense of its value, while, on the other hand, the economic confusion and frustration of the time encouraged many people to look to something besides hard work and the hope of material success as the focal point in their lives. These conflicting attitudes toward the gospel of work were part of a general uncertainty of economic values and goals, an uncertainty in large measure precipitated, and certainly highlighted, by the Depression. Desperately needing a sense of security, many faced the Depression by clinging to the old, established symbols and faiths such as the gospel of work; others looked for security in values less dependent on the material world.

Resignation, Acceptance, and the Search for Security

Uncertainty, ambivalence, and conflicting values are apparent also in the popular-magazine fiction of the thirties. While numerous stories complacently perpetuate the traditional rags-to-riches myth of success, a substantial minority avoid the stereotyped pattern of fairy-tale escape and make an obvious effort to adjust the myth of success to the reality of the times. Many of these stories question the desirability of the frantic struggle for success and reflect a conscious and pointed search for nonmaterial values. An analysis of the happy endings in the stories reveals that, while material success is still the most common reward for the hero, other rewards appear much more frequently than in comparable stories of the twenties. In the popular stories of the twenties, material advancement provides the happy endings more frequently than all other rewards combined. The popular-story formula required a happy ending, and popular writers had difficulty conceiving of happy endings that did not include material success. In many stories of the thirties, by contrast, readers are expected to identify with characters who have become aware of the shallowness or precariousness of material success and are searching for something else. Most frequently the "something else" is security, acceptance by others, love, close family ties, peace of mind, or simply the strength to accept defeat. Essentially what these stories offer their readers is a set of guidelines for adjusting their desires and values to a world of confusion and economic collapse. Since rags-to-riches success had lost most of its viability as a realistic goal, many magazine stories attempt to diminish its allure as a popular ideal and to enhance the appeal of other values.

Among the stories which set out deliberately to devaluate the image of success, one finds a wide range of antisuccess morals: success corrupts the character; it subverts personal relationships; it causes neuroses and ulcers; it isolates individuals from other people; and in general its lure blinds people to worthwhile goals. Often there is a conflict between success and some other specific value which is offered as an alternative to success. Particularly numerous in this group are stories in which the obsessive pursuit of success threatens to destroy the marriage and family life of misguided characters. The preponderance of stories portraying a conflict between success and marriage would seem to corroborate the observation frequently made by social historians of the period that the institutions of marriage and the family became much more highly valued in the thirties than in the twenties. No doubt this emphasis on the value of marriage and the family developed in part because financial hardship made marriage difficult or impossible for many young people starting out in the Depression years. But many of the popular stories imply also that family life took on more importance because it was viewed as one specific value which might compensate for the growing disillusionment with the pursuit of economic success.

A typical portrayal of the conflict between success and family relations is found in a *Saturday Evening Post* story about the head of a large industry

His success is insecure because he has recently taken over the position and also because the Depression is damaging the firm's business. He spends all his time working and worrying until it becomes obvious that he is losing his wife. She accuses him of shutting her out and is on the verge of leaving him when he finally comes to his senses and puts his work into its proper perspective.[34] Thus, the story demonstrates the stupidity of exchanging domestic happiness for a position of uncertain and excessively demanding business success. Similar cautionary tales stressing the evils of a fanatic devotion to work and success abound in the popular fiction of the thirties. Typical examples are a story in which a young man drives himself obsessively until his wife retaliates by refusing to wait dutifully at home for his return and another in which a career woman "cursed with ambition" never marries and drives herself to an early old age.[35]

The Depression also produced some notable variations in the old poor-boy-wins-dream-girl theme—variations which reflect a search for values more stable and less material than economic success. The stock plot of the poor-boy-wins-dream-girl story of the twenties, of course, centered around the poor boy's successful efforts to make himself worthy of the girl by raising himself to her economic level. Among the stories of the thirties, an interesting and fairly frequent variation of this plot portrays the rich girl's descent to the poor boy's level rather than his ascent to hers. Essentially, this variation on the established boy-wins-girl formula amounts to an adjustment of a favorite myth to what seemed realistically possible in the Depression; at the same time it makes the implicit assertion that love is a much more important value than success. Illustrating this theme of downward mobility is a story in which a young man, trained as a statistician, finds himself manning a pushcart for a grocery store. He can find no better job because of the Depression, and when he meets a girl from a rich family, he is afraid to tell her what his job is. The difference in their status seems to him an insurmountable problem. But the girl learns of his lowly job and brings herself down to his level by taking a job as a waitress.[36] The author does not minimize the problem created by the difference in status, but his reversal of the standard solution of the problem is calculated to de-emphasize the importance of material success and emphasize the importance of love.

In stories which hinge on the heroine's descent to the poor boy's level, there is generally no outright rejection of material success as a value. But there is an implicit recognition of the fact that the rags-to-riches view of success was becoming an increasingly untenable myth. Accompanying this recognition is an apparent attempt to reflect the reality of the Depression by basing the happy ending on downward mobility rather than upward mobility. Material success is portrayed as less important than love, but not necessarily in conflict with it. In another variation of the poor-boy-rich-girl story, however, love and personal integrity come into conflict with the pursuit of material success, and a happy resolution of the conflict requires the renunciation of economic success. Thus, in a reversal of the stereotyped pattern of the twenties, the poor boy wins the dream girl by eschewing material success rather than by achieving it.

This twist on the old pattern can be illustrated by a *Saturday Evening Post* story, titled "Money Player," in which an amateur tennis player almost yields to the temptation to give up his engineering studies for a lucrative advertising job. The situation at the beginning of the story is virtually identical to the stock situation in the poor-boy-wins-dream-girl story so common in the twenties. The destitute hero is struggling to put himself through school by working in a gas station. He is in love with a wealthy girl, who seems well out of the reach of anyone from his background. As a tennis star, however, he has a name that he could profit from if he chose to. The crisis in the story comes when the dream girl's father, an automobile manufacturer, offers the hero a very impressive salary merely for driving an experimental car to his tennis matches. Though he has scruples against such a deal, the hero accepts the offer on the grounds that it will elevate him to the dream girl's social and economic level. Up to this point, the story fits the typical Horatio Alger pattern: a rich man serves as the benefactor of a deserving poor boy, and the rich man's daughter is on hand as a potential crowning reward. But then the pattern is broken in all its essentials. The rich man is shown to be a self-interested scoundrel who exploits the hero by betting large sums of money on his tennis matches; the dream girl makes it clear that she is disappointed in the hero for having sold himself; and the hero realizes that other things are more important to him than conventional success. The final resolution, then, has the hero renouncing all association with his "benefactor" and returning to the gas station, "back where he started from." Only then does he get his real reward: the dream girl confesses her love and agrees to marry him after he has completed his education.[37] This ending, which resolves the question of values by rejecting economic advancement in favor of love and integrity, represents a significant departure from the

conventional poor-boy-rich-girl story, in which material success is portrayed not only as all-important in its own right but also as a prerequisite
for love and personal fulfillment.

Another important recurring pattern among the popular antisuccess
stories is a theme of acceptance or resignation. Stories reflecting this theme
portray the quest for material success as perilous and unpredictable, while
a kind of security is found in the contented acceptance of things as they
are, even if they are not very good. The adventurous, entrepreneurial spirit
of the self-made man is submerged by a fear of mobility and a passion for
stability. In such stories the goal is not *getting ahead* but the much more
modest hope of *getting along,* of surviving under difficult circumstances
and finding some foundation for continuing the struggle.

The emphasis on accepting the status quo and struggling along with
things as they are required a major departure from that most indispensable
element of the magazine-story formula—the happy ending. No sudden
success, no easy solution of the problems climaxes these stories; the happy
endings are happy only in the sense that the characters manage to accept
hardship and cope with it well enough to avoid going under completely.
In other words, the stories reflect an attempt to adjust to existing conditions
by drastically scaling down the characters' dreams and expectations so
that they are not glaringly at odds with the hard economic facts. In some
cases the stories explicitly caution against desiring too much, portraying
not ambition but acceptance and contentment as the ultimate virtues.
Readers of such stories were no longer encouraged to strive and succeed;
they were exhorted to adjust and accept.

A typical treatment of this struggling-along theme is found in a story
which contrasts a steady, plodding businessman with the ambitious career
woman whom he wants to marry. Too absorbed in her career to think of
marriage, she becomes more and more successful during the boom years
of the late 1920s, but is ruined by the crash. Meanwhile, the story's hero
goes along contentedly earning fifty dollars a week and asking philosophically,
"What's the use of wasting our lives chasing the almighty dollar—which is
getting more elusive every day?" At the end of the story, he is married to
someone else and still struggling along. The author's blessing on them is
that "They'll get along even if times get no better."[38] The reader's sympathies are strongly with the hero of the story, who has placed moneymaking in its proper perspective and wants merely the security of love,
a family life, and enough money to get along on.

The tone of resignation in this example is characteristic of the stories which define success as simply getting along and accepting the status quo. Like the inspirational books that emphasize mental attitude or peace of mind as the key to success, the stories of resignation imply that one way of insuring a measure of happiness is not to expect too much. In effect, they advise their readers to define success subjectively and not in terms of external achievement. In keeping with the philosophy of positive thinking, some stories are quite cheerful in their resignation. One lighthearted tale, which strikes the reader as a parody of positive thinking though an unintentional one, is titled "The Lucky Stiff." The hero is a casualty of the Depression, out of work and barely surviving. He experiences a series of catastrophes, each of which he rationalizes into a blessing. He misses a job opportunity in Uruguay, but reasons (however mistakenly) that he is lucky because of the "bad" climate. He has an automobile accident, but fortunately he is not seriously injured. He learns that he will have to suppor the family of his jobless brother and thinks only of how providential it is that he has the money saved to do it.[39] The hero is fortunate, then, or successful, in the sense that he is surviving and is able to convince himself that his circumstances are not as desperate as they could be. There is no fairy-tale ending to appeal to the reader's fantasies of success; there is instead an appeal to his capacity for cheerful acceptance of things as they a

The theme of resignation is portrayed more somberly in a story which deals with the trials and failures of an apple grower in the Midwest. His life is portrayed not as an idyllic life of agrarian pleasures, but as a hard and rather primitive struggle, demanding backbreaking work and yielding failure and frustration. He seems to be nearing the limits of his endurance as the story develops toward its climax, and he faces a choice between staying on the farm and giving up to try something else. Largely because of the influence of his wife, he decides to stay and fight longer. Once this decision is made—a resolution which does not change external circumstances but merely the state of mind of the hero—the story ends on a note of placid acceptance. The hero and his wife stand in the moonlight looking at the beauty of their farm, and though they are still in desperate straits, they are essentially content.[40]

Paradoxically, the farm in this story represents both a place of dispiriting hardship and a place of relative security. The alternative to staying on the farm is to move to the jungle world of the city and there enter into the competition for success. The story explicitly establishes a conflict

between the city and the country, and explicitly rejects the city in favor
of the country. "The town was no place for Tom," the author says. "He
had lived too long in the free, pure air. . . ." Though life on the farm is
primitive and difficult, at least the problems are a familiar part of the
hero's heritage. As in *Of Mice and Men,* where Lennie and George view
their dream farm as a retreat, the farm in this story is isolated from the
battle for success in the city and offers the serenity of a life close to nature.

This story is by no means an isolated example of the quest for security
or of the tendency to identify the farm with security. A substantial number
of other stories from my sampling reflect a similar combination of disillusionment with business success, acceptance of the hard facts of the
Depression, and affirmation of rural values over those of the city. In one
story the return-to-the-farm motif is portrayed through the career of a
wheat rancher who, "beaten, numb, hopeless," is forced to leave his land
periodically, but always comes back.[41] In another example a bankrupt
stockbroker and his wife escape the city and go west to settle on a farm.
When the stockbroker, who is the villain, chooses to borrow enough money
to go back to his vaguely sinister financial dealings in the city, his wife
leaves him and marries one of the natives of the rugged West.[42] The implication is that a character who is unwilling to exchange the pursuit of success
in the financial world of the city for the simple and healthy life on a farm
has grossly misplaced values and is, thus, unworthy of respect and love.

Most of the return-to-the-farm stories do not completely idealize the
farm; the rural life is portrayed as hard and frustrating. There is no promise
that the dream of success will be realized on the farm. On the contrary,
upward mobility seems to have been abandoned as a goal or value in these
stories. Security is a very strong value, however, and in a strange, negative
way the farm is a symbol of security. On the farm, life is relatively stable.
If conditions get no better, at least they remain about the same, or get
worse only very slowly; and the same cannot be said for the highly competitive and uncertain commercial-industrial world of the city. The fear of
mobility in such stories is, in some cases, a fear of *physical* as well as
economic mobility. One of the sources of insecurity in the machine age
is the instability that accompanies life in a physically mobile culture.

Clearly, all the stories which might be classified as stories of resignation—
those urging contentment with modest goals, those calling for a stoic acceptance of unbearable hardship, and those portraying an escape to the farm—
represent a significant disillusionment with the promises and values associated

with the myth of success. They reveal a more or less conscious effort to
bring the fictional portrayal of success and failure more nearly in line with
the actual conditions under which Americans were living in the Depression
years. And they attempt to invest with meaning ideals such as peace of
mind, security, and love which are not dependent on material success.
From a political viewpoint it is significant that the stories of resignation,
based though they are on a sometimes profound disillusionment with the
promises of American capitalism, betray no hint of radical political thinking.
Indeed, just as the proliferation of stories recapitulating the old rags-to-
riches myth served to assuage discontent by appealing to a romantic hope
for the future, the stories calling for a tragic acceptance of harsh reality
sometimes seem especially contrived to forestall any thought of radical
change in the system. Either alternative—a dreamy and idealistic faith in
the future or a resigned adjustment to the present—implies passiveness
rather than action and involves no threat to the established order.

In assessing generally the significance of the materials considered here—
from the success books of the positive thinkers like Carnegie to the popular
stories of resignation—it can be said that they all provide evidence that
significant changes in popular attitudes toward the traditional myth of
success were developing during the Depression years. By the 1950s it had
become a commonplace for social scientists to observe that Americans
were no longer motivated primarily by the old individualistic drive for
success. The "new middle class" of C. Wright Mills, the other-directed
character type of David Riesman, the "organization man" of William
Whyte, and the "status seeker" of Vance Packard were conceptualizations
which shared the observation that security, adjustment to the group, and
the attainment of status in the eyes of others had largely replaced the
ideal of individual achievement as the prime goal of most Americans.
There can be no doubt that the Depression contributed significantly
toward the development of this new mood. The Depression years were
a time of transition, when the tension was strong between the traditional
dream of individual success and the new ideals of adjustment, security,
and peace of mind. Politicians, journalists, film makers, and popular-story
writers tirelessly evoked the romantic image of rags-to-riches success. At
the same time, however, the public made best sellers of books like Pitkin's
Life Begins at Forty and Lin Yutang's *The Importance of Living,* both of
which repudiated many fundamental assumptions of the conventional
myth of success. And, as we have seen, the popular magazines printed a

growing proportion of stories that portray disillusionment with, or outright hostility toward, the dream of material success. Even the professional
spokesmen for success, including Dale Carnegie and other writers in the
positive-thinking school, denied either explicitly or tacitly many of the
basic assumptions behind the traditional myth of success. They denied the
old assumption that character was the key to success. Tacitly, they denied
that a forceful man could control the external world through sheer strength
of will. They denied the importance of hard work and the desirability of
aggressive, individual self-assertion. Though these were time-honored ideals,
they were not compatible with the new emphasis on positive thinking
and getting along with other people through the cultivation of personality.

The growing emphasis in the thirties on security rather than advancement, on mature contentment rather than youthful desire, on personality
rather than character, on getting along with others rather than surpassing
them, on leisure rather than arduous labor, on spiritual well being rather
than material wealth, on love, marriage, and the home rather than the job—
all this suggests that many ordinary Americans came out of the Depression
not only unsure that the dream of success was within their grasp, but also
more doubtful than before that it was worth pursuing.

Notes

1. Warren Susman, "Introduction," *Culture and Commitment: 1929-1945,*
p. 18.
2. Dale Carnegie, *How to Win Friends and Influence People,* p. 73.
3. Napoleon Hill, *Think and Grow Rich,* p. 37.
4. Ibid., p. 36.
5. Carnegie, p. 54.
6. Ibid., p. 72.
7. Frank Welsh and Frances Gordon, *Thinking Success into Business,* p. viii.
8. A. Whitney Griswold, "New Thought: A Cult of Success," *American Journal
of Sociology,* XL (1934), 309.
9. Louis Schneider and Sanford Dornbusch note that the psychological emphasis
in inspirational literature was not strong until the 1930s: "Psychological and psy-
chiatric orientations, previously of small significance, enter the literature in the
1930's and remain important." (*Popular Religion: Inspirational Books in America,*
p. 41).
10. Albert Fancher, *Getting a Job and Getting Ahead,* p. 14.
11. Roger Babson, *What Is Success?,* pp. 14-30.
12. Carnegie, p. 111.

13. Ibid., p. 144.
14. Ibid.
15. Hill, p. 248.
16. Carnegie, p. 96.
17. Ibid., p. 160.
18. Hill, p. 27.
19. Carnegie, p. 77.
20. Walter B. Pitkin, *Life Begins at Forty,* p. 82.
21. Ibid., p. 88.
22. Ibid., p. 70.
23. James D. Hart, *The Popular Book,* p. 255.
24. Ibid., pp. 252-54.
25. Lin Yutang, *The Importance of Living,* p. 1.
26. Ibid., p. 3.
27. Ibid., p. 2.
28. Ibid., p. 110.
29. Ibid., p. 145.
30. Ibid., p. 12.
31. Henry P. Link, *The Return to Religion,* p. 167.
32. Ibid., p. 37.
33. Ibid., p. 38.
34. Lucian Cary, "The Last Run of the Ivy Hounds," *Saturday Evening Post,* November 5, 1932, pp. 18-19, 77.
35. Margaret Cameron, "Empty House," *American Magazine,* February, 1931, pp. 62-65, 157-59; Faith Baldwin, "Has Her Cake and Eats It Too," *Ladies Home Journal,* August, 1933, pp. 8-9, 42.
36. David Garth, "See You Sunday," *American Magazine,* July, 1935, pp. 68-72, 134.
37. Lucian Cary, "Money Player," *Saturday Evening Post,* July 2, 1932, pp. 10-11, 62-64.
38. Faith Baldwin, "Money in the Bank," *Ladies Home Journal,* February, 1935, pp. 14-15, 55-58.
39. Rex Regan, "The Lucky Stiff," *Liberty,* May 9, 1931, p. 37.
40. Martha Hays Weymouth, "Decision by Moonlight," *American Magazine,* February, 1938, pp. 38-41, 144-45.
41. James Stevens, "A Man and a Half," *American Magazine,* May, 1933, pp. 71-74, 96.
42. Bruce Hutchison, "Anne's Heart Comes Home," *Liberty,* June 18, 1938, pp. 30-34.

6 / Dream or Nightmare: Direct Literary Attacks on the Myth of Success

On the popular level, the Depression experience created considerable uncertainty and ambiguity in America's attitudes toward the traditional myth of success. There was a strong impulse to escape reality and continue to feed on the old rags-to-riches fairy tale. But, on the other hand, there were clear signs of disillusionment with the dream of success. Among major novelists and dramatists, including Steinbeck, Farrell, O'Neill, Nathanael West, and others, the disillusionment with the dream of success was more profound and complete. Their portrayal of illusory dreams, their sympathy with failures and losers, and their general hostility toward the values of American bourgeois culture are recurring motifs which make up a very important part of the mood of the thirties.

Disillusionment with the myth of success is apparent in many literary works of the thirties as one specific facet of a general disillusionment with American capitalism. At the same time, the Depression experience also produced a number of novels and dramas in which a direct frontal attack on the myth of success is the central theme. In these works one finds a deliberate, unequivocal, sometimes impassioned, often embittered attempt to expose the absurdity, the danger, the viciousness, and the hollowness inherent in the dream of material success. In these works, there is little of the ambiguity that one finds in the pre-Depression works of such writers as Fitzgerald, Dreiser, and Lewis. The hostility toward the myth of success is generally clear-cut, and the literary weapons tend to be direct and even heavy-handed rather than subtle.

In Nathanael West's *A Cool Million, or The Dismantling of Lemuel Pitkin* (1934), the weapon is burlesque. In probably the broadest and most

derisive parody of the Alger myth in all of American literature, West
attacks with bitter mockery the naive idea that the virtuous and the industrious succeed in America. In several plays of the thirties, including
Clifford Odets' *Awake and Sing* (1934) and *Golden Boy* (1937), the
attack takes the form of a conflict of values, in which the compulsive
and misguided pursuit of material success subverts other values. Two hard-
hitting novels, Jerome Weidman's *I Can Get It for You Wholesale* (1937) and
Budd Schulberg's *What Makes Sammy Run?* (1941), attack the myth of
success through the portrayal of two thoroughly unsavory antiheroes, both
self-made men who are ruthless in their climb to the top.

Though these works differ in many of their attitudes, they are similar
in their implication that the American dream of material success had become a nightmare. Most of them are clear outgrowths of the Depression
experience, and that experience seems to have convinced many writers
once and for all that the individualistic pursuit of material success could
neither be escaped in a competitive society in which survival was not easy
and worldly accomplishment was still worshiped, nor could it be viewed
as a humane, dignified, and fulfilling quest. In the 1940s and 1950s novels
and dramas devoted to tarnishing the image of success continued to appear
in large numbers, and many were popular successes. But the prevailing
attitudes and themes of these works were already familiar in the thirties,
and it seems likely that the Depression experience had much to do with
creating them. Those writers who witnessed and chronicled what appeared
to be the collapse of American capitalism in the thirties had attacked the
myth of success from almost every conceivable perspective by the end of
the decade. Later writers, for the most part, simply continued to devalue
an already tarnished image.

Burlesquing the Alger Myth

In Nathanael West's four short novels, all written in the 1930s, the
persistent theme is man's frustration in a world of puerile illusions, false
fronts, and cheap dreams. West had a profound understanding of how the
vehicles of American popular culture—magazines, radio, popular books,
newspapers, the movies—pandered to the universal human impulse to
fight misery with dreams. In his world, however, the dreams are never
ultimately satisfying; they are tantalizing, frustrating, and finally destructive. The dream always turns into nightmare. In his last and most ambitious

novel, *The Day of the Locust* (1939), as we have seen, West turned to
America's dream capital, Hollywood, for a nightmarish glimpse into the
falsity, the self-delusion, the frustration, and the violence which Hollywood
so aptly symbolized. If it is appropriate that West should have turned his
energies to Hollywood, the dream factory, it is also appropriate that he
should have focused on the most persistent of all our dreams—the great
American dream of success. His fictional commentary on the myth of
success was *A Cool Million* (1934), his second novel.

A *Cool Million* is not a great novel, nor even a very good one. It is
obvious and contrived, and its parody of the pretentious Alger style is
accurate and consistent enough to be tiresome. In the context of a study
of the American dream of success, however, the novel is important and
revealing. Its broad, mocking, sometimes bitter parody of the American
success story suggests that in West's view the myth of success had become
not merely a harmless delusion, but a grotesque and dangerous lie that
needed to be exposed. Fitzgerald in the twenties had seen the corruption
and some of the mockery in the dream, but he had portrayed even Gatsby's
corrupt dream with sympathy and some fascination. West wrote *A Cool
Million* during the depths of the Depression (late 1933 and early 1934)
and out of a deep awareness of the deprivation and suffering which was
so acute for many Americans in those years.[1] He apparently felt that only
broad mockery and grotesque parody could do justice to the absurd contradiction between the bleak economic conditions of the Depression years
and the naïve optimism of the American myth of success.

The basic strategy of the novel is to turn the Horatio Alger success
story upside-down. Subtitled *The Dismantling of Lemuel Pitkin,* the book
describes an extended, melodramatic reversal of the familiar rags-to-riches
story. Lemuel has all the qualities and trappings of the typical Alger hero.
He is a poor but honest farm boy with boundless faith in his prospects for
making his fortune in the land of opportunity. He has a widowed mother
whose mortgage is about to be foreclosed and a girlfriend who represents
the flower of American womanhood. According to the myth, of course,
he should go into the world and make his fortune through honesty, industry,
pluck, and luck, later returning to save his mother's home from foreclosure.
Instead, through bad luck, gullibility, and ineptness in coping with a hostile
world, he progresses from one disastrous failure to another. But he does
not merely fail; he loses along the way his teeth, an eye, a leg, a thumb,
and his scalp. These ghastly physical emasculations are grotesque symbols
reflecting West's vision of the debilitation and destruction that could result

from the struggle for success in the America of the 1930s. Lemuel's feminine
counterpart, Betty Prail, makes a similar progress. She undergoes several
rapes, again symbolic of what happens to the helpless and the innocent
in a corrupt and violent society, and is eventually imprisoned and commercially exploited in a thriving business enterprise—Wu Fong's whorehouse.

In the course of its picaresque description of Lemuel's career, the novel
takes special aim at several of the most cherished pieties of the cult of
success. The ideal of America as a land of opportunity and the principle
of self-help, with its accompanying callousness toward the unfortunate,
are parodied early in the novel when the president of the Rat River National
Bank and former President of the United States, Shagpoke Whipple, refuses
to lend Lemuel and his mother the money they need to prevent the foreclosure of the mortgage on their home. He says that he would not lend
the money even if he could because Lemuel is too young to borrow and
needs the experience of succeeding on his own. He prefers to give hackneyed
advice instead of lending money: "Don't be discouraged. This is the land of
opportunity and the world is an oyster." America "takes care of the honest
and industrious and never fails them as long as they are both." From time
to time, also, West turns his mockery specifically on the ideal of perseverance and positive thinking. At one point, after numerous catastrophes—
including two jailings and the loss of his teeth and an eye—Lemuel begins
to feel that perhaps he is a failure. But Betty indignantly scolds him for
losing faith: "To make an omelette you have to break eggs. When you've
lost both your eyes, you can talk. I read only the other day about a man
who lost both of his eyes yet accumulated a fortune."[3] Lemuel is inspired
by similar words of comfort and encouragement as he proceeds from one
disaster to another. When he is shot at the end of the novel, he is still a
faithful believer in the clichés preached by Betty and Shagpoke.

Despite his slapstick burlesque of Algeresque plot situations and his
consistent parody of Alger's style, West manages to convey a sense of the
reality of the Depression. He captures the awful disjointedness of the times
by describing the grotesque and the terrible in pretentious but matter-of-
fact language, as if ghastliness were accepted as the normal order of things.
When Lemuel arrives in New York toward the end of the novel, for instance,
he is emaciated, dismembered, and tattered: he has one eye, one leg, no
teeth, no scalp, and little clothing. West says, "Instead of merely having no
hair like a man prematurely bald, the gray bone of his skull showed plainly
where he had been scalped by Chief Satinpenny."[4]   And yet, he is scarcely

noticed when he joins "the great army of unemployed" in New York:
"Times had grown exceedingly hard with the inhabitants of that once
prosperous metropolis and Lem's ragged, emaciated appearance caused no
adverse comment."[5] In fact, even Lem is superior to most of the unemployed.
He bathes regularly and visits employment agencies, "refusing to be discouraged or grow bitter and become a carping critic of things as they are."[6]
The same kind of cool, acquiescent tone is employed in the account of
Wu Fong's strategy for weathering the Depression. Finding himself over-
stocked with girls, he is forced to give up his "House of All Nations" in
favor of a more specialized establishment. By converting his house into
"an hundred per centum American place," he reduces his overhead and,
at the same time, capitalizes on the Hearst "Buy American" campaign.
West writes, "Although in 1928 it would have been exceedingly difficult
for him to have obtained the necessary girls, by 1934 things were different.
Many respectable families of genuine native stock had been reduced to
extreme poverty and had thrown their female children on the open market."[7]
The matter-of-fact tone and the mock-gentility of the language in such
passages serve as West's icily ironic method of registering his own horrified
awareness of what the Depression was doing to America.

It has been customary for critics to dismiss *A Cool Million* rather summarily on the grounds that it attacks heavy-handedly and pointlessly an
unworthy target. Some of the early reviews suggested that the book was
less than uproarious because it burlesqued a myth of the past that nobody
took seriously any longer.[8] Later critics have frequently echoed the same
objection. In a recent critical study, for instance, Randall Reid argues
that in attacking the American success story West had chosen a subject
too ridiculous to require or permit parody.[9] Heavy-handedness aside,
West's attack on the American myth of success can be explained and,
to a certain extent, justified on two related counts. In the first place,
when the novel was published, the rags-to-riches myth was not, as some of
West's critics have assumed, a long-forgotten stupidity of the American
past; it was still a persistently appealing popular myth. In the second place,
it was not, in West's mind, a harmless delusion but a dangerous obsession
containing the seeds of a native American fascism. West feared that those
who clung to the illusory dream of success could be exploited all too
easily by right-wing demagogues seeking power.

Though the vehicle for West's attack on the myth of success was a
broad mockery of Horatio Alger, the myth's most notorious spokesman,

his intent was not only to show the absurd incongruity of Alger's ideals
in the Depression years, but also to suggest that Americans in the 1930s
were compounding their problems by deluding themselves with those
ideals. West immersed himself in the Horatio Alger books in order to get
the feeling of the Alger style. He was also highly cognizant of the falsities
and illusions fostered by his own contemporary popular culture, however,
and much of his mockery in *A Cool Million* attacks the popular magazines
and inspirational books of the thirties rather than Alger himself. In one
of his inspiring speeches, for instance, Shagpoke Whipple insists:

> Shipping clerks are still becoming presidents of railroads. . . .
> Despite the Communists and their vile propaganda against
> individualism, this is still the golden land of opportunity.
> Oil wells are still found in people's back yards. There are still
> gold mines hidden away in our mountain fastnesses.[10]

To eliminate any doubt of the relevance of such a parody to the 1930s,
one need only realize that West could have found precisely the same sentiments and virtually the same words in almost any issue of *American
Magazine* or *Saturday Evening Post* and in countless how-to-succeed books
of the Depression years. Such titles as "Gold in Your Back Yard," "Dreams
Do Come True" (an actress' success story), "$1,000,000 on Ice" (a skater's
success story), and "It Pays to Keep Your Eyes Open" (in which a museum
curator explains that "wherever you are, you can find treasures under
your feet") suggest the wealth of contemporary material that a parodist
of the cult of success could draw on in the thirties.

Nor was Lemuel Pitkin's character pointless and irrelevant to the times.
His innocent and simpleminded acceptance of grinding poverty and vicious
exploitation, his refusal to become "a carping critic of things as they are,"
his hope for the future, his unbounded faith in the American capitalist
system despite what it has done to him—these are the qualities of docile
acceptance which the inspirational books and popular magazines seemed
intent on instilling in the victims of the Great Depression. As we have observed, much of the popular literature of the period encouraged an escape
into dreams and illusions, and even the popular stories which were most
cognizant of the ravages of the Depression tended to preach stoic acceptance
as the only means of coping with hopeless conditions. West does not recom-
mend any specific course of action, radical or otherwise, in *A Cool Million.*

But he does demonstrate the stupidity and the grotesque consequences
of innocent optimism and quiet acceptance of things as they are.

As a warning against the potentialities for demagoguery and fascism
inherent in the dream of success, the novel is something of a landmark.
Antedating Sinclair Lewis' *It Can't Happen Here* by over a year, it is one
of the first fictional outcries against the fascistic tendencies that West,
and later many others, saw developing in America. West saw the threat
as a native, homespun fascism related directly and indirectly to the American
myth of success.

The most important character in relation to this theme of incipient
fascism is Shagpoke Whipple. He is the one who preaches the gospel of
success that Lemuel and Betty believe in so implicitly, and he is the one
who organizes an American fascist party, which he calls the National
Revolutionary Party. Mixed up with his rags-to-riches clichés is a narrow
America-Firstism, a suspicion of all intellectualism or sophistication,
of all things not American, white, and Protestant, and of Radicalism and
the International Jewish Bankers. This Americanism feeds on the worship
of Lincoln, Henry Ford, and other rags-to-riches heroes, using their example as a justification for self-help and rugged individualism. "The story
of Rockefeller and of Ford is the story of every great American," Shagpoke
tells Lemuel, "and you should strive to make it your story. Like them,
you were born poor and on a farm. Like them, by honesty and industry,
you cannot fail to succeed."[11] Throughout the novel, Shagpoke repeatedly
preaches that to give anything less than devoted allegiance to America's
myth of success and her self-made heroes is to be subversive and dangerous.

West's implication is that under the guidance of a skillful and sincere
manipulator, like Shagpoke, the gullible and self-deluding people of
America, like Lemuel and Betty, could easily be marshaled into the van-
guard of a narrow, bigoted, and violent party of superpatriots. In West's
nightmarish projection, all Shagpoke has to do in order to triumph is to
unify his followers under the banner of native Americanism (their uniform
consists of leather shirts and coonskin caps), pander to their exalted
dreams of success, and supply enemies to blame when the dreams end in
frustration and failure. He plays on the frustration and bitterness of those
who have been victimized by the Depression and channels their hatred
toward two convenient scapegoats: the Jewish international bankers and
the "Bolshevik labor unions." Using such appeals, it is an easy matter for
Whipple to incite his followers to frenzied action, and West includes a

scene, foreshadowing the mob scene in *The Day of the Locust,* in which
the frustration and hostility of the crowd erupt into mass violence. The
crowd robs and loots and eventually kills and mutilates. "The heads of
Negroes were paraded on poles. A Jewish drummer was nailed to the door
of his hotel room. The housekeeper of a local Catholic priest was raped."[12]

In the final scene of the novel, the National Revolutionary Party has
triumphed, largely as a result of the martyrdom of Lemuel Pitkin, and
Shagpoke enshrines Lemuel as a legendary hero of the Party. It is Pitkin's
Birthday, a national holiday, and Shagpoke speaks in his honor to a crowd
of a hundred thousand. Though dead, says Shagpoke, Lemuel still speaks
"of the right of every American boy to go into the world and there receive
fair play and a chance to make a fortune by industry and probity without
being laughed at or conspired against by sophisticated aliens. . . ."[13]
Shagpoke's message is that the American dream can fail only if a con-
spiracy of foreign and alien elements is allowed to subvert it. West's message is that the American dream in the 1930s was bankrupt as a possibility
and dangerous as a hope because of its simple-minded, naïve, black-and-
white view of the world and because of the frustration caused by the creation of expectations that reality could not fulfill.

In 1935, a year after the appearance of *A Cool Million,* Sinclair Lewis
sounded his alarm against fascism in *It Can't Happen Here.* Though not
uniformly praised by the critics, *It Can't Happen Here* became a best
seller and a hot topic of conversation for several months. It is a measure
of the difference between the two works that Lewis' novel should become
a best seller while West's book was scarcely read. The latter, properly read,
is deeply unsettling and challenging to the patriotic American because it
exposes the danger inherent in that most cherished of all our myths—the
American myth of success. Lewis' novel, though suspicious of super-
patriotism, the Rotary Club, and the DAR, is essentially a defense of
the American system against the enemies without who would destroy it.
In many ways, Lewis' attitude is closer to Shagpoke Whipple's than it is
to West's. As one critic writes of Lewis, "He does not put his revolutionaries
in a distinctive American form; the sadistic and perverted secret police, the
racial persecutions, the concentration camps, the methods of torture are
all recognizably German in origin. In other words, Lewis has not taken
the trouble to visualize a native fascist movement and its probable road
to power."[14] West did visualize such a movement. While Lewis allowed
his readers the comfortable horror of imagining how the American spirit

of freedom and democracy could be subverted by alien elements, West forces his readers to realize that the very essence of "Americanism" is fraught with potential danger.

West's disillusionment with American culture is obviously much more profound than Lewis'. He mocks both the shallow materialism and the childish idealism inherent in the myth of success and implies that Americans of the 1930s still suffered badly from both weaknesses. His tone of bitter and cynical derision reflects the extent of his alienation from the deeply rooted traditions and popular myths of his culture.

Conflicting and Misguided Values

Though less cynical than West, Clifford Odets was also deeply disillusioned with the dominant values of his culture, and he repeatedly attacked the American myth of success as a distillation of his society's most spurious, inhumane, and destructive values. As a playwright who came into prominence and wrote his best plays in the Depression years, he was acutely aware of the confusion of values occasioned by the economic crisis. In such plays as *Awake and Sing, Paradise Lost,* and *Golden Boy,* his recurring theme is the quest of ordinary people, beset by poverty and a crippling economic crisis, for a set of standards by which to live a decent and satisfying life. Unlike West, Odets does not mock the idealism of the American dream. Indeed, his own idealistic faith in man's ultimate ability to find self-realization, despite the difficulties, is the central underlying attitude of some of his best-known plays, including *Awake and Sing* and *Paradise Lost.* At the same time, Odets felt that the materialism of modern society, the ambition to accumulate money and possessions, was one of the great obstacles to that self-realization. Thus, he repeatedly portrays the conflict between material success and other values. Deeply cognizant of the Depression's effects, Odets showed how hardship, deprivation, and frustration could intensify the dream of success. He also demonstrated the ultimately unsatisfying and sometimes destructive quality of a narrow pursuit that tended to subvert other values.

Odets' most explicit treatment of the theme of success is in *Golden Boy,* which was first produced by the Group Theatre in 1937. Typical of the antisuccess literature of the thirties, it is impassioned and direct. Lacking in subtlety and not devoid of clichés, it is nevertheless a dramatically

powerful indictment of the American dream of fame and fortune. In Odets'
version of the myth of success, the ambitious pursuit of money and fame is
utterly destructive; it leads not to happiness and self-realization, but to
brutality and eventually death both for the ambitious protagonist and his
victim. Early in the play, Joe Bonaparte's father asks the heroine, Lorna,
to "help Joe find truthful success." This is the central problem in the play,
and the central tragedy is that this "truthful success" is not to be found
in a society which is materialistic, viciously competitive, and economically
crippled.

The conflict between "success" and self-realization is objectified by
means of the simple but effective symbols of prizefighting and music.
Throughout the play, music represents the humane, spiritual, cultural
values, while prizefighting represents the battle for economic supremacy.
For Joe, an accomplished violinist, music has been a solace and a source
of identity and self-realization. But the world is a battleground, as Joe
sees it, and music is no weapon with which to fight the battle: "You can't
get even with people by playing the fiddle. If music shot bullets, I'd like
it better—artists and people like that are freaks today."[15] Joe turns to
boxing, then, because he believes that, unlike music, it is relevant to the
world in which he lives. Prizefighting becomes the symbol of how the
struggle for success is carried on in a competitive society. It is an appropriate symbol because it epitomizes both the primitive, brutal nature of the
struggle and the glittering and spectacular rewards that motivate the partici-
pants to join the battle. Joe himself is aware of the symbolic significance of
boxing. He comments that the whole essence of prizefighting is to show
the opponent, "I'm better than you are—I'll prove it by breaking your
face in."[16]

In giving up music for prizefighting, essentially what Joe decides is to
accept his world on its own terms. If existence in his world is dominated
by the boxing glove and not by the violin, it seems pointless to play the
violin. It is significant that Joe's decision to enter into the prizefighting
world is made on the eve of his twenty-first birthday. Odets' implication
is that to be initiated into manhood in our culture is to renounce the
harmony symbolized by music and join the battle for the physical, material
spoils of life. That material comfort and the spiritual-cultural values represented by music are mutually exclusive in the Depression-scarred world
in which Joe lives is suggested by the repeated image of the violinists and
other musicians standing on Broadway and 48th Street with no work and

no money. "Fiddlers, drummers, cornetists—not a dime in a car-load,"
Roxy says. "Bums in the Park!" Joe's choice, then, is between genteel
poverty and violent competition for success.

In a sense, Joe is forced into his choice by the society and circumstances
in which he lives. But unlike Dreiser's Carrie Meeber or Farrell's Studs
Lonigan, he is by no means a passive character. He has a burning ambition
which he directs frankly, openly, and self-consciously toward the achievement of fame and fortune in the ring. Contrary to the pieties of the conventional myth of success, Odets leaves no doubt that this ambition is a
destructive force. It springs not from a youthful and idealistic desire to
produce, but from deprivation, shame, frustration, and seething hatred.
Odets' attitude toward Joe's ambition is concisely summarized in an exchange between Lorna Moon and Mr. Bonaparte. Lorna says, "You could
build a city with his ambition to be somebody." Mr. Bonaparte, who is
the best spokesman for the humane values that Odets affirms in the play,
answers sadly, "no . . . burn down!" Joe is not a builder, but a destroyer
who eventually puts "the fury of a lifetime" in a blow that kills another
man in the ring.

Odets' analysis of the nature and source of Joe's violent ambition provides a cogent commentary, similar to that of Wright in *Native Son* or
West in *The Day of the Locust,* on the explosive situation that can develop
when a society taunts its young people by creating materialistic dreams
and desires which frequently cannot be satisfied. Joe Bonaparte feels the
frustration which comes from a background of poverty complicated by
the economic Depression. Perhaps worse, he feels the shame and insignifi-
cance that a society which worships material success can breed in its poor
and its failures. Mr Bonaparte understands the shame ("Joe like-a to be
fame, not feel ashame"), and Joe himself specifically mentions it as a
source of his ambition: "This is my profession! I'm out for fame and
fortune, not to be different or artistic! I don't intend to be ashamed of
my life!"[17] Odets implies that instead of weakening the commitment to
the dream of material success, a time of deprivation and frustration like
the Great Depression was likely to create an intensified ambition to fulfill the dream.

If success means brutality and death as Odets envisions it in *Golden
Boy,* it also means prostitution and exploitation.[18] Harold Clurman has
suggested that Joe's choice of prizefighting over music was intended to
represent the compromise that Odets himself made with commercialism

when he went to Hollywood. Whether or not it has autobiographical origins, the idea of selling oneself for money and fame or, conversely, the use of others as mere objects for personal gain, is a dominant motif in the play. Joe's pursuit of the American dream of success brings him none of the freedom and self-realization that the myth promises; it merely puts him in a position to be used by others in exchange for a few material possessions. In the competitive capitalist system, Joe is a commodity, not a person. Joe complains that Moody "treats me like a possession! I'm just a little silver mine for him." And he is bitterly aware of the fact that Eddie Fuseli, who wants to "buy a piece of Joe," uses him "like a gun."[19] The symbolic significance of Fuseli's exploitation of Joe is clear, but not particularly profound or disturbing. Fuseli is the character most thoroughly committed to the struggle for material success, and he is also one of a long list of gangster characters of the thirties who reflect the darkest and most sinister side of the American dream—those who become full-fledged outlaws in their aggressively individualistic struggle for success.

Even more damning, however, is Odets' portrayal of the way in which Moody and, in the beginning, Lorna attempt to exploit Joe. Moody is not a money-hungry cad. He is an ordinary man who is engaged, like Ralph in *Awake and Sing* or Ben in *Paradise Lost,* in the characteristic Odetsian struggle to make a decent life for himself in a competitive world. The tragedy is that only by using another man can be realize his dream of a home and a decent life for himself and Lorna. He sees the situation in simple, realistic terms: "We have to make that kid fight! He's *more* than a meal ticket—he's everything we want and need from life!"[20] If we continue to interpret Joe's entry into prizefighting as symbolic of the larger battle for gain in a competitive system, the conclusion seems inescapable: the pursuit of personal success in a capitalistic society is certain to involve the exploitation of others, even by ordinary, otherwise decent, people who are simply trying to reap their share of the rewards.

Odets uses some of his minor characters to help establish the pervasiveness of the worship of material success in American society and to reinforce his theme of exploitation. Siggie, Joe's brother-in-law, says frankly, "My God is success." He insists on celebrating after Joe kills the Chocolate Drop because "it's a night of success! Joe's in those lofty brackets from now on!"[21] Roxy Gottlieb, who owns 20 percent of Joe, is also exhilarated because he sees more profit in the future. Of all those present in the final scene—Siggie, Roxy, Fuseli, Moody, Mr. Bonaparte, and Frank, Joe's brother—only the latter two have any conception of the enormity of what Joe has done. Fuseli is interested only in gaining complete owner-ship of Joe, and even Moody is able to dismiss the dead man with scarcely a qualm. "Nobody's fault," he says. "Everybody's sorry—we give the mother a few bucks. But we got the next champ! Bottoms up!"[22] All the characters who have a stake in Joe's boxing career betray a callous unconcern for the man who was killed, and they have no inkling of the emotional state of the man who has done the killing. Even such basic perceptions and sensitivi-ties have been subverted by the overriding passion for success.

Odets leaves no doubt of the "true" values by which the "false" standard of material success should be judged. Through the symbol of music, through the character of Mr. Bonaparte and Frank, and through the final resolution that Joe arrives at just before his death, Odets proposes several alternatives to the violent struggle that Joe has sold himself into. He offers little hope, however, that these values could prevail in the grasping and economically chaotic environment of America in the Depression years. Mr. Bonaparte affirms all the values represented by the violin—real accom-plishment, harmony, sacrifice, and art—as well as love, nature, and com-passion. But despite his wisdom he has little influence. Many of the other characters consider him an old fool who doesn't accept reality and who doesn't even, as Roxy says, "understand our language." It is figuratively true, of course, that Mr. Bonaparte does not speak the same language as most of the others, and it is probably not without significance that he is the one character who speaks with a heavy accent throughout the play. The implication is that neither his language nor his values have been Americanized. As an organizer for the CIO, Frank represents another alternative to Joe's battle for fame and fortune: he fights for a cause, not for money. He explains his motivation in terms which relate him to the symbol of music. His music, he tells Eddie and Roxy, is "The satisfaction of staying where you belong, being what you are . . . at harmony with millions of others!"[23] For Frank and for Odets there is harmony or music in the acceptance of one's identity as one of the masses. Frank's philosphy of "staying where you belong" and "being what you are" is an explicit renunciation of the American dream of creating a new identity by rising from one social level to another.

After Joe's ambition causes him to kill, he comes to a partial realiza-tion of the importance of the harmony that Frank considers so essential. But the realization comes too late for him. He has become increasingly shallow, callous, and obnoxious from the time he sold himself into prize-fighting; and when he kills the Chocolate Drop, he is as good as dead himself. He says,"I murdered a man. Lorna, I see what I did. I murdered myself, too!"[24] He partially recovers himself when he realizes that his ambition to conquer the world has been destructive. He and Lorna vow, in her words, to "find some city where poverty's no shame—where music is no crime!—where there's no war in the streets—where a man is glad to be himself, to live and make his woman herself!"[25] But there is no going back to the dream of love and harmony. Joe's hands are ruined so that he cannot play the violin any longer, and his values are irrevocably perverted, as his last words reveal: "That's it—speed! We're off the earth—unconnected! We don't have to think!! That's what speed's for, an easy way to live!"[26] Joe is still looking for salvation in speed, and speed has been established much earlier as a symbol of his driving desire for fast success. Like Jay Gatsby's yellow roadster, his car is a symbol of false, materialistic goals, as well as power and motion. His last words, then, indicate that he is still cockeyed—still unable to distinguish the true from the false and still unable to focus his eyes clearly on one goal at a time. It is perfectly appropriate that his car should speed him to his death and that death should come before his love for Lorna is fulfilled. Love might be a solution for Joe, but it demands, as Edward Murray comments, "both selflessness in the lovers and stability in the environment."[27] In the brutally competitive, unstable, materialistic world that Odets describes in this play, there is little reason to hope that love could prevail.

Unlike Nathanael West's derisive mockery of the myth of success in *A Cool Million, Golden Boy* was well received by the general public and, on the whole, by critics as well. As Harold Clurman points out in his history of the Group Theatre, the play was the greatest box-office success in the group's history, earning enough in 248 New York performances and later in a highly successful London tour to sustain the group for two seasons.[28] Following its stage success, it was also well received in a film version. Odets was dealing with an American myth that could touch the experience and understanding of a wide audience, and in the gloomy Depression years there was increasing sympathy with the critical attitude that Odets assumed toward the myth of success.

Though *Golden Boy* was the only play in which Odets treated the theme of success explicitly and in depth, *Awake and Sing* (1934) and *Paradise Lost* (1936) reflect some of the same attitudes toward material success and the quest for a life of dignity and meaning. Both plays are, like *Golden Boy,* highly critical of the insidious corrupting influence of the meretricious dream of material success, but both end on a more ideal-istic and optimistic note than *Golden Boy. Paradise Lost* concerns the struggle of a middle-class family to maintain some semblance of dignity and integrity in the face of the devastating effects of the Depression on their way of life. As in *Golden Boy* false images of success get in the way of contentment and true self-realization. The son of the family, Ben, is plagued by extravagant, delusory dreams of fabulous monetary success and, in turn, by self-pitying disillusionment and guilt over not amounting to anything. His sister Pearl withdraws almost entirely into a dream world. The whole family, which seems representative of the American middle class at large, has the bewildering sense that its ideal of success and all its most cherished faiths and beliefs are being denied by the upheavals and dislocations of the Depression. Still, through Leo, the head of the family and an idealist who understands the falsity of material success, Odets brings a note of affirmation to the conclusion of the play. At the end Leo is bankrupt; the paradise lost is the comfortable life Leo provided for the family before losing everything. But his last speech is an idealistic vision of a hopeful future when men are no longer corrupted by selfish individualism, love prevails, and "no man fights alone."

Awake and Sing portrays the struggles and frustrations of a lower-middle-class family engaged in the same quest that Odets portrayed so frequently—the search for a life of dignity, self-respect, and fulfillment. Ralph, the idealistic son, looks sadly at his father's life in the play's last scene and says, "Let me die like a dog, if I can't get more from life."[29] Once again, however, Odets poses a difficult question: what goals, what incentives, what avenues are available to a young man in quest of a full and decent life? And once again he rejects the American dream of personal, material success as tantalizing, delusory, shallow, and ultimately destruc-tive of true fulfillment. Beginning with his first speeches in Act I, Ralph's cry is, "All I want's a chance to get to first base!" Odets suggests, however, that in an environment of severe competition as well as economic Depres-sion, there is little opportunity for a young man like Ralph to "get to first base" economically. Through Jacob, the voice of wisdom in the play, Odets comments bitterly on the discrepancy between the irresistible prom-ises and the gloomy unfulfillment of the myth of success. "In my day," Jacob says, "the propaganda was for God. Now it's for success. A boy don't turn around without having shoved in him he should make success. . . . He dreams all night of fortunes. Why not? Don't it say in the movies he should have a personal steamship, pyjamas for fifty dollars a pair and a toilet like a monument? But in the morning he wakes up and for ten dollars he can't fix the teeth."[30] Aside from the discontent and frustration created by such delusory dreams, the desire for material success, as in *Golden Boy,* subverts other values, including love and family harmony. Bessie's cynical acceptance of monetary values, which she says are the only standards that matter in America, has caused her to become callous, grasping, and insensitive to the emotions of her children. Uncle Morty, who boasts of being a self-made success, is pompous and utterly self-interested. As in *Paradise Lost,* however, Odets does suggest that it is possible to escape the corrupting influence of materialistic values. Through Jacob's teachings and his sacrificial suicide, Ralph becomes settled in the conviction that he does not want "life printed on dollar bills." He idealistically believes that he will be able to change the world because "life's different in my head." Thus the play ends on a note of hope and not despair.

The critique of American capitalism which Ralph has learned from Jacob has clear Marxian overtones. But, as has been pointed out, the play probably reflects less of Marx than it reflects of that native strain of American idealism and optimism which has frequently come into conflict with our materialism.[31] Jacob argues that in Russia the quality of life is better because "in Russia they got Marx." But when he later tells Ralph to "Do what is in your heart and you carry in yourself a revolution," his thinking is closer to Emerson's than to Marx's.

Self-Made Antiheroes

While Nathanael West attacks the myth of success by means of derisive burlesque and Odets dramatizes its shallow, bourgeois materialism and its abrogation of the search for a life of dignity, love, and decency, Jerome Weidman in *I Can Get It for You Wholesale* and Budd Schulberg in *What Makes Sammy Run?* portray the absolute corruptiveness of the American dream of success by showing the form it takes in two antiheroes—Weidman's Harry Bogen and Schulberg's Sammy Glick. Both novels were the first efforts of young Jewish writers who came to maturity during the Depression years and who had observed the vicious battle for success among New York garment manufacturers (in Weidman's case) and Hollywood screen writers (in Schulberg's case). Though neither novel is widely read today, both were taken seriously, if not uniformly praised, by the critics when they first appeared; and both were best sellers among the general reading public.[32] According to the vision of these two young writers of the Depression years, the American self-made man was no longer a symbol of America's best ideals; he was the very embodiment of petty selfishness and corruption.

The portrayal of the American self-made man as corrupt, self-interested, and unscrupulous was not new to the 1930s. Dreiser's Frank Cowperwood, to take one earlier example, is openly committed to the lobster-eat-squid morality, which recognizes that a man succeeds by superior strength and cunning, not by honesty and virtue. Still Cowperwood is portrayed as a hero, even a superman, not an antihero. In Harry Bogen and Sammy Glick there is none of the heroic, nothing of the superman. Cowperwood's heroic stature, his almost superhuman magnetism, has been lost, and in its place are petty viciousness and cynical toughness. Nor do Weidman and Schulberg treat their characters with the combination of distaste and sympathetic fascination that Fitzgerald has for Gatsby. The only fascination lies in the realization that such overwhelming ambition, such unadulterated selfishness, and such a sure instinct for the exploitation of others could exist in one person. Though neither Bogen nor Glick is held up as typical of all successful men, both novels imply that the Bogens and the Glicks thrive in American culture and become the most spectacular successes. Unlike West's Lemuel Pitkin who is victimized by a silly myth that he takes literally, or Odets' Joe Bonaparte who is destroyed by a set of false values that he can neither accept fully nor rise above, Harry Bogen and Sammy Glick are not victims in any immediate sense, but predators. They destroy others but they prevail themselves and remain happy in their corruption. Ultimately they are victims, however, in the sense that their early lives of poverty, deprivation, and desire have bred in them not only a viciously selfish ambition, but also a total insensitivity to their spiritual impoverishment.

Both novels suffer from the zealous, almost obsessive, desire of their authors to lay bare the corruption of the self-made men they portray. This zeal results in the kind of heavy-handedness and repetition that critics have objected to in West's *A Cool Million*. On the whole, however, both novels are powerful and convincing outcries against the excesses inherent in the American dream of material success.

In a first-person narration which is reminiscent of Jason Compson's self-revelation in *The Sound and the Fury*, Weidman's Harry Bogen reveals himself to be utterly singleminded in his ambition for monetary success and utterly merciless in the methods he uses to achieve it. His first triumph sets the tone for his actions throughout the novel. Taking advantage of the desperation of the shipping clerks in New York's garment district, he enlists the aid of a Communist "friend" to organize a shipping-clerk strike. Once the strike has succeeded well enough that the owners are ready to make concessions, Harry betrays the strikers and offers the owners a delivery service which makes it possible for them to fire their shipping clerks. This launches Harry as an entrepreneur, and he wastes no sympathy on those who happen to have been victimized.

From this start Harry makes a spectacular climb to the top in the garment industry, double-crossing partners, dodging income taxes, and using people with uncanny skill. Within two years, he has established himself as one of the most prosperous manufacturers in the ladies' ready-to-wear industry. His crowning accomplishment comes near the end of the novel when his firm is facing bankruptcy. He leads his partner, Babushkin, a talented dress designer who is too meek to be a good businessman, into a legal trap. When the crisis is resolved, Babushkin is on his way to jail and Harry, whose irresponsible spending has caused the bankruptcy, is unscathed and looking forward with exhilaration to the prospects ahead of him.

In the revelation of Harry's motives and inner thoughts, Weidman reverses many of the conventional themes of writers who have treated the dream of success in fiction. Harry does not have feelings of uncertainty and inner conflict between the desire for material success and the need for something more spiritually rewarding, nor does he achieve economic success only to find himself lonely and unsatisfied. He judges everything consistently in terms of self-interest and monetary values. He feels guilty not when he uses someone as a stepping-stone or ruins a business partner's life, but when he softens and runs the risk of betraying his self-interest. When he suspects himself, for instance, of being attracted to Ruthie Rivkin, a nice Jewish girl from his own social class, he is disgusted with his softness: "And the hell of it was that I didn't think it was the ten thousand dollars Mother said they were passing out to the guy that carried her to the altar, either."[33] According to Harry's "morality," to be interested in Ruthie because of her $10,000 would be legitimate, but to be attracted to her as another human being is sentimentality.

Conversely, he is proud of his unscrupulousness and always feels complimented when it is recognized by someone else. In an exchange with his mother, he is frankly pleased when she accuses him of being ironhearted:

I shrugged. But I was pleased. The old girl knew her onions, all
right. "Maybe," I said. "But that's the way you have to be in
business. If *you* haven't got the iron heart, it's the next guy."[34]

The climactic "moral" triumph comes for Harry after his victimization
of Babushkin. Because he has promised his own mother and Babushkin's
wife that he would do nothing to hurt his partner, he feels enough guilt
to be aware of it as a minor irritation that he would like to be rid of. And
when he reads about the whole affair in a trade paper, he realizes that he
is rid of it. He no longer feels guilt about Babushkin. He tests himself by
thinking of Babushkin's wife and child. "Instead of feeling worried or
scared, I felt happy. I felt so good that I laughed out loud. I had finally
arrived."[35] For Harry Bogen, to "arrive" means to be free from the last
vestiges of his rudimentary conscience. He has achieved his ideal of an
absolute, unmitigated commitment to the gospel of success, and in doing
so, Weidman suggests, he has willingly rid himself of the last traces of
humanity.

Weidman is more interested in depicting Harry Bogen as a phenomenon
than in analyzing what has produced him, but he implies some of the social
and psychological factors that have contributed to Harry's warping. He
is the product of a culture that worships success, and, like Odets' Joe
Bonaparte and Bessie Berger, he has learned that the only success that
really matters in his culture is economic success. His mother, who like Joe
Bonaparte's father is the novel's main spokesman for humane values,
wants the respect and dignity she would have if Harry were a lawyer. But
Harry sees no dignity in starving ("You know what lawyers are making
today? You know how many of them are starving?"), and he is convinced
that the world respects only money and the power that it represents. The
pressure to succeed economically dominates him so completely that he is
ashamed of his lower-middle-class background and bitter that he was once
only a shipping clerk. This shame is particularly obvious when he resorts
to elaborate schemes to avoid being seen with Ruthie Rivkin, the plain
Jewish girl from the Bronx. As a child of the Depression he has a vivid
understanding of the meaning of poverty and deprivation, and he is completely devoid of that nostalgic pride in his humble origins which, according
to the myth, the self-made man is supposed to have.

Though Harry succeeds without any flagrant violations of the law, he
lives by essentially the same tough-guy ethic that is portrayed in so many
of the gangster and detective novels of the thirties. The idealism that has

traditionally been associated with the American dream of success is completely missing in Harry Bogen. Cynical toughness, many writers of the
thirties implied, was one way of responding to and coping with strangling
economic conditions which contradicted the more idealistic American
dream of unlimited opportunity for all. Harry Bogen's code of toughness
is obvious from the time he double-crosses the shipping clerks: "The hell
with them. If they didn't like being shipping clerks, let them take a crack
at something else. The way I did."[36] Throughout the novel, Harry uses
this ethic of cynical toughness as a protection against guilt. In his mind
guilt implies softness, and softness is equivalent to failure.

Though *What Makes Sammy Run?* was not published until 1941, it
grew out of Schulberg's own experiences as a screen writer in Hollywood
during the Depression years. As an embodiment of bitter ambition, obsessive desire, and merciless egotism, Schulberg's Sammy Glick is easily a
match for Harry Bogen. Sammy never allows himself to be diverted from
the scrambling, hustling, conniving battle to succeed in Hollywood. He
has no self-doubt, no fear, no scruple, and apparently no limit of energy.
Like Harry, he has a merciless and uncanny skill in using other people for
his own self-aggrandizement. Early in the story, the narrator describes
him as "a much more predatory animal than a wildcat,"[37] and his whole
career is proof that the description is accurate. Beginning as an office boy
in the Alger tradition, Sammy launches his career in Hollywood by selling
and taking full credit for a story that belongs to a talented young writer
who is too naïve and weak to avoid being victimized. Once established,
Sammy puts the fraud, the vanity, and the shameless piracy of Hollywood
to his own uses, plagiarizing stories, selling ghostwritten screenplays as
his own, and impressing himself upon producers by bluff and flattery.
Using these methods, he rises with dizzying rapidity from beginning writer
to single-credit writer, to boy wonder, to producer's assistant, to producer
to head of a major studio.

Sammy's success comes on the strength of no talent and no creative
ability; all he knows is how to push. One of the Sammy Glick watchers
in the novel speculates on what would happen if Sammy used his energy
and drive to create something, instead of devising "ways of reaching the
top without creating anything." The answer is suggested in the careers of
those who do devote their energies to creating rather than playing the
politics of success. Julian Blumberg, whose story Sammy has stolen to
get his start in Hollywood, comes close to starving before his talents are

recognized. Al, the narrator, who fares only slightly better, eventually gives up the struggle and returns to newspaper work in New York. This quality of noncreativity and nonproductiveness, which is as obvious in Harry Bogen as it is in Sammy, distinguishes these characters of the thirties from earlier self-made men in American literature, including Dreiser's Frank Cowperwood and Lewis' Sam Dodsworth. Cowperwood is a financial genius with overpowering magnetism, and Dodsworth is both an inventive designer and a capable manufacturer of automobiles. Both Weidman and Schulberg suggest that in the America of the 1930s, spectacular success came not from productiveness and talent nor even magnetism and superior strength, but from piracy, fraud, exploitation, the relentless desire to push, and always the willingness to sacrifice everything else to the all-consuming passion for success.

Since they can conceive of no goal except material success, neither Harry nor Sammy is consciously aware of any sacrifice. The narrator of Sammy's story, however, comments periodically on the pleasures that are denied to men like Sammy. "You can't have your brothers and eat them too,"[38] the narrator says. Like other self-made men, Sammy is completely unequipped to enjoy leisure time: "He was working at it, he was working at having fun. Recreation never seemed to come naturally to him. In fact the only activity that did, seemed to be that damned running." Even sex is not an honest passion that is important to Sammy apart from his obsessive running. The narrator speculates, "He seemed to be a lusty little animal, but I think if Zanuck offered to give up his job to Sammy on the condition that Sammy never touch a woman again our hero would have gone impotent before you could say general-manager-in-charge-of-production."[39]

Both Weidman and Schulberg, like Dreiser and Fitzgerald, treat the interrelationship of success and sex as major motifs in their novels. In Harry Bogen and Sammy Glick, however, there is none of the romantic yearning for the Golden Girl that one finds in Jay Gatsby or Clyde Griffiths. The element of romance is stripped away to reveal the crudity and selfishness that lie underneath. To Harry Bogen "love" and sex are strictly business arrangements. He spends money on women, and in return they give him sex or the prestige of being seen with someone who can symbolize his success. Since Ruthie Rivkin offers him neither sex nor prestige, he breaks off his involvement with her. Since Martha Mills, a well-known Broadway actress, promises both, she becomes his Golden Girl, and he spends thousands

of dollars on jewelry and automobiles to buy her favors. In the last sentence
of the novel he exults, "Two years ago I was just another poor slob from
the Bronx. And to-night I'm going to sleep with an actress."[40] The pinnacle
of success is symbolized by the sexual conquest of the Golden Girl.

Sammy Glick is also incapable of separating sex from his ruthless and
all-consuming desire for wealth and power. He shows "the same selfishness,
cruelty, and power" in his sexual affairs that he devotes to his scramble
for success in the film industry; and one of his female acquaintances who
thinks that sex is "the friendliest thing two people can do in the whole
world" comments perceptively, "but somehow I've always felt that if I
ever went to bed with *him*—even if he didn't pay me—I'd feel like I was
doing it for money."[41] Yet at the end of the novel when he meets his
Golden Girl, Laurette Harrington, Sammy's emotions are deeper and more
complex than any that Harry Bogen experiences. Sammy's attraction to
Laurette is predictable since she is beautiful, impressive, and the daughter
of one of the wealthy New York owners of Sammy's studio. Like the
Fitzgeraldean Golden Girl she represents cultivation and social position,
and Schulberg uses language reminiscent of Fitzgerald in describing her:
"He had finally found a woman worthy of his ambition, she was the golden
girl, the dream, and the faster he ran the farther ahead she seemed to be."
Once he wins her Sammy says, " 'The night I made her I thought I was
the greatest guy in the world.' "[42] As a wealthy and socially prominent
woman, then, Laurette represents a coveted goal. But as the boss's daughter
she also represents a practical means of furthering his career, and it is no
coincidence that Mr. Harrington gives Sammy control of the studio and
permission to marry Laurette in the same interview. In Sammy's mind,
the marriage symbolizes the perfect merging of sexual success and economic
success.

As opportunistic as it sounds, however, Sammy has not contrived this
perfect arrangement in an entirely cold-blooded and mechanical way. In
his relationship with Laurette, he experiences an emotion that passes for
love. Kit Sargent, an acute observer and interpreter of Sammy, tells the
narrator, "Sammy isn't making a mechanical play for her because he thinks
he can use her. It's all mixed up together. The fact that her name is
Harrington must be just as sexually exciting as that moist red mouth or
those snooty bubs of hers."[43] On their wedding night when he is cuckolded
by Laurette, who sees the true nature of his attraction to her, Sammy's
emotion is genuine, if brief. The narrator realizes, "It was no fake. He was
devastated. Kit was right. He had fallen in love with position, with the

name and power of Harrington, and it came to him not as something sordid and cold but as love, as deep respect for Laurette's upbringing and attraction to her personality and desire for her body."[44] Since Sammy's whole being is charged with the obsession to succeed, it is inevitable, Schulberg suggests, that Sammy should be unable to distinguish love from ambition.

As his title suggests, Schulberg's central concern in *What Makes Sammy Run?* was to analyze what produces the terrifying and all-consuming ambition of men like Sammy Glick. It becomes apparent very early in the novel that the question raised in the title is not merely a rhetorical question. Though the question is obviously one that cannot be answered fully, Schulberg poses it seriously and pursues the answer relentlessly. His narrative strategy is essentially that used by Fitzgerald in *The Great Gatsby.* Al Manheim is a narrator-observer-commentator who is as fascinated by Sammy Glick as Nick Carraway is by Gatsby. His interest in Sammy, in fact, becomes an obsession, which drives him to discover everything he can about what produced the phenomenon that he sees before him.

Schulberg approaches the riddle of Sammy Glick as Fitzgerald approaches Gatsby—by characterizing him as both an individual and a figure in a myth much larger than himself. From the beginning Sammy's story is described as an American story, and Sammy is seen against the backdrop of the American myth of success. When Sammy makes his first triumph, the narrator says, "It was America, all the glory and the opportunity, the push and the speed, the grinding of gears and the crap."[45] And throughout the development of Sammy's character, the reader is forced to see his ruthless ambition in specific relation to the most cherished ideals of American culture. He is placed in the tradition of the American self-made man, characterized as having "a brand-new Horatio Alger mind," associated with American individualism, and criticized for his pose of benevolent paternalism, which is "a little too much like the tycoon who spends the first part of his life sucking and crushing and the last part giving away dimes and Benjamin Franklin advice." In the novel's last sentence, the record of where Sammy ran and of what made him run is offered by the narrator as "a blueprint of a way of life that was paying dividends in America in the first half of the twentieth century."[46] We must come to terms with Sammy as a warped and grotesque antihero, but also as an American, representing not a violation and perversion of American ideals of success, but a twentieth-century distillation and fulfillment of them without the veneer of refinement that makes them palatable. Kit puts it in Freudian terms, speculating that "the thing that makes Sammy so fascinating for us is that he is the id of our whole society," free of the restraints of the superego. As the id is the core of our basic appetites, Sammy represents pure desire, not covered by Oxford manners, polite sociability, or Christian morals. He is ambition and corruption in the raw, "the thing itself, the id, out in the open. It might not be very pretty, but there it was."[47]

Throughout the development of his career, then, we are made to realize that one reason why Sammy runs is that he is an American, and running is an American tradition. The full extent of the society's influence on Sammy is not clarified, however, until toward the end of the novel when Manheim investigates Sammy's childhood and adolescence. Then it becomes clear why he runs so fast and scrambles so much, and it becomes even more inescapably apparent that Glick's evil is America's evil and not the province of one warped individual. Sammy is a product of New York's lower East Side ghetto, where the family has lived in marginal poverty before the Depression and in grinding poverty afterward. In this environment, he learned to run and to fight—to fight the Catholic boy who "felt called upon to avenge Christ every day" and to run for whatever rewards he could get his hands on. All the suffering he has endured as a child growing up in this world later becomes the motivating force behind his bitter and ruthless ambition. On the basis of his research into Sammy's background, Manheim redirects his hatred:

> I thought of Sammy Glick rocking in his cradle of hate,
> malnutrition, prejudice, suspicion, amorality, the anarchy
> of the poor; I thought of him as a mangy little puppy in
> a dog-eat-dog world. I was modulating my hate for Sammy
> Glick from the personal to the societal.[48]

With this understanding of what makes Sammy run, the reader is left at the end with a dreary picture of the price Sammy will have to pay for his way of life—not a "sudden pay-off but a process, a disease he had caught in the epidemic that swept over his birthplace like the plague . . . the symptoms developing and intensifying: success, loneliness, fear."[49] By the time he is established as a studio manager, Sammy has already felt this last symptom: he has had occasion to fear the bright young men pushing from below. In other words, he has begun to pay the price that anyone has to pay for success in a ruggedly competitive system. At the end, Sammy is no less terrifying than he has been all along, but his story has become not merely

a chilling delineation of the evil within one warped individual, but an indictment of a society that worships success and still permits the kind of poverty
and deprivation that engulfs Sammy in his childhood.

Harry Bogen and Sammy Glick are two of the best-known self-made
heels in the literature of the thirties. But they are not isolated attacks on the
American self-made man. Lesser-known works portrayed similar warped
personalities and a similar disillusionment with the society which produced
them. John Howard Lawson's *Success Story,* for instance, one of the plays
produced by the Group Theatre in the early thirties, has a protagonist who
is irredeemably corrupted by his struggle for business success. In fiction,
Elizabeth Seifert's *A Great Day* (1939) is a detailed account of a day in the
life of an unprincipled self-made millionaire who has made his success by
the fraudulent sale of patent medicines. Agnes Turnbull's *Remember the
End* (1938) is a similar exposé of the career of a young Scot who ignores
the welfare of others and sacrifices his own artistic instincts and human
relationships in his struggle to reach the top in the Pennsylvania steel industry.
Harry Lee's *No Measure Danced* (1940) describes the ruthless opportunism
of a female business executive who gains success at the expense of everything else. Though these works cannot measure up to the relentless power-
fulness with which Schulberg and Weidman portray cynical, ruthless ambition, they share the desire to expose the American self-made man as no
longer a hero, but an unprincipled villain who succeeds by the exploitation
of others and the suppression of his own better nature.

Whether the tone is crusading, derisive, alarmed, angry, bitter, awed, or
indignant, all the works emphasized in this chapter have the effect of tarnishing the image of success. The quest for material success is shown to be a
farcical nightmare for the innocent and the weak like Lemuel Pitkin, a brutal
and self-destructive obsession for the confused and the uncertain like Joe
Bonaparte, and an exercise in self-interested ruthlessness for the tough and
the unprincipled like Harry Bogen and Sammy Glick. And yet if the dream
of success has become a nightmare, if individualism and ambition are bankrupt
as ideals for sensitive and humane young men, still the America envisioned
by these writers could offer no incentives, no values, no source of dignity
and respect to replace the dream of success. This is the central dilemma
emphasized in these attacks on the myth of success. In a viciously competitive
and economically crippled world, individual success seemed impossible or
not worth the battle. Yet American society continued to tantalize its young
people with images of material success so attractive that they blotted out

other values. The Joe Bonapartes, the Harry Bogens, and the Sammy Glicks could not achieve success and remain human, but at the same time they could not deny success without denying the only source of fulfillment that seemed to matter in their society. According to the values they had absorbed from their culture, there was no other way to achieve the identity the status, and the power that they passionately needed. Their obsessive ambition, which has nowhere constructive to go, points up the brutality and the predation that can result when a society creates materialistic dream that it can satisfy only for the grasping few.

As viewed by these writers of the thirties, the deprivation accompanying poverty and economic Depression brought to the surface the worst possibili inherent in the traditional American myth of success. When the nation was young and expansive, perhaps it inspired creative ambition, a sense of promise, and an idealistic dream of self-realization through tangible achieve ment. But in the world invoked by these writers of the Depression years— a world of broken dreams, cramped possibilities, and limited rewards— the old ideals take on new and frightening form. The old individualism has hardened into ruthless self-interest and openly callous toughness. Ambition derives not from an idealistic sense of promise but from seething frustration hatred, and a cynical acceptance of the world's viciousness. The imposing stature of the self-made man has shrunk to the wiry, petty figures of Harry Bogen and Sammy Glick. In general, the quest for success is no longe a dream implying self-realization and fulfillment; it has become a nightmare implying physical and spiritual impoverishment.

Notes

1. James Light, *Nathanael West: An Interpretative Study*, p. 109.
2. Nathanael West, *A Cool Million,* in *The Complete Works of Nathanael West,* pp. 149-50.
3. Ibid., p. 214.
4. Ibid., p. 248.
5. Ibid., p. 246.
6. Ibid., p. 247.
7. Ibid., p. 202.
8. See, for instance, Lewis Gannett, "A Cool Million," *New York Herald Tribune* (June 21, 1934), p. 19; and "A Cool Million," *New York Post* (June 23, 1934), p. 7.
9. Randall Reid, *The Fiction of Nathanael West,* p. 107.
10. West, p. 174.
11. Ibid., p. 150.

12. Ibid., 245-46.

13. Ibid., p. 255.

14. D. F. Dooley, *The Art of Sinclair Lewis*, p. 193.

15. Clifford Odets, *Golden Boy*, in *Twenty Best Plays of the Modern American Theatre*, edited by John Gassner, Act I, p. 789.

16. Ibid., Act III, pp. 810, 811.

17. Ibid., Act I, p. 786; Act II, p. 807.

18. In *Clifford Odets: The Thirties and After*, Edward Murray discusses the prostitution motif at some length, relating it to Eddie Fuseli's homosexuality and to the hint of sexual perversion which he thinks is present in the characterization of Tokio.

19. Odets, *Golden Boy*, Act III, p. 812.

20. Ibid., Act I, p. 788.

21. Ibid., Act III, p. 817.

22. Ibid.

23. Ibid., p. 817.

24. Ibid., pp. 815-16.

25. Ibid.

26. Ibid.

27. Murray, p. 59.

28. Harold Clurman, *The Fervent Years*, pp. 196-97.

29. Clifford Odets, *Awake and Sing*, in *Famous American Plays of the 1930's*, Act III, p. 93.

30. Ibid., Act II, p. 59.

31. Charles Kaplan, "Two Depression Plays and Broadway's Popular Idealism," *American Quarterly*, XV (Winter, 1963), 579-85.

32. *What Makes Sammy Run?* had sold close to 2.5 million copies by 1965 and *I Can Get It for You Wholesale* had sold just over 2 million. See Alice Payne Hackett, *Seventy Years of Best Sellers, 1895-1965*.

33. Jerome Weidman, *I Can Get It for You Wholesale*, p. 140.

34. Ibid., p. 224.

35. Ibid., pp. 366-67.

36. Ibid., p. 84.

37. Budd Schulberg, *What Makes Sammy Run?*, p. 14.

38. Ibid., p. 303.

39. Ibid., pp. 75-76.

40. Weidman, p. 370.

41. Schulberg, p. 95.

42. Ibid., pp. 279, 298.

43. Ibid., p. 275.

44. Ibid., p. 297.

45. Ibid., p. 39.

46. Ibid., p. 303.

47. Ibid., p. 212.

48. Ibid., p. 249.

49. Ibid., p. 302.

/ Conclusion

Perhaps the most evident general conclusion that emerges from a study
of what happened to the American dream of success when it collided with
the grim reality of economic crisis is that attitudes toward the dream became endlessly complex, confusing, and contradictory. The Depression
era was a time of uncertainty and ambivalence—of cynicism and idealism,
of the reaffirmation of old faiths and the search for new ones, of softness
and toughness, of optimism and despair, of realism and fairy-tale illusions.
It was a time of upheaval, when American values seemed to be in the process
of shifting but not in a clear-cut direction. As the Lynds said of Middletown
America was still facing both ways, "caught in its institutional conflicts,
caught between past and future, and now knowing which way to move."[1]
Certainly it was a time of challenge and crisis for the American dream of
success, but the response to that challenge was not uniform; it was conservative and radical, angry and accepting, disillusioned and millennial.

In popular literature, the central contradiction is that one finds endless
reaffirmations of faith in the conventional myth of success, but also some
disillusionment, tarnishing of the image, and efforts to define new goals.
Popular magazines and how-to-succeed guidebooks tirelessly retold the old
story of the poor boy who makes good and, often with a sense of urgency,
reaffirmed the importance of the values which had always been identified
with the American success story and which now seemed threatened.
Cautionary tales demonstrated the indispensability of ambition, industry,
and other traditional virtues; and "proof" abounded that America was still
a golden land of opportunity, although immigration figures (in the early

thirties more people left than entered the country) suggest that the Promised Land image was suffering as it had never before in our history.

Such writings leave the vivid impression that the Depression years were preeminently an age of illusions. Traditionally given to extravagant expectations of the world, Americans demonstrated a strong tendency during the Depression crisis to cling to their expectations even if this meant ignoring or distorting objective reality. In other words, the American dream tended to become the American illusion when the reality of Depression conditions clashed with the myth of unlimited opportunity and fabulous success. A growing proportion of success stories in the Depression years offered escape to a dream world and provided mythological support for traditional ideologies, but unlike the conventional American success story, were not intended to provide realistic models which the aspiring young man could emulate. Tacitly, the creators of success fantasies in the thirties recognized that myth and reality were separate and distinct, with little interplay between them.

Despite the tendency to cling to the old symbols, however, the impact of the Depression was reflected in certain shifts in attitude and adjustments in the myth. Many of the popular stories scaled down the goals of their characters to bring them more nearly in harmony with what seemed realistically possible. And, much more frequently than in the twenties, the stories emphasized nonmaterial rewards such as peace of mind, love, family harmony, and respect. In some stories of the thirties there were substantial modifications in the standard formula for magazine fiction, including departures from that most fundamental ingredient of the formula—the happy ending. In the popular-magazine fiction of the twenties, there is seldom a variation from that basic formula in which the protagonist, after a period of conflict or development, triumphs in some way at the end—the most typical rewards being economic success, romance, or a combination of the two. In a number of popular stories of the thirties, there is no happy ending, no success, no triumph, in fact, no progression or mobility at all. Instead, the stories portray a static quality of acceptance of things as they are.

Another of the contradictions of the Depression years was a reaffirmation of the gospel of work while, at the same time, a new gospel of leisure was given considerable currency. Among those intent on perpetuating America's traditional myth of success, no doctrine was more piously reemphasized than the belief in the ennobling and sanctifying value of hard work. The economic crisis which cut men off from their work had the effect of sharpening the already intense American belief in work not only as a practical economic necessity but as a quasi-religious source of salvation. Yet some of the most popular inspirational books of the decade, most notably Walter Pitkin's *Life Begins at Forty* and Lin Yutang's *The Importance of Living*, attack the gospel of work and the whole struggle for worldly success as perverse and dehumanizing relics of the past. They urge the renouncement of vain striving and the affirmation of spiritual contentment, the enjoyment of leisure, and the savoring of life's small pleasures.

This increasing emphasis on leisure can be related to the ascension of a new type of hero in the popular-magazine fiction and biographical articles of the thirties. As the businessman lost ground as a fictional hero and a subject of biographies, he was replaced by little men and professionals from various spheres, but particularly by figures from the world of entertainment and sports. In the nineteenth century and through the 1920s, when the businessman was still king, the idols held up for worship and imitation in popular literature tended to be creators of wealth, builders of tangible, physical things. During the Depression era, it was apparent that the "idols of production" were beginning to be displaced by the "idols of consumption."[2] Actors, writers, singers, and other heroes related either directly or indirectly to the world of entertainment and leisure became predominant in mass-magazine fiction and biography. This shift in popular idols symbolizes a significant turning point in the evolution of American society. As long as American society was expansive, wide open, still in the process of being physically built, the idols of production were appropriate heroes. But once the process of growth had leveled off and the process of bureaucratic organization and solidification had set in, there was less to admire in the producers and more time to devote to entertainment and the enjoyment of leisure. In the twenties the cult of prosperity, the growth of advertising, and the sometimes frantic pursuit of pleasure were signs of the developing emphasis on leisure and consumption. Yet the idols of production, the businessmen and industrialists, were still the dominant popular heroes. Ironically it was in the Depression decade, when leisure was forced by unemployment, and for many there was little money for entertainment, that the idols of consumption captured the popular imagination. The economic crisis of those years dramatically established the fact that there were distinct limitations to our ability to find rewards in work and production. In searching for new idols, one direction Americans looked to was the sphere of entertainment and leisure.

Another of the central paradoxes of the period was related to the increased emphasis on security which the precarious economic conditions of the thirties helped to foster. In one sense the quest for security was consistent with important doctrines of the traditional myth of success. It implied an emphasis on hard work, getting ahead, economic stability, and saving for the future. On the other hand, some of the antisuccess literature of the period rejects the pursuit of success on the grounds that self-made success is highly precarious and insecure. To be mobile in a competitive system could be dangerous as well as rewarding, and many popular stories of the thirties imply that the security of accepting one's present status is preferable. This fear of mobility is one of the keys to understanding the influence of the Depression upon our mythology of success. In *People of Plenty* David Potter comments on the psychological ravages caused by a mythology of success which presents an unattainable ideal as if it were a reality. He suggests that we should, and may, begin to think of mobility as optional and not obligatory as our society gets closer to being fully developed and there are fewer opportunities to be exploited.[3] On the popular level, clear signs of this new attitude toward mobility appeared in the 1930s.

The shift in emphasis from inner-direction to other-direction and from character to personality, both of which are very obvious in Carnegie's *How to Win Friends and Influence People* and other how-to-succeed guidebooks of the thirties, is related to this quest for security. The very nature of the complex, bureaucratic corporate system of twentieth-century America, of course, placed a premium on belonging, fitting in, getting along with other people rather than overwhelming them. At the same time, the anxiety created by the Depression contributed to a heightened awareness of the loneliness and insecurity that might well accompany the spectacular success of the inner-directed rugged individualist. In the twenties, Bruce Barton could still glorify the inner-directed man who had a sublime contempt for public opinion—a man whose motto might be, "Never explain; never retract; never apologize; get it done and let them howl!" In the Depression years, few philosophers of success were prepared to give such rash advice. The general tenor of their advice is summarized in Carnegie's title, where first priority is given to the art of winning friends. Their emphasis tends to fall heavily on finessing one's way carefully upward by means of tactful manipulation and an ingratiating personality. This insinuating approach was viewed as a safer procedure than attempting to power one's way to success by magnetism and strength of character.

Implicitly, the philosophy of positive thinking which often accompanied this emphasis on personality was an admission that actual control of the external world through the individual will was a thing of the past and less important in any event than control of one's own thoughts. The paradox in the theory of positive thinking is that, while it promises results in the outside world (Napoleon Hill's title *Think and Grow Rich* is a typical example), it offers no concrete explanation of how external reality can be altered by the power of the mind. The real promise, then, is simply that if one tries, he can manipulate his own mind. He can be successful if he defines "success" properly, if he controls his desires and resigns himself to what he has. While faith is maintained in the subtle manipulation of people, tacitly the focus on one's own mental condition represents an erosion of the legendary optimism of the rugged individualist who had boundless confidence in his ability to change the world. This optimism was perhaps appropriate to an age of physical expansion and relative simplicity. It was not appropriate to an age of complex corporate organization, and certainly not to an age of dispiriting economic breakdown.

One clear and uncontradictory impression left by the popular literature of the thirties is that, among the general populace, the Depression decade was not a period of radical political ideas. Despite the uncertainty and ambivalence, the ordinary American maintained enough faith in the fundamental promise of the American dream, the assurance that every man was free to work for a better future for himself or his children, to preclude any widespread sentiment in favor of a radical overhaul of the system. Even among popular stories which honestly portray the ravages of the Depression—the poverty, the desperation, the utter powerlessness to do anything—there is no hint of radical ideology. The typical message of such stories is that the true hero is not the man who rebels and strikes out against deprivation and hardship, but the man who stoically accepts the status quo and does not lose faith in a better future.

Among the major novelists and playwrights of the Depression years, disillusionment with the traditional American dream of personal success was thoroughgoing and profound. As a realistic possibility, the dream of fame and fortune seemed to be a casualty of a system of competitive capitalism that had gone bankrupt. As an ideal, it was portrayed as delusory, corrupt, materialistic, and destructive. Many writers of the Depression decade who attacked the myth of success did so not only because of its

bourgeois shoddiness and its hollow, materialistic content, but also because
of the dangers inherent in the idealism, the hopefulness, and the desire
which have always been at the heart of the American dream. Steinbeck
suggests in *The Grapes of Wrath* that dreams of paradise in California
yield bitter frustration and must be exorcised before effective communal
action can be taken. Farrell suggests in the *Studs Lonigan* trilogy that the
puerile dreams that Studs' shoddy culture has bred in him are barriers to
action in the real world and, thus, ultimately agents in his destruction.
Nathanael West's *The Day of the Locust* dramatizes the correlation between
frustrated dreams and violent action, while *A Cool Million* suggests that
the myth of success could become the core of a native American fascism.
Odets' Joe Bonaparte, Weidman's Harry Bogen, and Schulberg's Sammy
Glick all exemplify the ruthlessness and brutality which can result when
the extravagant expectations of the American dream are combined with
the poverty and deprivation of economic Depression and social inequality.
Certainly West's cynicism, Hemingway's professed toughness, Caldwell's
cool and matter-of-fact humor, Dos Passos' pessimism, and Farrell's
objective naturalism would seem inconsistent with an idealistic belief in
a dream. In *The End of Ideology* Daniel Bell points to the years of crushing economic Depression as the beginning of the end of millennial hopes
and idealistic impulses in the modern world.[4] Yet it is another measure
of the two-facedness of the Depression era that it was also a time when
idealistic, even messianic, thinking was at a peak. As Malcolm Cowley has
written, it was an Age of Faith when apocalyptic and millennial ideas
were at least as commonplace as cynicism and despair.[5]

The faith of the thirties was to an extent, of course, a Marxian faith.
But except for the orthodox and now mostly forgotten party-line proletarian novelists, our writers did not merely substitute the Communist dream
for the American dream. Their idealism was largely an indigenous American
idealism, and their real hope was to define a new American dream out of
a synthesis of the new sense of communalism and the traditional American
belief in personal freedom, equality, and the dignity of the individual.
This new American dream is perhaps best represented by Steinbeck. In
Of Mice and Men, the dream of Lennie and George is compounded of a
deep longing for communion with others and an equally deep need for
the kind of freedom, independence, and dignity that is found at the heart
of Jeffersonian agrarianism. Similarly, in *The Grapes of Wrath* Steinbeck
emphasizes both the need for communal action and the importance of
maintaining individual dignity. This synthesis of the communal and the

individual is implicit in many of the utterances of Tom Joad and the
preacher, Jim Casy. Near the end of the novel, Tom restates Casy's idea
that no individual has a soul of his own, "but on'y a piece of a big one."
He adds:

> Then it don' matter [if they kill him] . Then I'll be all
> aroun' in the dark. I'll be ever' where—wherever you look.
> Wherever they's a fight so hungry people can eat, I'll be
> there. . . . I'll be in the way kids laugh when they're
> hungry an' they know supper's ready. An' when our folks
> eat the stuff they raise an' live in the houses they build—
> why, I'll be there.[6]

There is something of Emerson in Tom's reference to the universal soul
that all men share, something of Jefferson in his image of the self-sufficient
farmer, and, of course, something of Marx in his dream of communal action
to improve the lot of hungry and oppressed people. Clearly, Steinbeck is
searching for a dream that is American but, at the same time, humane and
relevant to twentieth-century problems.

Clifford Odets' idealism derives from a blend of essentially the same
principles. Central to Odets' plays is the quest for a life of dignity and self-
realization. Sometimes the quest is stated in terms that echo deeply rooted
American traditions of freedom and self-reliance, as in Jacob's Emersonian
admonition to Ralph to "Do what is in your heart and you carry in yourself
a revolution" (*Awake and Sing*). But a crucial part of Odets' dream for
the future is a vision of brotherhood and love. Leo Gordon's last speech
in *Paradise Lost* is an impassioned formulation of this vision:

> Yes, I want to see that new world. . . . Oh yes, I tell you the
> whole world is for men to possess. Heartbreak and terror are
> not the heritage of mankind! The world is beautiful. No fruit
> tree wears a lock and key. Men will sing at their work, men
> will love. Ohhh, darling, the world is in its morning . . . and
> *no man fights alone*![7]

In this passage, Odets' faith in the future is more buoyant than Steinbeck's,
and it is not particularly consistent with the tone of a play which portrays
the wholesale dissolution of the ideals and way of life of middle-class
Americans. Nonetheless, it reflects a long tradition of irrepressible American

optimism and the unwillingness of Americans, even those like Odets who portrayed his share of the seamy side of the Depression, to give up their dreams of the future. Like William Saroyan, whose idealism sometimes seems dreamy, sentimental, and inconsistent with the poverty and hardship he describes, Odets had an abiding faith in the resiliency of the human spirit.

It should be emphasized that, in their efforts to define a new American dream, our writers of the thirties were generally insistent on a balance between the two ideals of individual dignity and group cooperation. Most of the important Depression-era writers who toyed with Communism— including Richard Wright, Nathanael West, Odets, Steinbeck, and Dos Passos—were much too cognizant of the needs of the individual and of their own needs as artists to be comfortable within the party or to be fully accepted by party-line critics. On the other hand, the social faith of the thirties, the longing for communion with others and an escape from isolation, was strong enough to encompass writers who had been alienated and uncommitted in the twenties. Hemingway echoes the faith of the thirties in *To Have and Have Not* when Harry Morgan makes his deathbed admission that "No matter how a man alone ain't got no bloody f---ing chance." By the latter years of the decade, Thomas Wolfe had also become committed to the faith of the thirties. Included in *You Can't Go Home Again* (1940) are an anticapitalist section titled "The Party at Jack's" and an antifascist story called "I Have a Thing to Tell You." Wolfe concludes with a "credo" in which he gives eloquent expression to the apocalyptic vision of a new American dream. He rejects the narrow, self-oriented American dream of success and fame, calling it "the enemy." Yet he expresses an exuberant faith in the realization of the American dream of the future:

I believe that we are lost here in America, but I believe we shall be found. And this belief . . . is for me—and I think for all of us—not only our own hope, but America's everlasting, living dream. I think the life which we have fashioned in America, and which has fashioned us was self-destructive in its nature, and must be destroyed. I think these forms are dying, and must die, just as I know that America and the people in it are deathless, undiscovered, and immortal, and must live.

> I think the true discovery of America is before us. I think
> the true fulfillment of our spirit, of our people, of our
> mighty and immortal land, is yet to come. And I think
> that all these things are certain as the morning and in-
> evitable as noon.[8]

This is the voice of anger and disillusionment with the bankrupt American dream of individual success, but it is also the voice of idealistic faith in a new realization of America.

The millennial hope for the true realization of America seems to have intensified the anger and disillusionment with which our writers exposed the broken promises of the dream of success and the shallowness of material acquisitiveness as an ideal. Writers of the twenties had attacked the myth of success as had earlier muckrakers like David Graham Phillips, but not without admiration for the self-made man and even some pandering to the dream. In the thirties the myth was attacked from all angles and often with deep conviction. By the end of the decade there was not much that had not been said in the name of tarnishing the image of success. Post-Depression writers continued to tarnish the image as is evidenced by such works as Arthur Miller's *The Death of a Salesman* (1946), Frederick Wakeman's *The Hucksters* (1946), Charles Gorham's *The Gilded Hearse* (1948), Bernard Malamud's *The Natural* (1952), and Sloan Wilson's *The Man in the Gray Flannel Suit* (1955). But for the most part the anti-success themes of these writings had been anticipated, if not fully exploited, in the thirties.

Despite the continued outpouring of literary attacks, however, the myth of success is by no means dead as a popular ideal in modern America. How-to-succeed guidebooks still appear in large numbers, Dale Carnegie self-improvement courses still attract patrons, newspapers still run features on successful men and women, politicians still gain sympathy by romanticizing their humble origins, and one still hears the old arguments about the importance of self-help, industry, and ambition. New mind-power "systems" surface periodically (like the current EST fad) and earn fortunes for their inventors. Even *Playboy,* the best known of the men's magazines, is at least as success oriented as it is sex oriented. As a guidebook complete with glittering images of success and with authoritative instructions on where to go, what to wear, what to buy, and how to be sexually successful, it serves the special needs of the affluent, consumer-oriented, other-directed young man of the midtwentieth century.[9]

In general terms it can be said that the myth of success came out of the Great Depression tarnished, altered, and challenged, but not totally rejected and replaced. From the beginning of our history, the myth of success has penetrated American culture much too completely for a single crisis, even one as harrowing as the Great Depression, to deal it the death blow. Our major novelists and dramatists of the thirties were virtually unanimous in their disillusionment with the dream of success. But those who define the temper of the thirties entirely in terms of the social consciousness and leftist tendencies of our major writers and intellectuals have left us with an incomplete picture of the period. Intellectuals had attacked the myth of success before the Depression and they have since, but middle America has never totally given it up, partially, it seems, because the American experience has not provided anything comparable with which to replace it. Since the Great Depression, no new popular ideal has yet established itself as a replacement for the ideal of the self-made man; no myth of similar proportions has emerged, and it seems unlikely that any American ideal will ever match the remarkable resiliency of the myth of success.

Notes

1. Robert and Helen Lynd, *Middletown in Transition*, p. 510.
2. Leo Lowenthal uses these terms in his article, "The Triumph of Mass Idols," in *Literature, Popular Culture, and Society*, pp. 109-36.
3. David Potter, *People of Plenty*, p. 109.
4. Daniel Bell, *The End of Ideology*, pp. 369-70.
5. Malcolm Cowley, "The 1930's Were an Age of Faith," *New York Times Book Review*, December 13, 1964, pp. 4-5, 14-17.
6. John Steinbeck, *The Grapes of Wrath*, pp. 373-74.
7. Clifford Odets, *Paradise Lost*, in *Six Plays of Clifford Odets*, pp. 229-30.
8. Thomas Wolfe, *You Can't Go Home Again*, pp. 741-42.
9. The central symbol in *Playboy*, of course, is the Playmate. And since the Golden Girl, representing the twin ideals of success and sex, has been a recurring symbol in our literature of success, it seems appropriate that a single magazine should finally devote itself to both obsessions, and that it should be enormously popular and influential.

Bibliography

I. Primary Sources*

A. NOVELS AND PLAYS

Anderson, Sherwood, *Poor White.* New York: Huebsch, 1920.

Brooks, John, *The Big Wheel.* New York: Harper and Brothers, 1949.

Cain, James M., *The Moth.* New York: Alfred A. Knopf, 1948.

Caldwell, Erskine, *God's Little Acre.* In *The Caldwell Caravan: Novels and Stories by Erskine Caldwell.* Cleveland: World Publishing Co., 1946.

———— *Tobacco Road.* New York: Scribner, 1932.

Cantwell, Robert, *Land of Plenty.* New York: Farrar, Straus, 1934.

Chandler, Raymond, *The Big Sleep.* New York: Ballantine, 1972.

Conroy, Jack, *The Disinherited.* New York: Convici-Friede, 1934.

Dahlberg, Edward, *Bottom Dogs.* New York: Simon and Schuster, 1930.

Dos Passos, John, *Adventures of a Young Man.* New York: Popular Library, 1939.

———— *U. S. A.: A Trilogy.* New York: Modern Library, 1939. One volume containing *1919, 42nd Parallel,* and *The Big Money.*

Dreiser, Theodore, *An American Tragedy.* New York: Boni and Liveright, 1925.

———— *The Financier.* New York: Harpers, 1912.

———— *Sister Carrie.* New York: Doubleday, Page, 1900.

* Popular magazine short stories, articles, and features are cited in full in the notes and will not be listed again here.

Fallada, Hans, *Little Man, What Now?* New York: Grosset and Dunlap, 1933.

Farrell, James T., *Studs Lonigan: A Trilogy.* New York: The Modern Library, 1935.

One volume containing *Young Lonigan, The Young Manhood of Studs Lonigan,* and *Judgment Day.*

——— *A World I Never Made.* Cleveland: World Publishing Co., 1936.

Fitzgerald, F. Scott, *The Great Gatsby.* New York: Scribner, 1925.

——— *The Last Tycoon.* New York: Scribner, 1941.

——— *The Stories of F. Scott Fitzgerald.* Edited by Malcolm Cowley. New York: Scribner, 1951.

——— *Tender Is the Night.* New York: Scribner, 1934.

Gorham, Charles O., *The Gilded Hearse.* New York: Creative Age, 1948.

Halper, Albert, *Union Square.* New York: Viking Press, 1933.

Hammett, Dashiell, *The Maltese Falcon.* New York: Knopf, 1930.

——— *The Thin Man.* New York: Knopf, 1932.

Hart, Moss, and Kaufman, George, *You Can't Take It with You.* New York: Farrar, Straus, 1937.

Hemingway, Ernest, *In Our Time.* New York: Scribner, 1925.

——— *To Have and Have Not.* New York: Scribner, 1937.

Lawson, John Howard, *Success Story.* New York: Farrar, Straus, 1932.

Lewis, Sinclair, *Arrowsmith.* New York: Harcourt, Brace, 1925.

——— *Babbitt.* New York: Harcourt, Brace, 1922.

——— *Dodsworth.* New York: Harcourt, Brace, 1929.

——— *It Can't Happen Here.* New York: Harcourt, Brace, 1935.

McCoy, Horace, *They Shoot Horses, Don't They?* New York: Simon & Schuster, 1935.

Malamud, Bernard, *The Natural.* New York: Harcourt, Brace, 1952.

Marquand, John, *The Late George Apley.* Boston: Little, Brown, 1937.

Odets, Clifford, *Awake and Sing.* In *Famous American Plays of the 1930's.* New York: Dell Publishing Co., 1959.

——— *Golden Boy.* In *Twenty Best Plays of the Modern American Theatre.* Edited by John Gassner. New York: Crown Publishers, 1939.

——— *Paradise Lost.* In *Six Plays of Clifford Odets.* New York: Random House, 1939.

O'Hara, John, *Hope of Heaven.* New York: Harcourt, Brace, 1938.

O'Neill, Eugene, *Hughie.* New Haven: Yale University Press, 1959.

——— *The Iceman Cometh.* New York: Random House, 1946.

————— *Long Day's Journey into Night.* New Haven, Conn.: Yale
   University Press, 1956.
————— *The Plays of Eugene O'Neill.* 3 vols. New York: Random House,
   1955.
————— *A Touch of the Poet.* New Haven: Yale University Press, 1957.
Rice, Elmer, *The Adding Machine.* New York: Doubleday, Page, 1923.
Saroyan, William, *The Daring Young Man on the Flying Trapeze and Other
   Stories.* New York: Random House, 1934.
————— *The Time of Your Life.* In *Famous American Plays of the 1930's.*
   Edited by Harold Clurman. New York: Dell Publishing Co., 1959.
Schulberg, Budd, *What Makes Sammy Run?* New York: Random House, 1941.
Steinbeck, John, *In Dubious Battle.* New York: Covici-Friede, 1936.
————— *The Grapes of Wrath.* New York: Bantam Books, 1939.
————— *Of Mice and Men.* New York: Covici-Friede, 1937.
Tarkington, Booth, *The Plutocrat.* Garden City, N.Y.: Doubleday, Page, 1927.
Wakeman, Frederic, *The Hucksters.* New York: Rinehart, 1946.
Weidman, Jerome, *I Can Get It for You Wholesale.* New York: Simon
   and Schuster, 1937.
West, Nathanael, *The Complete Works of Nathanael West.* New York:
   Farrar, Straus, and Cudahy, 1957. Contains *The Dream Life of Balso
   Snell, Miss Lonelyhearts, A Cool Million,* and *The Day of the Locust.*
Wilder, Thornton, *Heaven's My Destination.* New York: Harper and Brothers,
   1935.
Wilson, Sloan, *The Man in the Gray Flannel Suit.* New York: Simon
   and Schuster, 1955.
Wolfe, Thomas, *You Can't Go Home Again.* New York: Harper and
   Brothers, 1940.
Wright, Richard, *Native Son.* New York: Harper, 1940.

B. GUIDEBOOKS AND OTHER NONFICTION PRIMARY SOURCES

Babson, Roger, *What is Success?* New York: Fleming H. Revell Co., 1923.
Barton, Bruce, *The Man Nobody Knows.* New York: Grosset and Dunlap,
   1924.
Brande, Dorothea, *Wake Up and Live!* New York: Simon & Schuster, 1936.
Brophy, Loire, *Men Must Work.* New York: Appleton-Century Co., 1938.
Bryan, Julian Scott, *From Father to Son.* New York: Farrar, Strauss, 1937.

Carnegie, Andrew, *The Gospel of Wealth and Other Timely Essays.*
New York: The Century Co., 1900.

Carnegie, Dale, *How to Win Friends and Influence People.* New York:
Pocket Books, Inc., 1936.

Chalfant, Allan B., *What's Holding You Back?* New York: McGraw-Hill,
1937.

Clemens, Samuel, *"The Late Benjamin Franklin."* In *The Complete Humorou*
Sketches and Tales of Mark Twain. Edited by Charles Nieder. Garden
City, N. Y.: Hanover House, 1961.

Congdon, Don (ed.), *The Thirties, A Time to Remember.* New York: Simon
and Schuster, 1962.

Conwell, Russell, *Acres of Diamonds.* New York: Harpers, 1915.

Cotton, John, "Christian Calling." In *The Puritans: A Sourcebook of*
Their Writings. Edited by Perry Miller and Thomas H. Johnson. New
York: Harper and Row, 1963.

Davis, Howard L., *The Young Man in Business.* New York: John Wiley and
Sons, Inc., 1931.

Emerson, Ralph Waldo, *"Wealth."* In *The Selected Writings of Ralph*
Waldo Emerson. Edited by Brooks Atkinson. New York: Modern
Library, 1940.

Fancher, Albert, *Getting a Job and Getting Ahead.* New York: McGraw-
Hill, 1931.

Franklin, Benjamin, *Advice to a Young Tradesman.* In *A Benjamin Franklin*
Reader. Edited by Nathan G. Goodman. New York: Thomas Y. Crowell,
1945.

Gebler, Robert T., *Full Speed to Success.* Philadelphia: Lippincott,
1934.

Harding, Warren G., "Business Sense in Government," *Nation's*
Business, VIII (November, 1920), 13-14, 69.

Hill, Napoleon, *Think and Grow Rich.* New York: Crest Books, 1963.

Hoover, Herbert, *American Individualism.* Garden City, N. Y.: Doubleday,
Page and Co., 1922.

James, William, *The Letters of William James.* Edited by Henry James.
Boston: Little, Brown, and Co., 1920.

Laird, Donald and Eleanor, *The Technique of Handling People.* New
York: Whittlesey House, 1943.

Lin, Yutang, *The Importance of Living.* New York: Reynal and Hitchcock,
1937.

Link, Henry C., *The Return to Religion.* New York: Macmillan, 1936.

Mather, Cotton, *Essays to Do Good.* Boston: American Tract Society, 1710.

Piper, Henry D. (ed.), *Think Back on Us . . . . A Contemporary Chronicle of the 1930's by Malcolm Cowley.* Carbondale, Ill.: Southern Illinois University Press, 1967.

Pitkin, Walter B., *Life Begins at Forty.* New York: McGraw-Hill, 1932.

Raymond, Ernest, *The Super-Science of Success.* Privately printed by the author, 1933.

Rischin, Moses (ed.), *The American Gospel of Success: An Anthology from Cotton Mather to Michael Harrington.* Chicago: Quadrangle Books, 1965.

Welsh, Frank M., and Gordon, Frances L., *Thinking Success into Business.* Chicago: Albert Whitman Co., 1932.

Wilson, Woodrow, *The New Freedom.* New York: Doubleday and Co., 1913.

II. Secondary Sources

A. BOOKS

Allen, Frederick Lewis, *Only Yesterday.* New York: Harper and Brothers, 1931.

——— *Since Yesterday.* New York: Harper and Brothers, 1940.

Arnold, Thurman, *The Folklore of Capitalism.* New Haven: Yale University Press, 1941.

Barber, Bernard, *Social Stratification.* New York: Harcourt, Brace, and World, 1957.

Bell, Daniel, *The End of Ideology.* Glencoe, Ill.: The Free Press, 1960.

Bendix, Reinhard, and Lipset, Seymour, *Social Mobility in Industrial Society.* Berkeley, Calif.: University of California Press, 1959.

Boorstin, Daniel, *The Image, or What Happened to the American Dream.* New York: Atheneum. 1962.

Cady, Edwin H., *The Gentleman in America.* Syracuse, N. Y.: Syracuse University Press, 1949.

Carpenter, F. I., *American Literature and the Dream.* New York: Philosophical Library, Inc., 1955.

Cawelti, John G., *Apostles of the Self-Made Man.* Chicago: University of Chicago Press, 1965.

Chenoweth, Lawrence, *The American Dream of Success: The Search for Self in the Twentieth Century*. North Scituate, Mass.: Duxbury Press, 1974.

Childs, Marquis W., and Cater, Douglas, *Ethics in a Business Society*. New York: Harper, 1954.

Clurman, Harold, *The Fervent Years*. New York: Hill and Wang, 1957.

Commager, Henry Steele, *The American Mind*. New Haven, Conn.: Yale University Press, 1950.

Curti, Merle, *The Growth of American Thought*. New York: Harper, 1951.

Dooley, D. F., *The Art of Sinclair Lewis*. Lincoln, Neb.: University of Nebraska Press, 1967.

Edgell, David, *William Ellery Channing*. Boston: The Beacon Press, 1955.

Engel, Edwin A., *The Haunted Heroes of Eugene O'Neill*. Cambridge, Mass.: Harvard University Press, 1953.

Gabriel, Ralph H., *The Course of American Democratic Thought*. New York: Ronald Press, 1940.

Gardener, Ralph D., *Horatio Alger, or the American Hero Era*. Mendota, Ill.: Wayside Press, 1964.

Geismar, Maxwell, *The Last of the Provincials*. Boston: Houghton Mifflin, 1947.

Gerber, Philip L., *Theodore Dreiser*. New York: Twayne Publisher, Inc., 1964.

Hart, Hornell, *Recent Social Trends in the United States*. New York: McGraw Hill, 1933.

Hart, James D., *The Popular Book*. Berkeley, Calif.: University of California Press, 1961.

Hearn (née Hindman), Pamela K., *Eugene O'Neill's Treatment of Religion, Love, and Illusion*. Unpublished master's thesis, Southern Illinois University, 1962.

Heilbroner, Robert, *The Quest for Wealth*. New York: Simon and Schuster, 1956.

Hofstadter, Richard, *Anti-Intellectualism in American Life*. New York: Alfred A. Knopf, 1963.

Kirkland, Edward, *Dream and Thought in the Business Community*. Ithaca, N. Y.: Cornell University Press, 1956.

Light, James F., *Nathanael West: An Interpretative Study*. Evanston, Ill.: Northwestern University Press, 1961.

Lisca, Peter, *The Wide World of John Steinbeck.* New Brunswick, N. J.: Rutgers Univeristy Press, 1958.

Lowenthal, Leo, *Literature, Popular Culture, and Society.* Englewood Cliffs, N. J.: Prentice-Hall, 1961.

Lynd, Robert and Helen, *Middletown in Transition.* New York: Harcourt, Brace, 1937.

Lynn, Kenneth S., *The Dream of Success: A Study of the Modern American Imagination.* Boston: Little, Brown and Co., 1955.

Madden, David (ed.), *Proletarian Writers of the Thirties.* Carbondale, Ill.: Southern Illinois University Press, 1968.

———— *Tough Guy Writers of the Thirties.* Carbondale, Ill.: Southern Illinois University Press, 1968.

Millgate, Michael, *American Social Fiction: James to Cozzens.* Edinburgh: Oliver and Boyd, 1964.

Mills, C. Wright, *White Collar.* New York: Oxford University Press, 1951.

Murray, Edward, *Clifford Odets: The Thirties and After.* New York: Frederick Ungar Publishing Co., 1968.

Newcomer, Mabel, *The Big Business Executive: The Factors That Made Him,* New York: Columbia University Press, 1955.

Nosow, Sigmund, and Form, William H. (eds.), *Man, Work, and Society: A Reader in the Sociology of Occupations.* New York: Basic Books, Inc., 1962.

Packard, Vance, *The Status Seekers.* New York: D. McKay Co., 1959.

Potter, David M., *People of Plenty.* Chicago: University of Chicago Press, 1954.

Raleigh, John H. (ed.), *Twentieth Century Interpretations of The Iceman Cometh.* Englewood Cliffs, N. J.: Prentice-Hall, 1968.

Reid, Randall, *The Fiction of Nathanael West.* Chicago: University of Chicago Press, 1967.

Rideout, Walter B., *The Radical Novel in the United States, 1900-1954.* Cambridge, Mass.: Harvard University Press, 1956.

Riesman, David, *The Lonely Crowd.* New Haven: Yale University Press, 1950.

Rogoff, Natalie, *Recent Trends in Occupational Mobility.* Glencoe, Ill.: The Free Press, 1953.

Schneider, Louis, and Dornbusch, Sanford M., *Popular Religion: Inspirational Books in America.* Chicago: University of Chicago Press, 1958.

Snowman, Daniel, *America Since 1920.* New York: Harper and Row, 1969.

Sorokin, Pitirim, *Social and Cultural Mobility.* Glencoe, Ill.: The Free Press, 1959.

Susman, Warren (ed.), *Culture and Commitment: 1929-1945.* New York: George Braziller, 1973.

Swados, Harvey, *The American Writer in the Great Depression.* Indianapolis, Ind.: Bobbs-Merrill, 1966.

Thorp, Margaret Farrand, *America at the Movies.* New Haven, Conn.: Yale University Press, 1939.

Tipple, John, *Crisis of the American Dream.* New York: Pegasus, 1968.

Warner, W. Lloyd, *American Life: Dream and Reality.* Chicago: University of Chicago Press, 1953.

———— and Abegglen, James, *Occupational Mobility in American Business and Industry, 1928-1952.* Minneapolis: University of Minnesota Press, 1955.

Weber, Max, *The Protestant Ethic and the Spirit of Capitalism.* Revised edition. New York: Scribner, 1958.

Wecter, Dixon, *The Hero in America.* New York: Scribner, 1951.

Weiss, Richard, *The American Myth of Success.* New York: Basic Books, 1969.

White, William Allen, *A Puritan in Babylon: The Story of Calvin Coolidge.* New York: Macmillan, 1938.

Whyte, William H. Jr., *The Organization Man.* New York: Simon and Schuster, 1952.

Wish, Harvey, *Contemporary America: The National Scene Since 1900.* Revised edition. New York: Harper, 1955.

———— *Society and Thought in Modern America.* New York: Longmans, Green, 1952.

Wylie, Phillip, *A Generation of Vipers.* Revised edition. New York: Rinehart, 1955.

Wyllie, Irwin, *The Self-Made Man in America.* New Brunswick, N. J.: Rutgers University Press, 1954.

B. ARTICLES

Bell, Daniel, "Crime as an American Way of Life," *Antioch Review,* XIII (Summer, 1953), 131-54.

Branch, Edgar M., "Studs Lonigan: Symbolism and Theme," *College English,* XXIII (December, 1961), 191-96.

Cawelti, John, "The Concept of Formula in the Study of Popular Literature," *Journal of Popular Culture,* III (Winter, 1969), 381-90.

Chase, Stuart, "American Values: A Generation of Change," *Public Opinion Quarterly,* XXIX (Fall, 1965), 357-61.

Cowley, Malcolm, "The 1930's Were an Age of Faith," *New York Times Book Review,* December 13, 1964, pp. 4-5, 14-17.

———— "While They Waited for Lefty," *Saturday Review,* June 6, 1964, pp. 16-19, 61.

Day, Cyrus, "The Iceman and the Bridegroom," *Modern Drama,* I (May, 1958), 3-9.

Fielden, Kenneth, "Samuel Smiles and Self-Help," *Victorian Studies,* XII (December, 1968).

Fortune Magazine, Fortune Quarterly Survey II, October, 1935, pp. 56-58+; Quarterly Survey IV, April, 1936, pp. 104-105; Quarterly Survey V, July, 1936, pp. 83-85, 148+; Quarterly Survey VI, October, 1936, pp. 130-32, 210+; Quarterly Survey VII, January, 1937, pp. 86-87, 150+.

Galloway, D. D., "Nathanael West's Dream Dump," *Critique,* VI (Winter, 1963-64), 46-64.

Griswold, A. Whitney, "New Thought: A Cult of Success, *"American Journal of Sociology,* XL (November, 1934), 309-18.

———— "Three Puritans on Prosperity," *New England Quarterly,* VII (1934), 475-93.

Harrison, J. F. C., "The Victorian Gospel of Success," *Victorian Studies,* I (1957), 155-64.

Hart, John E., "Albert Halper's World of the 30's," *Twentieth-Century Literature,* IX (January, 1964), 185-95.

Holmes, John Clellon, "15 ¢ Before 6:00 P.M.: The Wonderful Movies of the Thirties," *Harper's* (CCXXXI), Dec. 1965, 51-55.

Johns-Heine, Patrick and Gerth, Hans S., "Values in Mass Periodical Fiction, 1921-40." In *Mass Culture.* Edited by Bernard Rosenberg and David White, Glencoe, Ill.: The Free Press, 1957, pp. 226-35.

Kaplan, Charles, "Two Depression Plays and Broadway's Popular Idealism," *American Quarterly,* XV (Winter, 1963), 579-85.

/Index

About the Author

Charles R. Hearn, associate professor of American Studies at Southeast Missouri State University, specializes in twentieth-century American literature and popular culture. His other works include a biographical article on Ellen Speyer for *Notable American Women, 1607-1950.*